D1029341

The Franciscan
Concept of Mission in the
High Middle Ages

The Franciscan
Concept of Mission in the
High Middle Ages

E. Randolph Daniel

The University Press of Kentucky

ISBN: 0-8131-1315-6

Library of Congress Catalog Card Number: 74-7874

Copyright © 1975 by The University Press of Kentucky

A statewide cooperative scholarly publishing agency
serving Berea College, Centre College of Kentucky,
Eastern Kentucky University, Georgetown College,
Kentucky Historical Society, Kentucky State University,
Morehead State University, Murray State University,
Northern Kentucky State College, Transylvania University,
University of Kentucky, University of Louisville, and
Western Kentucky University.

Editorial and Sales Offices: Lexington, Kentucky 40506

to my parents,
Mr. and Mrs. Leon S. Daniel

Contents

Acknowledgments

Recognition is due first to Professor C. Julian Bishko of the University of Virginia who originally suggested that I consider Joachim, interested me in the expansion of Latin Christendom, guided my dissertation, and set a model of thoroughness I have tried to attain.

My uncle, the late Earl L. Crum, who was professor of classics at Lehigh University, first stimulated my interest in classical literature. Professor Ernest McGeachy of Davidson College and Professors John H. Leith of Union Theological Seminary in Virginia and George H. Williams of Harvard University laid the foundations for me in ancient history and in the history of the Christian church and its thought.

As a Junior Fellow at the Southeastern Institute of Medieval and Renaissance Studies I had the opportunity to study under Professor Richard W. Southern, president of St. John's College, Oxford University, whose guidance and support have been invaluable.

Professor Marjorie Reeves, who was at St. Anne's College of Oxford University until her retirement, has kindly discussed various aspects of Joachim and Joachitism with me in addition to reading portions of this manuscript. I hope this study will advance, in some small way, the study to which she has contributed so much.

Professors Dabney Park of Florida International University and Richard Pope of Lexington Theological Seminary read and criticized helpfully an earlier version of this manuscript.

Père Jacques Bougerol, O.F.M., of the Collegio S. Bonaventura at Grottaferrata, Rome and Professor Ewart Cousins of Fordham University have encouraged and advised me in my work with St. Bonaventure. Among American historians, interest has been growing in the Franciscans and Joachim. My correspondence and contacts with them have stimulated further reflection and refinement of my own work. Among these are Professor Charles T. Davis of Tulane University; Professor Delno West of Northern Arizona University; Professor David Burr, Virginia Polytechnic Institute and State University; and Dr. Carolly Erickson of Berkeley, California.

Miss Dorothy Leathers typed extensive portions of the text and footnotes. My wife, Frankie, has read the manuscript repeatedly, patiently corrected it, and typed much of it. Ellen and Stuart have played without protest around stacks of books, microfilm, and manuscript pages.

I am grateful for two research grants plus a travel grant from the University of Kentucky Research Foundation which have enabled me to conduct research both in this country and abroad. Father Dennis McGuckin, O.F.M., formerly librarian at Holy Name College in Washington, D.C., not only permitted me to use its superb collection of *franciscana* but also assisted me with microfilming and locating materials. Father George, O.F.M., of St. Leonard's College in Dayton, Ohio has graciously allowed me to use its holdings freely. In addition I have been assisted by Alderman Library, the University of Virginia; Margaret I. King Library, the University of Kentucky; Harvard University Libraries; the Boston Public Library; the Library of Congress; the Catholic University of America Library; and the Library of the University of Cincinnati. I have consulted manuscripts and obtained microfilms from the British Museum; the Bodleian Library at Oxford University; the Bibliotheek der Rijksuniversiteit te Utrecht; the Zentral Bibliothek of Zürich; the Biblioteca Medicea Laurenziana and the Biblioteca nazionale of Florence; the Bibliothèque nationale and the Bibliothèque mazarine in Paris; the Knights of Columbus *Manuscripta* project at St. Louis University; and the Vatican Library in Rome.

Illis bona, mihi imperfecta.

I must also recognize use of material from articles of mine which appeared as follows: "Apocalyptic Conversion: The Joachite Tradition Alternative to the Crusades," *Traditio* 25 (1969):130-42; and "The Desire for Martyrdom: A Leitmotiv of St. Bonaventure," *Franciscan Studies* 32 (1972):74-87.

Introduction

One of the conceptual foundations of the medieval West was the *societas christiana*. Anyone who had not been baptized and did not confess the true faith was automatically an outsider. Communication across such divisions was superficial at best, and Latin Christians were always suspicious and fearful of the hostility of Jews, Muslims, heretics, or pagans.

When the West began to expand and develop dynamically in the High Middle Ages, the problem of the non-Christian had to be faced. The growth of international commerce, conquest, and colonization east of the Elbe and southward from the Pyrenees and Cantabrian mountains, the restrictions on and persecutions of Jews, and the Holy War were all aspects of the response of Latin Christendom to the presence of unbelievers.

Voluntary conversion by means of missionaries was, therefore, only one side of a polygon. Beginning with the wanderings of the Irish *peregrini* and Pope Gregory I's decision to send missionaries to the Anglo-Saxons, there had been a continuous history of individual and organized efforts to win Scandinavians, Slavs, and Jews for the faith. The mission of the Franciscans was not unique nor was it an isolated phenomenon.

Many different trends occurred simultaneously in Europe during the eleventh through the fourteenth centuries. The rediscovery of Aristotle and the development of scholasticism helped spur Peter the Venerable, Ramon de Penyafort, Roger Bacon, and Ramon Llull to attempt to devise an apologetical and philosophical theology which missionaries, trained also in non-Christian languages, could employ to demonstrate the truth of Christianity to learned Jews or Muslims. Roger Bacon was himself a Franciscan; Ramon Llull founded

Miramar to train Friars minor and apparently became a tertiary. But neither Bacon nor Llull was able to exert any appreciable influence on the Order. Franciscan missionaries recognized the language problem; friars became prominent in the universities; but the Order never established missionary colleges.

Abbot Joachim of Fiore and the Joachites moved in a qualitatively remote world from the schoolmen's devotion to the application of logic. They understood history as the realization of God's plan, and anticipated its culmination in the near future when Muslim persecution, the mystical antichrist, and attacks by heretics would precede the advent of the Holy Spirit. At that time, the Spirit would pour out the *spiritualis intelligentia* on two orders of *uiri spirituales,* and send these monks out to realize the *plenitudo gentium* so that all Israel might then be saved. When the monastic order of the third *status* was fully realized, it would flourish in a world where all except a few peoples on the fringe were enlightened Christians and inner spiritual peace was matched by an end to conflict and warfare.

Joachim's vision of a consummation of history attracted some Friars minor in Naples and its vicinity as early as the 1240s. Gerard of Borgo San Donnino succeeded mainly in casting suspicion on Joachim, but John of Parma and Hugh of Digne were prominent and widely influential brothers. There is too little evidence, however, to determine the nature of their influence.

Peter John Olivi fused Joachitism with the Franciscan ideology of mission, and certain individuals as well as groups of Spiritual friars were strongly influenced by him. In addition, the literary circulation of Joachitism was relatively extensive within the Franciscan Order. But few Joachites were actually missionaries, and as late as the early fifteenth century, Joachitism was still confined to individuals and certain groups rather than broadly diffused.

If St. Francis had been able to assess the Franciscan ideology of mission at the beginning of the fifteenth century, he would have found it remarkably consistent with his own thinking. The root of the Franciscans' understanding of their mission was their conviction that God had sent St. Francis and the Order to renew the life of Christ and the apostles in this *nouissima hora.* The friars' eschatology compelled them to concentrate on the imitation of Christ and within this, it obliged them to focus their attention on the passion.

This *imitatio crucis* in turn defined the friars' role as Franciscans: they were to summon all people to repent and to prepare themselves for the end of history and the final judgment.

Fundamentally, therefore, there was only one mission, and that mission did not substantially change whether the friars were dealing with the Christian or the non-Christian. Of course, St. Francis recognized that friars going to the Muslims would encounter more hostility and harsher conditions than those going, for example, to Germany—at least after the initial establishment of the Order north of the Alps—but the point remains that whether they were serving among Christians or non-Christians, the friars believed their mission to be the same: they were to call their auditors to penitence.

St. Francis and the Order maintained that the example of a holy and spiritual life was a more effective incentive to repentance than preaching. The requirements listed for missionaries consistently emphasized spiritual maturity and moral attainment. For missionaries in orders, some education was necessary, but lay friars could operate as missionaries if they lived a sufficiently holy life.

The *imitatio crucis* had to be both internal and external. Matthew 16:24 was a key text both for Franciscan spirituality and the friars' ideology of mission: "If any man will come after me, let him deny himself, and take up his cross, and follow me." A Franciscan had to deny himself, mortify his body, suffer patiently and joyfully, and desire to die for the sake of God and his neighbor. The desire for martyrdom was a spiritual state, attained only when a friar loved God more than himself, and other people as much as himself. The friar who wanted to reach perfection had to desire to imitate Christ's death as well as his life. The Franciscans were well aware of the theological questions raised against the desire for martyrdom, but their *imitatio crucis* justified it.

Franciscan eschatology, spirituality, and their correlate, the friars' ideology of mission, took shape in the life and writings of St. Francis. The desire for martyrdom motivated him and most of the early missionaries to go on their journeys. The full expression of this ideology, however, was the work of St. Bonaventure. In its Bonaventurian formulation, this concept of mission prevailed throughout the following century and a half. Angelo of Clareno, the Spiritual, and Bartholomew of Pisa were familiar with it. The anonymous *Tract-*

atus de martyrio sanctorum is a lengthy defense of martyrdom, inspired by the Franciscan ideology of mission.

The history of most monastic and religious orders has been one of relaxation and reformation. The majority of historians, however, have contended that the Franciscan Order moved away from St. Francis's ideal of poverty in order to serve the church more efficiently. They maintain that the apostolate and clericalization required modification of the observance of poverty.

Since my study posits the continuity of the ideology of the Franciscan mission, it necessarily argues a different view of the Order's evolution. The friars understood their mission in terms of service to the Order's ideal, and it is inconceivable that a modification of that ideal—especially a modification involving the apostolate—could leave the ideology of mission untouched.

This study suggests, accordingly, that while many Franciscans wanted to relax the observance of the Rule and sought to justify their relaxations, the Order as a whole maintained St. Francis's ideal. Poverty was a vital and necessary part of the Franciscan *religio*. Both Spiritual and Conventual Franciscans agreed on this, even when they struggled bitterly over its actualization.

Of course, history tends to focus its attention on change, innovation, and development. But in consequence, the question of poverty has often been emphasized to the exclusion of other aspects of the Franciscan ideal. It should be borne in mind that medieval men themselves insisted on tradition and emphasized precisely those characteristics that were most conservative. If we are to understand their institutions as they conceived them, we must be prepared to deal equally with those elements that remained stable and those that fluctuated. The Franciscan mission was not a subsidiary to the mainstream of the Order's development, but central to it: while it encouraged poverty, it also created mystics; moreover, it both occasioned and was itself sustained by an intense desire to be martyred in its service.

Abbreviations

Full references will be given on the first usage in each chapter. The following abbreviations are used for periodicals, journals, and collections.

AF: Analecta franciscana, 10 vols. (Quaracchi, 1885-   ).
AFH: Archivum franciscanum historicum.
AHR: American Historical Review.
ALKG: Archiv für Literatur-und Kirchengeschichte des Mittlelalters, ed. H. Denifle and F. Ehrle, 7 vols. (Berlin and Freiburg im-Breisgau, 1885-1900; repr. Graz, 1956).
AST: Analecta sacra tarraconensia.
L'attesa: L'atesa dell' età nuova nella spiritualità della fine del medioevo, Convegni del centro di studi sulla spiritualità medievale, 3 (Todi, 1962).
BFAMA: Bibliotheca franciscana ascetica medii aevi (Quaracchi, 1949-   ).
BSFS: British Society of Franciscan Studies.
CC: Corpus Christianorum.
CSEL: Corpus scriptorum ecclesiasticorum latinorum.
DAEM: Deutsches Archiv für Erforschung des Mittelalters.
DHGE: Dictionnaire d'histoire et de géographie ecclésiastique.
DO: St. Bonaventure, *Decem opuscula ad theologiam mysticam spectantia,* ed. PP. Collegii S. Bonaventurae (Quaracchi, 1965).
DTC: Dictionnaire de théologie catholique.
Fran. Studies: Franciscan Studies.
Franz. Stud.: Franziskanischen Studien.
Golubovich, Biblioteca: Girolamo Golubovich, *Biblioteca bio-biblio-*

grafica delle terra santa e dell' oriente francescane, vols. 1-5 (Quaracchi, 1906-27).

MF: Miscellanea francescana.

MGH QzG: Monumenta Germaniae historica: Quellen zur Geistesgeschichte.

MGH SS: Monumenta Germaniae historica: Scriptores.

MOFPH: Monumenta ordinum fratrum praedicatorum historica.

NZMW: Neue Zeitschrift für Missionswissenschaft.

OO: St. Bonaventure, *Opera omnia,* ed. PP. Collegii S. Bonaventurae, 10 vols. (Quaracchi, 1882-98).

Op Th sel: St. Bonaventure, *Opera theologica selecta,* ed. PP. Collegii S. Bonaventurae, (Quaracchi, 1964).

Opuscula: St. Francis, *Opuscula S. patris Francisci assisiensis, BFAMA* 1.

PL: J. P. Migne, *Patrologia Cursus Completus,* Series latina.

RS: Rerum britannicarum medii aevi scriptores.

SF: Studi franciscani.

Speculum minorum: Singulare opus . . . quod Speculum seu Firmamentum trium ordinum intitulatur (Venice, 1513).

ZKG: Zeitschrift für Kirchengeschichte.

ZMW: Zeitschrift für Missionswissenschaft.

The expansion of the Latin West carried it outside of Europe into Syria, Palestine, and, by means of traveling merchants and missionaries, through central Asia to India and China. It took many forms—military conquest and colonization, missionary work, commercial activity, religious crusades—all direct reflections of the trends that were operating in response to conditions within Latin Christendom during this time. From the tenth century, the population of the West had been steadily increasing in direct proportion to improved agrarian technology and the enlargement of arable fields, making migration attractive. Further, the manufacture of cloth, especially wool, gave western Europe an exportable product by which to sustain industry and commerce. Flanders, Tuscany, and Lombardy led the rest of Europe in the rise of commerce, manufacturing, and urbanism; ports such as Genoa, Venice, and Barcelona carried Latin goods to Constantinople and the ports of Syria and Egypt. Finally, the growing stability of monarchical, princely, or town governments enabled Latin Christians to mobilize their military resources against outside enemies rather than consuming them in internal strife.

Stability and cultural exchange in turn stimulated intellectual pursuits. Masters and students who congregated in the shadow of Romanesque and Gothic cathedrals formed the nucleus of growing universities.[1] Paris became the intellectual center of the West. Translations from Arabic, Hebrew, and Greek brought classical, Islamic, and Jewish philosophy and science to the attention of Latin scholars. Aristotelian logic and philosophy, interwoven with Neo-Platonism transformed the arts curricula and affected all branches of study. Contact with other civilizations combined with the stimulus of towns, universities, and more complex governments not only to introduce new concepts and customs to medieval Christians, but to create more sophisticated and articulate expressions of the old.[2]

Yet, the very vitality that made Latin Christians more aware of neighboring civilizations simultaneously encouraged them to react aggressively toward any people who seemed to be alien and dangerous. The Latin West saw itself as a *societas christiana*, comprising all people who had been baptized into and accepted the Catholic faith. Christian Rome was identified with imperial Rome and Latin culture was inseparable from the true faith. The political and constitutional importance of the notion of the *societas christiana* needs no emphasis, but the cultural role of this complex of ideas and values is equally significant for any understanding of the medieval attitude toward non-Christians. Every social or political group, from the family to a civilization, requires a shared constellation of concepts and values which at once unifies its members and distinguishes them from other groups. By conscious education or unconscious osmosis children absorb the group's bonds and attitudes. In the medieval West, Latin Christianity and culture alone determined the collective mores and feeling of solidarity among the members of the whole civilization. The multitude of familial, seigneurial, feudal, civic, and political communities stood together under the supreme *dominium* of Christ to whom the Father had given all power and who reigned in heaven surrounded by his saintly and angelic court. Through the church's priesthood and sacraments, Christ mediated the grace which alone enabled men to stand in God's favor. Monarchical *auctoritas* and *potestas,* authority and power, derived solely from Christ's plenitude. History was the unfolding of divine providence. The ancient belief that the welfare of society depended on God's favor had survived St. Augustine's *De ciuitate dei* almost unscathed. The heretic who obstinately defied and offended Christ was a traitor to the *societas christiana* and the communities it embraced. By angering God, he attacked the foundation on which the welfare of civilization rested. Violent disasters motivated medieval men and women to try to placate God as the flagellants did after the outbreak of the Black Death.

The attitude of Latin Christians toward non-Christians was a natural corollary of the *societas christiana.* Anyone who was not a *fidelis* automatically became an alien, and a potential—if not an actual—enemy. Economic, social, and political antagonisms were subsumed into this all-embracing religious and cultural intolerance and became inseparable from it. At best, a muted hostility characterized relationships between Latin Christians and those whom they regarded as infidels. A gulf of suspicion frustrated any mutual understanding.

Conversely, to accept the Roman faith meant much more than mere religious conversion. When Danes, Poles, Bohemians, and others adopted Catholicism, they were accepted into the *corpus christianorum.* In other words, they became participants in Latin civilization. (This acceptance is not to be confused with the attitude of nineteenth-century missionaries who believed that they were civilizing as well as Christianizing Africans and Asians. Conversion to Christianity in the nineteenth century simply included the acceptance of the superiority of European civilization; it did not incorporate those converted *into* European civilization. It was nationalism, not a *societas christiana* that fostered this attitude.)

In 1200 the term "religious alien" could be applied to various peoples in the Latin West. Jewish communities had been a source of intermittent friction since the days of the Roman Empire. Now the Peoples' Crusades stimulated a wave of popular anti-Semitism, and forced conversions and massacres continued sporadically from the twelfth through the fifteenth centuries.

Of greater concern to the Latin Christian were the heretics: the Cathari or Albigensians in southern France and the groups of dualists scattered in the Rhineland and Italy were viewed as a dangerous, cancerous growth promoted by the Devil.

Latin fear and suspicion extended even to those Christians whose loyalties were directed toward Constantinople rather than Rome. The long story of schisms and growing misunderstanding between the two halves of the Roman Empire cannot be dealt with in detail. Rivalry between popes and patriarchs, theological differences, conflicting liturgical practices, differences on economic, social, and cultural levels, and political jealousies between western and eastern Roman emperors combined with the linguistic gulf between Latin and Greek-speaking cultures to create suspicion, misconceptions, friction, and finally embittered enmity when the Fourth Crusade attacked, seized, and looted Constantinople in 1204. Still, common Christian faith prompted in the Latin a certain sympathy toward the Greeks, sympathy that the non-Christian could never enjoy.[3]

Of all threats to Christianity as a whole, none loomed so large or seemed so menacing as Islam. This was partly due to Western ignorance and misinterpretation of Islamic eschatology; but the statistics were indeed alarming: Christians had succumbed to Islam more readily and in much greater numbers than had Muslims to Christianity. Moreover, rumors circulated that there were alliances between Christian heretics and the Muslims creating a formidable coalition bent on destroying Christendom.

Ironically enough, in 1200 the strength of the Islamic Empire was already on the wane. Four decades of Christian conquest awaited the Christian victory at Las Navas de Tolosa in 1212. But now, Islam confronted Christianity from Asia Minor to the Pyrenees. The territorial extent and political, economic, and social sophistication of the Islamic Empire was formidable, and western Europe had only recently begun to achieve the level of commercial, industrial, urban, and intellectual activity that had long characterized Muslim countries. Worse, Islam was an aggressive faith whose proselytizing impulse and insistence that it alone possessed saving truth corresponded to fundamental characteristics of Christianity. It had conquered Syria, Palestine, Egypt, North Africa, and Spain, converting to itself peoples who had once been Christian. Salah-al-Din had recently retaken Jerusalem in 1187 and repelled Richard I the Lionhearted's armies. The peoples of the Iberian peninsula could testify to the difficulty of recovering even small areas from the Moors against whom they had been struggling since the eighth century.

The Crusade summons issued by Pope Urban II at Clermont in 1095 had channeled fear of the Muslims and outrage against them into a Holy War whose aims were to recover the Holy Land and aid the Byzantine Empire. The traditional notion of a pilgrimage was combined with the doctrine that to fight for the defense of the faith against the enemies of Christ was not only justifiable but positively meritorious, warranting at least popular martyrdom for those who died on the expedition.

But the Crusade's initial success was followed by repeated failures. Little by little, interest was aroused in alternative solutions to the problem posed by Islam. True pacifists, who rejected war on principle and absolutely or categorically denounced any use of force in dealing with non-Christians, were virtually unknown in the Middle Ages, although the use of force against pagans or forcible conversions had always provoked some criticism. It was clearly the failure of the Crusade that stimulated interest in converting the Muslims by peaceful means. Missions offered an avenue to this effect.

The medieval church had been encouraging missionaries since the sixth century, although it must be emphasized that the motivation of the first monastic missionaries was asceticism.[4] The Irish *peregrini* had regarded exile from their homeland and families as a form of extreme renunciation, and it is difficult to decide whether these sixth-century monks actually set out as missionaries, or whether their journeys simply gave them incidental opportunities to try to convert pagans. Initial motivation notwithstanding, the example set by men such as Saints Columba and Columbanus, and Pope Gregory I's decision at the end of the sixth century to send missionaries to Kent inspired Anglo-Saxon monks. And in the later ninth and tenth centuries, the Benedictine monks continued the labors of the Irish and English. In the latter half of the tenth century, the idea of pilgrimage reappeared among the disciples of St. Romuald: "For them . . . the love of exile was a form of self-renunciation, an opportunity of leaving all things; the world and its ease, the earthly country and, if God willed, life itself."[5] It is recorded that St. Adalbert, who worked among the Bohemians as bishop of Prague, and was martyred in 997 by the Prussians,[6] as "a rich young man . . . decided to go into exile—*peregrine profiscisci*—so as to become old in poverty under a foreign sun; [and] all hard and bitter things seemed sweet to him because of Jesus, his well-beloved."[7] Later Adalbert set out to work among barbarians, aware that he would receive martyrdom at their hands if he was unable to convert and baptize them.[8] Bruno of Querfurt also desired to be martyred as a missionary, his inspiration coming in part from Adalbert's example.[9] So by the eleventh century, the desire for martyrdom was linked with asceticism among the monastic missionaries.

Now, in the thirteenth century, when missionary activity drew interest as a means of peaceful conversion, three different approaches were conceived, each reflecting the world view and priorities of the men who subscribed to it: the philosophical approach; the belief in the imminent apocalyptic conversion of non-Christians; and, differing sharply from either of these, the Franciscan missionary ideal.

The basis of what is called here the philosophical approach was the assumption that learned non-Christians would accept Christianity if it could be proved to them that the search for rational truth bore witness to the validity of Christian claims. Its origins seem to have been in Christian Spain where the Reconquest had left Muslims and Jews under the rule of Castilian and Aragonese kings. Toleration of these non-Christian populations continued until the end of the medieval period and the existence of such communities provided a strong incentive to missionaries. Since these Moors and Jews lived within Christian kingdoms, missionaries were granted favorable conditions for preaching to or disputing with them.[10]

One reason that such a program was even thinkable is the fact that Al-Andalus and Christian Spain were engaged in an intellectual commerce from the early twelfth century. Toledo became a center where numerous scientific and philosophical works were translated from Arabic and Hebrew into Latin; only Sicily and southern Italy could compete with Castile and Aragon in transmitting classical, Arabic, and Jewish science and philosophy to the schools of a West eager for intellectual stimulants. The cultural role of Christian Spain was partly due to the vigor of Al-Andalus; Ibn-Rushd (known to the Latins as Averroes) and Moses ben Maimon, or Maimonides, were the outstanding Muslim and Jewish thinkers of the century. In fact, this commerce was one-way, flowing from the south to the north, but it does indicate that Christian Spain was receptive to the influences that worked upon it across religious and political boundaries. Since educated Muslims, Jews, and Christians all shared an Aristotelian and Neo-Platonic philosophical tradition, missionaries were able to use that philosophy as a base upon which to erect their arguments.

The existence of Muslims and Jews within Castile and Aragon and the general receptivity to intellectual exchange were complemented by a third element, St. Dominic's Order of Friars preacher. St. Dominic and St. Francis were contemporaries, and in many respects their Orders were similar; but the differences are important. Philosophy found a readier acceptance among the Black friars than among the Franciscans. Dominic had been trained in the liberal arts and theology at Palencia in preparation for a clerical career. The dominant aim of his life was to save the souls of infidels and heretics by preaching and disputation. His dedication to collective as well as to individual poverty was sincere, but Dominic well knew that it was necessary to train his friars in the arts and theology if they were to preach doctrinally, or successfully argue with opponents of the faith. Moreover, in order to study Muslim or Jewish philosophy and converse with infidels, the missionaries had to master Arabic and Hebrew. Therefore, Dominic merged mendicancy and study, demanding austerity but requiring every province to maintain a school. In addition, the abler scholars were sent to *studia generalia* located in such places as Paris, Bologna, and Cologne. The Dominican mission was rooted in asceticism and spirituality, but the influence of scholasticism was strong.

The philosophical program itself can be traced back at least into the first half of the twelfth century to Abbot Peter the Venerable of Cluny (1122-1156). Evidence indicates that early in 1142, Abbot Peter commissioned four translators (Robert of "Ketton," Hermann of Dalmatia, Master Peter of Toledo, and Mohammed, a Moor) to translate the Koran from Arabic into Latin along with a number of other works he desired to use in writing an apologetical treatise against Islam.[11] His purpose was to make available in Latin sufficient information about Mohammed and Islam so that this "heresy" might be refuted.[12] He wrote a letter to St. Bernard of Clairvaux and included a copy of the translations in hopes that he would agree to compose the refutation. There is no reply extant; we only know that Bernard refused. Peter later wrote his own *Liber contra sectam siue haeresim Saracenorum.* He began by admitting that it probably seemed strange for a Latin from France who had never been to North Africa or the Middle East and spoke a language foreign to his readers to approach Muslims. But he came, he said, "not as the Latins were wont to do—with weapons—but with words; not with force—but reason; not with hatred—but love, the kind of love that should exist between Christians and non-Christians, the same love with which the apostles approached the Gentiles, the love that God Himself had for those who did not serve him."[14] Peter argued that the opposition of one faith to another was fruitless, as was persecution and conversion under threat of execution. All informed men knew that truth was to be sought by reason. No learned man would want to hold an erroneous view, Peter said; since philosophy and the liberal arts sought to distinguish between the true and the false, it was within this framework of the rational pursuit of knowledge, held in common by Greeks, Persians, Arabs, and Latins, that he wished to defend the Christian faith.[15] Having established this much, Peter argued that Mohammed admitted the Old and New Testaments as God's revelation; he then tried to disprove the Muslims' charge that these testaments had been tampered with. His contention was that

Mohammed did not meet the qualifications established by the Old and New Testaments for true prophets and, therefore, Muslims should accept the Old and New Testaments rather than the Koran as the revealed word of God.

Peter's book seems to have been a pioneer effort, and he himself was aware that he would need missionaries to put his plans into action.[16] He apparently made no effort to create facilities for such men, however. Dominic's Order of Friars preacher, founded specifically to convert both heretics and non-Christians, provided the institutional means of accomplishing the program that Peter planned but only partially executed. Their programs were remarkably similar but there is no evidence that the Dominicans knew of Peter's project.

The Dominican program was largely confined to Castile and Aragon, where the man who put substance to Dominic's vision was apparently Fr. Ramon de Penyafort (1176-1280).[17] Ramon had studied in Barcelona, received the doctor of laws degree at Bologna in 1216, and returned to his native Catalonia where he joined the Dominican Order in 1222. Pope Gregory IX summoned him to the curia, and at the Pope's request he compiled the *Decretales Gregorii IX* (1230-1234). The Order elected him Master General in 1238 and he drew up a redaction of the constitutions before he resigned the generalship in 1240.[18] He devoted the rest of his life to the task of converting the Moors. The letter he wrote to his successor as Master General tells us both about the work the Dominicans were doing in Spain and Africa, and Ramon's deep interest in missions; in addition to instructing and preaching to Christians in their native languages, recovering apostates, defending the faith before Muslims, and working with or freeing Christian captives, the Dominicans had won fruit among the Muslims themselves, gaining the favor of some of the nobles, and more importantly, that of the King of Tunisia, whom Ramon calls Miramolin. Ramon believed that the gates were now open for the reaping of an inestimable harvest; many Saracens, especially in Murcia, were either open or secret converts to Christianity. But there were not enough harvesters.[19]

Ramon's interest in mission was an important factor in the establishment of special *studia* in Spain in which carefully selected friars could become well acquainted with Arabic or Jewish philosophy and languages. The records of these colleges are fragmentary, but the earliest was founded before 1245, and eventually there were five, located at Tunis, Murcia, Valencia, Barcelona, and Játiva.[20]

According to Petrus Marsilius, Ramon de Penyafort asked St. Thomas Aquinas to write a book against the errors of the infidels and Thomas replied with the *Summa contra gentiles*. Thomas stated that his purpose was to set forth the truth of the Catholic faith and to refute the errors that contradicted it, but two difficulties confronted such an undertaking. The first was insufficient knowledge of the errors themselves; the second was the refusal of the Muslims and pagans to accept either Testament as authoritative. It was necessary, therefore, to rely on natural reason, since all men assented to its conclusions; but in divine matters, natural reason was deficient.[21] Ramon's concept of mission was shared by Fr. Humbert of Romans (Master General 1254-1263, died 1277). In his *littera encyclica* of 1255, he reminded the friars that under his generalship he hoped to see the Greeks reunited with the Latin church, and Christianity preached to the Jews, Muslims, and other pagans. Significantly, he pinpointed the scarcity of linguistically qualified missionaries, and the *amor soli natalis,* the desire to remain in one's native country with its familiar language and customs, as the two obstacles impeding successful missionary activity. He appealed to those friars who had been inspired by God to learn Arabic, Hebrew, Greek, or any barbarian language and go as missionaries to write to him. In a *littera encyclica* written after the Chapter General of Paris in 1256, Humbert described in glowing terms the response to his appeal and the successes the friars had had among the heretics, the Maronites, the Cumans, the Muslims in Spain, and the Prussians.[22]

Humbert gave a more detailed but less optimistic exposition of his concept of mission in his *Opus tripartitum,* written for Pope Gregory X in anticipation of the Second Council of Lyons where Gregory hoped to lay the foundation for another Crusade. Humbert's thesis was that the *populus christianus* were burdened by three threats: outside enemies, the schism, and moral corruption within the church. Accordingly, his *Opus* is divided into three books, the first concerned with the Crusade against the Saracens, the second with the schism between the Latin and Greek churches, and the third with reform of the Latin church.[23]

Since the purpose of the *Opus tripartitum* was to defend the

Crusade, the first book is largely devoted to a recital of the spiritual and temporal injuries inflicted upon the Christian faith and faithful by the Muslims. In fact, it actually tends to discourage missionary work outside of Aragon and Castile in favor of taking up arms.[24]

Humbert's dedication to the philosophical missionary program becomes more obvious in the second book where he discusses the Greeks. Indeed, his entire attitude changes. The militant, pessimistic harshness with which he regarded the Muslims is replaced by a muted, but perceptible optimism, and a hostility that is tempered by genuine sympathy. While he laments the decline of learning among the Greeks, he commends their virtue; the Greeks may be schismatics, but the Latins are partly to blame for it. Noteworthy is his citation of the language barrier as one important reason for the schism's duration, and recommendation that Latins study the Greek language.[25]

The most famous product of the Dominican missionary *studia* was Ramon Martí, the Catalan; he joined the Order between 1243 and 1248 and in 1250 was assigned to study Arabic either at Murcia or Tunis. In 1264 he and four other Christian scholars were appointed to a commission whose task was to expunge blasphemous passages from the *Talmud*. Four years later he published his major work, the *Pugio fidei*, in which he sought to defend Christianity both against Judaism and Islam. After teaching for some years at Montpellier, he was assigned to the Hebrew studium at Barcelona in 1281 and remained there until 1285, a year before his death.[26]

The philosophical program of mission did influence Dominicans outside of Spain. As early as 1236 the Chapter General, meeting at Paris, ordered that brothers in all provinces should learn the languages of those peoples living around them.[27] In 1237, Philip, provincial minister of Syria and Palestine, wrote to Gregory IX that schools for the study of languages had already been set up in the convents of his province and that the friars were learning new languages, especially Arabic. Some friars had journeyed to Armenia to study the languages of that region.[28] We have no evidence, however, that any specialized missionary colleges were founded anywhere but in Spain, and of these, the duration is for the most part uncertain. Some of them did survive at least until the end of the century.

Meanwhile, William of Tripoli, another Dominican, was writing a tract for Gregory X at about the same time that Humbert was working on his *Opus tripartitum*.[29] He employed prophecies to prove that the demise of Islam was imminent and then marshaled evidence to prove that the Muslims were in many respects drawing close to the Christian faith. Both Humbert and William contrasted Christianity and Islam, but whereas Humbert concluded that the simpler teachings and more attractive promises of Islam made the success of Christian missionaries to the Muslims doubtful, William believed that the greater profundity of Christianity would attract the Muslims. William asserted that he had already baptized more than a thousand converts simply by preaching the word of God, resorting neither to philosophical arguments nor to the threat of force. He opposed the Crusade in almost pacifistic terms. His remarks about the superfluity of philosophical arguments and his belief in the efficacy of preaching would indicate that he saw no need for missionaries to learn any disciplines but languages and theology.[30]

The adherents of the philosophical approach to missions assumed that educated non-Christians were rational thinkers who could be converted to Christianity by logically valid arguments. But there were other men, like William, who believed rather that history was moving to its culmination and would climax with the miraculous conversion of non-Christians and a final age of universal peace and concord.

According to both Matthew and Mark, Jesus stated that the gospel must be preached to all the nations of the earth before the antichrist and the consummation of the world would come. "And this gospel of the kingdom shall be preached in all the world for a witness unto all nations; and then shall the end come" (Mt. 24:14); "And the gospel must first be published among all nations" (Mk. 13:10).

In his epistle to the Romans, Paul brought this synoptic tradition into his explanation of the role of Israel in God's plan of salvation. All but a few Jews had rejected the gospel, but their stubbornness had promoted the conversion of the Gentiles, and would stir the Jews to jealousy and emulation. Yet only when the "fulness of the Gentiles" *(plenitudo gentium)*, had entered the faith, would the whole of Israel be saved. This would occur about the time when antichrist would appear. Paul believed that his missionary journeys had already brought the gospel to the Gentiles in the East and he planned to go westward from Rome, so that all might hear it.[31]

In the Middle Ages, this final conversion of Israel was associated with the advent of Elijah and Enoch. Their preaching would convert the Jews after the "fulness of the Gentiles" had been won. Whether this would precede or follow the coming of antichrist was debated, but the apocalyptic conversion became a firm element in the tradition of last things. This eschatology helped to justify toleration of the Jews within Christendom; since God had reserved them until the end, they were not to be persecuted or forcibly converted.[32] Commentators on Matthew and Mark maintained the belief that the gospel had to be preached to all nations before the end would come.

The motivating force behind this tradition of apocalyptic conversion was the intense belief that history was coming quickly to an end. In the early church, most Christians believed that the Second Coming of Christ would occur in the very near future, but by the fourth century, the strength of this eschatology had waned. St. Augustine established the normative medieval view when he interpreted the thousand years described in Revelation 20:2-4 not in terms of a literal 1,000 year reign of the saints and martyrs with Christ on earth, but as an indefinite historical period between the incarnation and the Second Coming. This interpretation not only dismissed millennialism, but also placed the apocalyptic events at a completely unknowable future time. Augustine believed that five ages had already taken place between Adam and the incarnation. After Christ the sixth and final age had begun, but its duration could only be conjectured from God-given signs of the approaching end. As history neared its climax the world would become increasingly senile and decayed. Evil would flourish. Faith and love would diminish among Christians. The gospel would be preached to all peoples and the Jews converted. When these and other signs appeared, men might reasonably expect the imminent appearance of antichrist.[33] Over the following eight centuries, people repeatedly discerned these signs in the events and conditions of their own days. Pope Gregory the Great believed that he could discern them clearly. Christian of Stavelot speculated on the conversion of the Bulgars and Khazars.[34] Perhaps the approach of the year 1000 kindled some hopes. On the whole, medieval Augustinian apocalypticism lacked the eschatological intensity that had characterized the pre-Constantinian church,[35] but it contributed to and strengthened the tradition of last things and the notion of apocalyptic conversion. Further contribution to the notion of apocalyptic conversion was provided by various prophetic works. The *De fine mundi*, attributed to Methodius, was actually the work of a Mesopotamian Christian of the seventh century. It was soon translated into Greek and appeared in a Latin version near the end of the eighth century. Throughout the medieval period it remained one of the most popular of all prophetic texts. Undoubtedly stimulated by Arab conquest, the anonymous author traced the history of Islam and Christianity from Adam to a point where the Muslims would overwhelm the Christians. After this disaster, a Last World Emperor of the Romans would appear and turn the tables on the Arabs. The total defeat of Islam would herald the appearance of antichrist at whose approach, the Emperor would lay down his crown on Golgotha. The "Son of Perdition" would then reign in Jerusalem where Elijah and Enoch would confront him and convert the Jews. Antichrist would begin persecuting the faithful, but Christ would come in glory to slay him and consummate history in the final judgment.[36]

Much of the apocalyptic program of the Pseudo-Methodius was itself derived from the so-called Tiburtine Sibyl, composed 350. This text prophesied the appearance of a mighty Emperor named Constans during whose 112 year reign the pagans would be converted or destroyed, the Jews become Christian, and the hosts of Gog and Magog be totally crushed. Then Constans would go to Jerusalem to surrender his crown and antichrist would appear.[37]

Adso in his *Epistola . . . de ortu et tempore antichristi* predicted that the Jews would follow antichrist, but a remnant of them would be saved by the preaching of Elijah and Enoch.[38]

The works of Abbot Joachim of Fiore have their historical context here among these prophetic texts. But while most of the prophetic texts tended to strengthen the dominance of Augustinian eschatology in the Latin church, Joachim's apocalyptic program constituted a decisive departure from the normative medieval tradition. Much is yet unknown about Joachim's life. He was born in Calabria about 1135, probably the son of a notary. His father apparently wanted him to pursue a career at the royal court, but a journey to Palestine resulted in Joachim's conversion, and he returned to Italy determined to become a monk. He became Abbot of Corazzo, but in 1188 or 1189 withdrew to the Sila mountains where he founded the monastery of St. Giovanni in Fiore, the mother house of the Order of Fiore. It is not clear whether Corazzo was a Cistercian monastery when Joachim was abbot or whether he gave it to the Cistercian Order when he left to found Fiore; in any case, Joachim was deeply influenced by Cîteaux and its movement.

Joachim's career as a prophet or exegete began relatively late in his life. The dating of his works and even the genuineness of a few of them are still uncertain, but most of his surviving commentaries and treatises were completed before 1200. His *Tractatus super quatuor euangelia* apparently was begun after 1200 and probably left unfinished at his death.

Joachim never claims in his genuine works to be a prophet or a visionary. He asserted that God had given him the key to the true understanding of Holy Scripture, and his aim was to share this knowledge exegetically in his commentaries. Using a combination of typological and allegorical exegesis, Joachim constructed a framework within which history could be divided into parallel stages. Joachim is known for his Trinitarian division of history into three *status*, the third of which has millennial characteristics, but he also employed a more traditional two-stage scheme.

Joachim divided history since Abraham into two *tempora*, each of which he subdivided into seven separate time periods (or *etates*). The seven periods of the first *tempus* comprised all the events of the Old Testament. They directly paralleled the seven periods of the second *tempus* which comprised all history from the birth of Christ to the end of the world. Joachim believed that the two final time periods in the second *tempus* had not yet occurred. Joachim himself was living in the fifth; the sixth was about to begin, would endure for a brief length of time, and be followed by the seventh and final *etas*. [39] He equated the seven periods of the first *tempus* both with the seven seals of the Apocalypse, and a series of seven wars or persecutions that had occurred in Old Testament history. These were accordingly paralleled in the seven periods of the second *tempus* by the seven openings of the seals and seven wars or persecutions that had occurred—or were yet to occur—in modern history.[40]

Joachim believed that the sixth *etas* in the first *tempus* corresponded to the conquest of Babylon by the Persian Cyrus and the restoration of Jerusalem; its parallel in the impending sixth *etas* of the second *tempus* would correspond to Revelation 13:1: the New Babylon (the church) would be attacked by the beast with seven heads and ten horns, rising from the sea.[41] This sixth persecution was to be the first antichrist; for Joachim accepted the traditional belief in a final antichrist, linked with Gog, who would come at the end of the seventh *etas*.[42]

Joachim's understanding of apocalyptic conversion was largely determined by his attitude toward the Holy War and his fear of Islam, both of which strongly influenced his view of his own times and his expectations for the impending sixth *etas*. He identified the followers of Mohammed with the beast described in Revelation 13:3, one of whose heads was cut off and appeared to be dead, but gained new life.[43] The Christians might triumph, but the victory would not be finally decisive. Joachim believed that the seven heads of the dragon in Revelation 12:3 represented Herod, Nero, Constantius, Mohammed, Mesemothus, Salah-al-Din, and the first antichrist. The name *Mesemothus* probably refers to the Almohads or a ruler of that group, as far as can be determined.[44] So the fourth, fifth, and sixth heads all represent adherents of Islam; moreover, Salah-al-Din, the last of these, was a contemporary of Joachim. However much devastation the Arab conquest had caused in the fourth *etas*, or in the fifth, the sixth would see the flood tide of Saracenic power. "Complebitur autem sub sexta apertione que sub quarta esse cernimus inchoata."[45] Joachim expected the sixth *etas* to begin about the year 1200 and because of its horrors be swiftly consummated.[46]

Joachim's attitude toward Salah-al-Din is certainly understandable. Salah-al-Din had gained control of Egypt in 1169 and Damascus in 1174. Aleppo fell in 1183 and finally in 1187 Jerusalem itself surrendered.[47] The third Crusade, led by Philip II Augustus of France, Richard I the Lionhearted of England, and Frederick Barbarossa, the Roman Emperor, failed to defeat Salah-al-Din; he died in March 1193, still in control of Syria, Palestine, and Egypt.[48]

There are two references to Salah-al-Din in Joachim's writings. In the *Liber introductorius in Apocalypsim* Joachim identifies Salah-al-Din with the sixth head of the dragon and the king in Daniel 7:24 who was to be more powerful than his predecessors. "Recently (*nuper*) Salah-al-Din has begun to tread upon Jerusalem and, in order that our sins may be laid on Christian necks more heavily than is conceivable, he has grown strong." Joachim says that Salah-al-Din may fulfill the entire prophecy himself or another after him may complete it, but the whole is to be understood in the light of the dragon's sixth head in Revelation and the eleventh or little horn in Daniel's vision. Whether the little horn was to be Salah-al-Din or his successor, he was to humiliate three kings.[49]

According to the *Liber figurarum* the sixth king would bring together many kings and with them would war against the lamb, as God's unconscious instrument, killing not only the impious or false Christians but also many just believers who would thus become martyrs. Joachim believed that this persecution had already begun. It would be followed by a Christian victory that would prostrate the head of the dragon on which the sixth king reigned until it appeared virtually to be dead. But a few years later the head would revive, and the sixth king—Salah-al-Din if he lived that long or another—would assemble a much larger army than before and in a general battle give crowns of martyrdom to many of the elect.[50] Joachim's uncertainty about the future role of Salah-al-Din would indicate that both passages date from Salah-al-Din's lifetime.[51] Although Joachim does not deal with the third Crusade in either of them, both serve to clarify Joachim's conversation with Richard I in Sicily in which the abbot was required to make a forecast with regard to the success or failure of the expedition. This was shortly after Christmas Day of the year 1190 at Messina.[52] The conversation began with an exposition of Revelation 12:1-6, which describes the great red dragon with seven heads and ten horns standing before a woman who is about to give birth so that he can devour her child as soon as it is born. According to Joachim, the woman represented the church, the dragon was the devil, and his seven heads the seven chief persecutors of the church. In accordance with Revelation 17:10, the first five of these had fallen, one yet existed, and one was still to come. Richard's primary concern, of course, was the sixth, Salah-al-Din, and the seventh, antichrist. Joachim assured him that although Salah-al-Din was then oppressing the church of God and reducing to servitude Christ's tomb, the Holy City of Jerusalem, and the land on which the Lord had walked, he would shortly (*in proximo*) lose the kingdom of Jerusalem and be killed. His downfall would be such as had never been before from the beginning of the world. The homes and towns of his followers would become desolate, and Christians would go back to their lost pastures.[53]

At this point Joachim reportedly said to Richard: "The Lord has left all these things for you to accomplish. He will give you victory over your enemies and make your name eternally glorious while you glorify him, if only you persevere in what you have begun." [54]

Of course, it is possible that Joachim suited his remarks to the occasion in his conversation with Richard. The identification of Salah-al-Din with the sixth head of the dragon is consistent with his writings, but whereas the *Liber introductorius* makes no mention of an Islamic defeat, and the *Liber figurarum* predicts an Islamic defeat followed by an even stronger revival, in the interview Joachim promises Richard a decisive Christian victory, and predicts the crushing defeat and demise of Salah-al-Din. If a sequence could be established, it might be possible to see in these varying predictions the development of Joachim's ideas; but since only the interview can be precisely dated, such a progression is not currently demonstrable.

One must therefore conclude that up until 1194 Joachim's attitude toward Islam, more specifically toward Salah-al-Din and the Turks, included two opposing ideas held in tension. He saw the Saracens as a growing menace to the church that would reach its full development during the crucial years beginning in 1200. He did admit, however, that a major Christian military victory by means of a Crusade was possible even before 1200. So although the Crusade did not accord well with Joachim's apocalyptic expectations, at this point he had not yet rejected or become a critic of it. Within a few years, however, Joachim's attitude had changed. No doubt part of the reason was the failure of the third Crusade to halt the rise of Salah-al-Din. The emperor Frederick Barbarossa had led a large army across the sea, but very few had returned. Joachim lamented bitterly the number of Christian lives wasted by that expedition.[55]

But the principal factor behind his conviction that the Crusade was a futile enterprise was his understanding of the plan of God. He believed that the Saracen menace would reach its height during the impending sixth *etas*, the opening of the sixth seal. This would coincide with the transition from the second to the third *status*. In accordance with the requirements of the *concordia*, this transition incorporated many of the elements traditionally associated with the final end of the world, among them, the apocalyptic conversion of non-Christians.

The Crusades could no longer be victorious and Christians were only deceiving themselves by placing their faith in military means. The source of victory lay not in military power but in a faithful remnant. The full force of the Saracen tide was still to be felt. The pseudo-prophets would combine with the Saracens to persecute the true as well as the false believers. Joachim declares that he met a man in Messina in 1195 who told him that an embassy had been sent from the sect of the Patarenes to negotiate an alliance between the heretics and the forces of Islam. When the moment came, the alliance would be revealed. Among the forces that the *pagani* would bring would be the Turks from the east, the Ethiopians from the south, the Moors (*Meselmuti*) from the west, and some fierce pagans from the north. The Roman Empire had held these forces in check, but when the sixth angel sounded his horn, they would be unleashed to wreak vengeance.[56] Although these were the allies of the devil and members of the beast, they were nevertheless instruments of God, possessing an apocalyptic mission. So military power was useless against them. The Christians would triumph when the time came, not by battle but by preaching; not by means of weapons, but by the enduring faith and patience of those whose mission it would be to usher in the third *status*.[57]

Joachim placed these events in the transitional generations between the second and the third *status*, that is, in the fortieth, forty-first, and forty-second generations from the incarnation (roughly 1200-1260).[58] The persecution by the pseudo-prophets, Saracens, and antichrist would purify the *uiri spirituales,* monastic orders that would emerge during the transition.[59] Endowed with the eternal gospel, the *spiritualis intelligentia* or *doctrina spiritualis* proceeding from both Testaments as the Holy Spirit proceeds from the Father and the Son, these monks would convert the Gentiles, reunite the schismatic Greeks with the Latin church, and finally bring about the salvation of the Jews.[60] Thus, the third *status* would appear in full bloom *(fructificatio)* with a purified church under monastic leadership, embracing all men in an atmosphere of peace, freedom, and contemplation.[61] Only those peoples on the fringe of the earth would remain outside so that they could join with Gog and Magog in the armies of the last antichrist at the end of the third *status*.[62]

Thus Joachim added a third element to the traditional apocalyptic notion by positing the reunion of the Greeks with the Latin church. He made the monks, mystical representatives of the traditional Enoch and Elijah, the agents of this conversion. Finally, by placing these events in the sixth *etas*, or the crucial transitional generations between the second and third *status*, he brought to the tradition an immediacy and urgency that the older one had not possessed, founded as it was on the Augustinian concept of a sixth age extending from the incarnation until the indefinitely fixed end of the world.

Since Joachim was convinced that imminent persecution was only the necessary prelude to the millennial status, further Crusades could scarcely appear to be anything but futile. They could not prevent the sufferings to come nor achieve the peace that would follow the torment. Joachim criticized the Crusade not on negative grounds, but because of his vision—of the monks and *uiri spirituales*, purified by the fire of the Saracens and pseudo-prophets, filled with understanding by the Holy Spirit, agents of the Christian triumph. Their preaching would accomplish what no army could, the unification of Gentiles and Jews, with the exception of those peoples reserved to Gog. In the manner of Isaiah when he saw the mountain of the house of the Lord lifted up so that the peoples flowed up to it and peace was universal, Joachim was consumed by the vision of a world united under one faith.

The influence of Joachim on his contemporaries and the people of the first half of the thirteenth century is gradually becoming apparent, although evidence is still fragmentary and scattered. As the founder of the Florensian Order, he enjoyed some fame during the first two decades after 1200, although the Order soon faded into obscurity. The impression made by the condemnation of his treatise against the trinitarian doctrine of Peter Lombard in 1215 was to endure far longer, but to the eventual suspicion of his theology. His reputation as a prophet or as an exegete endowed with exceptional understanding spread widely by 1215 or 1220, but his thought seems to have been understood in terms of an imminent advent of antichrist preceding the end of the world. There is little evidence that his emphasis on the apocalyptic conversion of non-Christians became widely known during the period before 1240.[63]

One characteristic of later Joachitism was the production of spurious prophetic texts and commentaries attributed to Joachim himself. The earliest of these was also the most influential, the *Expositio in Hieremiam* or *Super Hieremiam.* It was long regarded as a genuine work of Joachim, and, indeed, if the number of extant manuscripts and printed editions is evidence, it was the most popular work circulating under the abbot's name. For a time, it was believed to be the work of a Franciscan, but more recently, it has been suggested that it came from a circle of Florensian or Cistercian Joachites in Calabria.[64] Since Gerard of Borgo San Donnino possessed a copy of it in 1248, it must have been written prior to this, but how much earlier is uncertain.[65] Although it preserves the essential elements of Joachim's thought, it is less complex, concentrating for the most part on Joachim's three-*status* scheme. It speaks in more precise chronological terms than Joachim himself, specifying the year 1260 as the end of the second *status.*[66] The *Super Hieremiam* also has a harsh polemical thrust. It threatens, where Joachim warned of the troubles to come. The most frequent targets of its barbs are the prelates of the church, including the pope, and the Roman Empire, especially the Emperor Frederick II.

The author of the *Super Hieremiam* believed as Joachim did that the third *status* would be preceded by a terrible persecution. However, whereas Joachim had emphasized the menace of the heretics and Saracens, the *Super Hieremiam* concentrates particularly on the Emperor Frederick II and the Germans.[67]

The *Super Hieremiam* bitterly criticizes the papal attempts to stimulate further Crusades. It was against the divine plan to contend further for Jerusalem; the Crusade would only serve to weaken Christendom. Moreover, the popes' concern with the Crusade prevented them from recognizing their proper task. The Empire had been a barrier protecting Christendom from the pagans. Sending the

Christian people to barbarous nations in the name of the cross, redistributing and altering powers could only weaken that barrier: with that obstacle removed, the persecuters would flow westward against the unprotected Christian church. Nevertheless, the author warns, he who cuts the hedge should beware the bite of the snake (*coluber*).[68] In other words, the threat is internal as well. Frederick II himself was the snake who would bite. Thus, the papacy must forget the earthly Jerusalem in order to concentrate on the welfare of the mystical city, the church. Indeed, the popes had persecuted rather than cooperated with those monks from whom the *uiri spirituales* would emerge to renew the church in the third *status.*[69]

The *Super Hieremiam* accordingly criticizes the Crusade for apocalyptic reasons. It borrowed from Joachim the alternative tradition of apocalyptic conversion. Peace would be won not by warfare but by the monks of the coming orders. Nevertheless, the polemical thrust of the *Super Hieremiam* distinguishes it sharply from Joachim's writings. The author attacks the Crusade because it is a policy contrary to that of his own circle. The bitterness of his words is foreign to Joachim's work. For Joachim, the third *status* was a vision of the future that gave meaning, albeit a painful one, to his own time. In the *Super Hieremiam* the author is concerned with the present and the past; his accumulating anger at errors and apparent wrongs determines the mood of his work.

Here then was the historical backdrop against which the Franciscan Order developed and grew, the philosophies that shared the stage with the Franciscan ideology of mission. History was coming to an end; there was much yet to be done. The Franciscan response to the situation was touched and challenged by both the scholastic and the apocalyptic approaches, but was quite different from either of these in tactics and intent. Whereas philosophical debate called for a rational approach to Christianity and Joachitism posited miraculous wholesale conversion, the Franciscans sought personal spiritual perfection that they might teach men by example how to prepare themselves for the final judgment.

BIBLIOGRAPHICAL ESSAY

On the medieval mission prior to the thirteenth century, see Kenneth S. Latourette, *A History of the Expansion of Christianity*, vol. 2, *The Thousand Years of Uncertainty* (N.Y. & London, 1938); James Addison Thayer, *The Medieval Missionary: A Study of the Conversion of Northern Europe, A.D. 500-1300* (N.Y. & London, 1936); Eleanor Duckett, *The Wandering Saints*, pb. ed. (N.Y., 1964); and Ludwig Bieler, *Ireland: Harbinger of the Middle Ages* (London, 1963). The most sympathetic histories of Slavic Europe are Francis Dvornik, *The Slavs: Their Early History and Civilization* (Boston, 1956) and idem, *The Making of Central and Eastern Europe* (London, 1949). Geoffrey Barraclough, *The Origins of Modern Germany*, pb. ed. (N.Y., 1963), pp. 249-81, and Walter Kuhn, "German Settlement in Eastern Europe from the Middle Ages to the Eighteenth Century," in *Eastern Germany: A Handbook*, ed. the Goettingen Research Committee (Wuerzburg, 1963), pp. 37-107, describe German colonization in Eastern Europe. No comparable studies exist in English for the Iberian peninsula as an entity, but see Robert I. Burns, *The Crusader Kingdom of Valencia: Reconstruction on a Thirteenth-Century Frontier*, 2 vols. (Cambridge, Mass., 1967) and Jaime Vicens Vives, *An Economic History of Spain*, trans. Frances M. Lopez-Morillas (Princeton, 1969).

On religious, cultural, and scholastic development in the Middle Ages, Charles H. Haskins, *The Renaissance of the Twelfth Century*, pb. ed. (Cleveland & N.Y., 1957) is the classic work from which other studies take their departure. The best synthesis of this period is R. W. Southern's *Making of the Middle Ages* (New Haven, 1965). Jean Leclercq, *The Love of Learning and the Desire for God*, trans. Catherine Misrahi, pb. ed. (N.Y., 1962) distinguishes monastic theology from that of the schoolmen and characterizes the underlying aims of both.

Walter Ullmann, *The Growth of Papal Government in the Middle Ages*, 3rd ed., (London, 1970) has described the evolution of the notion of the *corpus christianorum* through the Gregorian controversy. On religion as a bonding element see Joseph R. Strayer, "The Fourth and the Fourteenth Centuries," *AHR* 77(1972):1-14.

Cecil Roth, *History of the Jews*, pb. ed. (N.Y., 1961), pp. 135-232 is a good general sketch of medieval anti-Semitism. Jacob R. Marcus, *The Jew in the Medieval World: A Source Book: 315-1791*, pb. ed. (N.Y., 1969) contains translated source materials. James Parkes, *The Conflict of the Church and the Synagogue*, pb.

ed. (N.Y., 1969) traces the treatment of Jews under Roman Rule and the Germanic successor kingdoms. Yitzhak Baer, *A History of the Jews in Christian Spain*, 2 vols. (Philadelphia, 1959, 1966) is an excellent study of the Jewish communities in the Iberian peninsula. A. Lukyn Williams, *Adversus Iudeos: A Bird's Eye View of Christian Apologiae until the Renaissance* (Cambridge, Eng., 1935) summarizes the major apologetical treaties. On the first Crusade and massacres of the Jews, see Steven Runciman, *A History of the Crusades*, 3 vols. (Cambridge, Eng., 1951-1954; pb. ed., N.Y. & Evanston, Ill., 1964-1967), 1:134-41, and Norman Cohn, *The Pursuit of the Millennium*, 2d ed., rev. (N.Y., 1970), pp. 61-88.

On Latin Christians' attitudes toward Islam, see R.W. Southern, *Western Views of Islam in the Middle ages* (Cambridge, Mass, 1962); Norman Daniel, *Islam, and the West; The Making of an Image* (Edinburgh, 1962); and James Kritzeck, "A Mission to Islam," *NZMW* 20 (1964): 42-49.

The best narrative history of the Crusades is Steven Runciman, *History of the Crusades*. For individual topics the most complete studies can be found in Kenneth Setton, ed., *A History of the Crusades*, 2 vols. to date (2d ed., Madison, Wis., 1969). On the crusading idea, see Paul Alphandéry, *La chrétienté et l'idée de croisade,* 2 vols. (Paris, 1954, 1959).

Palmer A. Throop, *Criticism of the Crusade* (Amsterdam, 1940) is the only lengthy study devoted to criticism of the Crusade. Steven Runciman, "The Decline of the Crusading Idea," *Relazioni del X Congresso internazionale de scienze storiche* (Florence, 1955), 3:637-52, is largely dependent on Throop.

Although it is primarily a political narrative, Harold Livermore, *A History of Spain* (London, 1958) is probably the best treatment in English of the period of cultural exchange between Al-Andalus and Christian Spain. In Spanish the standard work is Ramon Menendez-Pidal, ed., *Historia de Espanasm,* 4 vols. to date (Madrid, 1935-   ). Charles-Emmanuel Dufourcq, *L'Espagne catalane et le Maghrib aux xiiie et xive siècles* (Paris, 1966) shows the interrelationship between commerce, politics, and religious contacts.

On eleventh-century efforts to convert the Muslims see D. M. Dunlop, "A Christian Mission to Muslim Spain in the Eleventh Century," *Al-Andalus* 17(1959):259-310; A. Cutler, "Who was the 'Monk of France' and When did he Write? A Note on D. M. Dunlop's 'Muslim Spain in the Eleventh Century,' " *Al-Andalus* 28(1963): 249-69; and idem, "The First Crusade and the Idea of Conversion," *The Muslim World* 55(1968):57-71, 155-66.

Haskins, *Renaissance*, contains the best summary treatment of the twelfth- century translators.

On the Dominican mission see Martin Grabmann, "Die Missionsidee bei den Dominikanertheologen des 13. Jahrhunderts," *NZMW* 1(1911):137-46.

Studies of the Missionary colleges include Berthold Altaner, "Die Heranbildung eines einheimischen Klerus in der Mission des 13. und 14. Jahrhunderts," *ZMW* 16(1926):89-107; idem, "Sprachstudien und Sprachkenntnisse am Dienste der Mission des 13. und 14. Jahrhunderts," *ZMW* 21(1931):113-36; idem, "Die fremdsprachliche Ausbildung der Dominikaner Missionare während des 13. und 14. Jahrhunderts," *ZMW* 23(1933):233-41; idem, "Zur Geschichte des Unterrichts und der Wissenschaft in der spätmittelalterlichen Mission," *ZMW* 26(1936):165-71; U. Monneret de Villard, *Lo studio dell'Islam in Europa nel xii e nel xiii secolo,* Studi e Testi 110 (Rome, 1944); J. M. Coll, "Escuelas de lenguas orientales in los siglos xiii y xiv," *AST* 17(1944):115-38; 18(1945):59-89; 19(1946): 217-40; M. Th. D'Alverny, "La connaissance de l'Islam in occident du ixe au milieu du xiie siècle," *L'occidente e l'Islam nell'alto medioevo,* 2 vols., Settimane di studio del centro italiano di studi sull'alto medioevo 12 (Spoleto, 1965), 2:577-602; and Robert I. Burns, *Christian-Islamic Confrontation,* pp. 1402-8, 1410-11.

In addition to the works cited in the Bibliographical essay on Joachim, see Herbert Grundmann, "Zur Biographie Joachim von Fiore und Rainers von Ponza," *DAEM* 16(1960):437-546; idem, "Lex und Sacramentum bei Joachim von Fiore," *Miscellanea mediaevalia* 6(1969):31-48; Antonio Crocco, *Gioacchino da Fiore* (Napoli, 1960); Beatrice Hirsch-Reich, "Joachim von Fiore und das Judentum," *Miscellanea mediaevalia* 4(1966):228-63; and Bernard McGinn, "Joachim and the Sybil," *Cîteaux commentarii cistercienses* 24 (1973):97-138.

II.

In These Last Days

"In these last days the grace of God, our saviour, has appeared in his servant Francis to all those who are humble and are friends of holy poverty. Revering the superabundant mercy which God revealed in him, they have been taught by his example to deny impiety and worldly desires totally, to love in conformity to Christ and to thirst unquenchably for future blessedness."[1]

With these words, Bonaventure began his *Legenda maior*. This was his understanding of the Order's mission as St. Francis lived it: to draw men to conversion and penitence in anticipation of the New Jerusalem—by renewing evangelical perfection in their own lives of renunciation, humility, and poverty.

Admittedly, Bonaventure's formulation of Franciscan eschatology must be approached with some caution; scholarship has come to distrust the works of his disciples because of the controversial stands that underlie much of their treatment of poverty. Bonaventure is among those credited with trying to gloss over and conceal the growing rifts within the Order. Franciscan eschatology itself was a controversial issue after Fr. Gerard of Borgo San Donnino published his *Liber introductorius in euangelium eternum* (1254), declaring St. Francis the herald of Joachim's third age which would commence in 1260.[2]

Some reservation notwithstanding, we may rightly approach Bonaventure and his disciples as the first to attempt to work out the Franciscan eschatology, and in fact, both sides of the later Spiritual-Conventual controversy borrowed from and were heirs of St. Bonaventure. Moreover, the renovationist eschatology set forth by St. Bonaventure and his followers is a direct development of the ideals that characterized the primitive Franciscan community.

Cajetan Esser, in his *Origins of the Franciscan Order*, cites the call to penance as the inner motivation precipitating the Franciscans' desire to live according to the form of the gospel. This desire was realized in apostolic preaching to Christians and non-Christians by word and example; on the common basis of poverty, manual labor, and mendicancy a genuine brotherhood was formed, binding its members together by fraternal love.[3]

Controversy over the role played by Joachite Apocalypticism in the development of Franciscan eschatology has tended to overshadow the fact that the Franciscan concept of mission is essentially an eschatology of renewal. It is this idea of renewal that distinguishes the Franciscan concept of mission sharply from the Joachite doctrine. Joachim emphasized evolution, progression;[4] even his most orthodox interpreters acknowledge his belief in a future age that would complete what was presently incomplete, whether this would be accomplished spiritually or institutionally. Joachim quite certainly believed that the apostolic church itself was qualitatively inferior to the coming *ecclesia* of the *uiri spirituales* by whom all mankind—except those reserved to antichrist—would attain a new level of spirituality and live together in universal peace during an indefinitely delimited period of history.[5]

Reform, on the other hand, implies original perfection, subsequent corruption, and the effort to renew and surpass the primeval state.[6] Individually or collectively, men may go forward, then slip backward before pushing further toward their goal; there is no miraculous divine intervention within history.

Gerhard Ladner has shown that the idea of reform originated in the Christian notion of baptismal regeneration and penance, and that in the patristic period it continued to be understood personally. Monasticism extended it to a communal level; Benedict of Aniane in the ninth century, and the Cluniac monks in the tenth made the concept of monastic reform familiar outside the religious order; in the eleventh century, Pope Gregory VII applied reform to the *ecclesia* as a whole; and during the twelfth the papal reformers made evangelical renewal a burning issue. Both the Gregorians and the reformist heretics looked back to the apostolic church as the original state of purity and pressed for the reformation of the corrupted church of their own day.[7]

Franciscan eschatology combined this idea of reform with an Augustinian understanding of history: the Order had been sent by God in the last age of the world to prepare humankind for the final apocalyptic events that would end history. By renewing the life of the crucified Christ and the apostles, St. Francis and his brothers would show men and women how to prepare themselves to face Christ at the last judgment.

Jacques de Vitry, the earliest outside source to comment on the friars, wrote in 1216: "These friars live . . . according to the form of the primitive church about which it was written: 'The multitude of believers was of one heart and one soul' (Acts 4:32) . . . I believe . . . that the Lord wants to save many souls by means of these simple and poor men as a reproach to the prelates who resemble 'mute watchdogs unable to bark' "(Isa. 56:10).[8] Jacques noted the evangelical quality of the friars' lives and believed that in "the twilight of this world which is sinking toward the West," God had sent the Friars minor to arouse the church and to renew the apostolic life as a protection against the imminent time of antichrist.[9]

This idea is echoed by the anonymous Franciscan *Catalogus sanctorum*: "Now in these last days when the end of the world approaches, Christ, the sun, has made Francis shine as a symbol of himself."[10] It is reechoed in the writings of Thomas of Celano: "[Now] . . . when evangelical doctrine has grown generally weaker throughout the world, [God has sent St. Francis] . . . in order that throughout the entire world universally, testimony might be offered to the truth by means of an apostolic example. And it has been done as God intended, because Francis's teaching has shown that the wisdom of this world is certainly foolishness and in a brief space of time, under Christ's leadership, the world has turned toward the true wisdom of God by means of the foolishness of preaching."[11]

Both Thomas of Celano and Jacques of Vitry were living in the period that traditional Augustinian eschatology defined as the sixth age, the period between the incarnation and the Second Coming of Christ. It had already lasted more than 1,200 years and only God could know how much longer it would continue. Despite its chronological vagueness, the concept of the sixth age shaped both Thomas's and Jacques's view of the world. Preceding the advent of antichrist, the world was becoming more and more corrupt. Sin had grown stronger while faith and love had weakened. The church itself has become corrupt and its effectiveness in proclaiming the gospel had diminished. All of these developments were leading naturally to history's end.

This view had been accepted tradition for centuries and was conventional and widespread at the beginning of the thirteenth century. Its very conventionality reinforced its impact on the medieval *Weltanschauung*. From the Age of Gold the world was edging toward clay, and men mourned the glories that had already passed. Not only had the best already been—but Augustinian eschatology held out only antichrist and the Last Judgment as the ultimate vision of things to come. The present world was corrupt and inferior; but the future could only be worse.

This view was accepted by the majority of churchmen and laymen, and by the pope himself: the world was senile, aged, sliding toward the last horrors. The purity of the primitive church had declined along with the heroic character of early Christians.

Into this crumbling ruin, God had sent St. Francis to renew the evangelical life: "And after the Lord gave me brothers, no one showed me what I ought to do, but the Most High himself revealed to me that I ought to live according to the form of the holy gospel."[12] Renouncing his rights and properties as the son of an Assisi merchant, St. Francis and his brothers believed themselves led by Divine inspiration to surrender self and possessions, and seek rather the eternal joys of the kingdom of God. In the face of the approaching Judgment, St. Francis and his friars had been called to renew the purity of the evangelical life as an example of God's wisdom. In a hopeless and transient world, they were to be the light to guide men toward eternal life.[13]

Thus conceived as the renewal of evangelical perfection, the Franciscan *religio* found its focus in the *imitatio Christi*, within which the passion came to hold the central position. In the Prologue to his *Legenda maior*, Bonaventure identified St. Francis as the angel in Revelation 7:2 who was to come after the opening of the sixth seal, ascending from the east bearing the sign of the living God. Gerard of Borgo San Donnino had made this same identification in his *Liber introductorius in euangelium eternum* when he said that Francis was to initiate Joachim's third *status*. But if Bonaventure adopted this identification from Gerard, he gave it a radically different interpretation. By identifying St. Francis with the angel of the sixth seal, St. Bonaventure sought to express Francis's significance within the framework of Augustinian eschatology. In Bonaventure's eyes Francis's uncommon level of sanctity made him an imitator of angelic purity and an example to the followers of Christ. He was an Elijah-type figure sent by God to prepare men in these last and most dangerous times for the coming of Christ in glory, even as John the Baptist had called men to repentance before the first coming of Christ in humility. For Bonaventure, this identification hinged upon and found its justification in the stigmata, "the symbol of the likeness of the living God, namely of Christ crucified." With it he sought to represent Francis's total conformity with Christ, particularly with the passion, and to symbolize Francis's role as a forerunner of Christ's Second Coming.[14]

Bonaventure expressed his understanding of the Order's role by using the image of the city. He thus described a triune goal: the mystical Jerusalem, which could be attained by ecstatic contemplation; the eschatological Jerusalem, which was the kingdom of God; and the *ciuitas dei*, which was the body of the elect. In other words, the friars were to be both contemplatives and missionaries, striving for union with God and inspiring others to seek to reform themselves according to the model of the evangelical life.

In 1259, two years after Bonaventure had been elected Minister General of the Order,[15] he journeyed to Mt. Alverna, where St. Francis had received the stigmata, to search for "inner peace." It was here that his *Itinerarium mentis ad deum* apparently began to take shape. Long meditation gave him to understand that the six-winged seraph who had borne the stigmata when it appeared to St. Francis was a symbol of Francis's absorption in contemplation, and of the steps by which Francis had arrived at his mystical ecstasy. Later, when Bonaventure wrote his *Itinerarium mentis ad deum,* he used the seraph as the key to the ladder by which peace might be pursued.[16]

He declared that the ascent to God was composed of seven steps. The first six were speculative and corresponded both to the six wings of the seraph and to the first six days of creation. Step by step they would lead the *uiator* first, to contemplate God through creatures;

second to behold Him in creatures; third, to see Him through the mind; fourth, to contemplate Him in the mind; fifth, to rise above the mind and behold God as unity; and finally, to see Him as triune and as incarnate in Jesus Christ. At this point the *uiator* would arrive at the threshold of inner peace and the entrance to the interior Jerusalem, ready for the sabbath of rest.[17] The intellect could go no further. The *uiator* had now to put aside rational operations; he was to "consult grace, not doctrine; desire, not understanding; the sigh of prayer, not studious reading; the bridegroom, not the teacher; God, not man; darkness, not brightness; not light but that fire which inflames totally and carries into God by ecstatic and most ardent affections. This fire is indeed God and his furnace is in Jerusalem."[18] The *uiator* who thus gave himself up to this fire would be inflamed by Christ through the fervor of His passion. For Christ was the way and the door through which the *uiator* would make this *transitus*. Mystical union could be attained only through the crucified. Ardent love of the passion meant single-minded desire to conform oneself to Christ's death. This longing had raised Paul to the third heaven just as it had been the dominant force that motivated St. Francis.[19] "He who turns his face fully toward the propitiatory [Christ], seeing him hanging on the cross, by faith, hope, love, devotion, admiration, exultation, appreciation, praise and joy, makes the *pasch,* that is, the crossing of the Red Sea from Egypt into the desert to taste the hidden manna and to rest with him, appearing externally dead, but perceiving within, in so far as is possible for a *uiator* [*secundum statum uiae*], the meaning of Christ's words from the cross: 'This day you will be with me in paradise.' "[20] This crossing was to be a spiritual exodus, an entrance into the supernal Jerusalem through the gate of the blood of Christ.[21]

In his earlier works, Bonaventure remained wholly within the traditional Augustinian eschatology of the sixth age. His *Collationes in Hexaëmeron,*[22] however—sermons preached to the friars at Paris in April and May 1273—reveal that Bonaventure eventually adopted a schemata similar to Joachim's twin series of seven *tempora*. Although he remained Augustinian in his eschatology, he now placed himself and the Franciscan Order within the sixth period of the second series of *tempora*, the period during which Joachim expected the first antichrist to appear.[23] Paris was at this time at the center of the controversy over the study of Aristotle and Averoes. Bonaventure regarded the teachings of Siger of Brabant and his colleagues as dangerous; he believed that radical Aristotelianism was a sign of an impending eschatological crisis. Against this threat of heresy he placed the example of St. Francis.[24]

Comparing the hierarchy of the militant church with that of the nine angelic orders, Bonaventure placed the contemplatives at the hierarchy's apex: in ascending order, the contemplatives were those who prayed (the Benedictine monks), those who were speculatives (the Dominicans and the Franciscans), and those who had attained mystical ecstasy. He equated the friars with the celestial cherubim—the second highest order of angels. The ecstatics he equated with the highest order of angels, the seraphim; for within this order of ecstatics the church was to come to perfection. Bonaventure apparently believed that this order did not yet exist within the militant church, and would not be realized until Christ had appeared and suffered in His mystical body. But the conferment of the stigmata indicated to Bonaventure that St. Francis had attained mystical ecstasy and the members of this future seraphic order would follow his example.[25]

Francis had made the *transitus*, reached the sixth speculative level described in the *Itinerarium mentis ad deum*, renounced the intellect, and passed via suffering and tribulation into ecstatic contemplation. In his *Itinerarium mentis ad deum*, Bonaventure equated all those who stood ready to make the *transitus* with the celestial cherubim.[26] Therefore, by placing the mendicants—particularly the Franciscans—on a plane with the cherubim in the *Collationes*, Bonaventure indicated that they were potential members of the seraphic order of ecstatics. Bonaventure neither excluded the Dominicans nor singled out the Franciscans; both orders were advised to look to Francis for guidance and example in seeking the mystical Jerusalem.

From his conversion until death Francis strove to renew the evangelical life according to the form of the gospel. He committed his Order to the same task: to renovate and embrace the evangelical perfection commanded by the gospel. As Bonaventure defined it in his *Questiones disputatae de perfectione euangelica*, evangelical perfection "begins with the reunciation of temporal goods through poverty; it proceeds to chastise the body through chastity, . . . it is consummated with the dedication of the interior, mental virtues through the abnegation of the will and the vow of obedience, in which man is rightly said to deny himself according to that saying of the Lord . . . 'If anyone wishes to come after me, let him deny himself and lift up his cross and follow me' " (Lk. 9:23).[27] The imitation of Christ and the apostles includes self-vilification, because Christ emptied himself for the sake of mankind;[28] renunciation of worldly goods, because Christ was stripped of all clothing;[29] obedience unto death, because the crucifixion exemplified perfect virtue.

In the early church God had sent men able to work miracles in order to confute the idolaters. Then he had raised up men who understood the Scriptures and the methods of disputing to combat the heretics. But in the last stages of the world it was avarice (*cupiditas*) that had to be opposed. So God had sent the lovers of poverty. The friars' mission was to spearhead the *ciuitas dei* in the struggle against evil, ever-increasing in anticipation of antichrist. [30]

The ultimate goal of the *ciuitas dei* was the New Jerusalem, described in the twenty-first chapter of Revelation: "and her light was like unto a stone most precious, even like a jasper stone, clear as crystal; And had a wall great and high, and had twelve gates . . . On the east three gates; on the north three gates; on the south three gates; and on the west three gates" (Rev. 21:11-13).

Probably it was David of Augsburg who first identified the gates of the eschatological holy city with the twelve chapters of the *Regula bullata.*[31] It became a dominant structural image of the *Expositio super regulam*, a commentary on the *Regula* generally considered to be the work of Bonaventure. Although it has been attributed to his disciple, Fr. John Pecham, there is no question that the *Expositio* adheres faithfully to Bonaventure's concept of the Order's role and life.[32] According to the *Expositio*, the first three chapters of the *Regula* correspond to the eastern side of the New Jerusalem and to its first three gates. Chapters four through six oppose the dangers coming from the north; chapters seven through nine oppose the threat of ruin from the west. The last three chapters symbolize the delightful breezes of the south. In the twelfth chapter St. Francis "opened the way for those thirsting for martyrdom, teaching them to join themselves to the infidels, leaving their homes."[33]

This is more than medieval fondness for number symbols; this identification of the New Jerusalem with the chapters of the *Regula bullata* actually describes the eschatological role of the Franciscan Order. Bonaventure saw St. Francis as a man intended by God to be a model for mankind as the sixth age drew toward its close. By his Rule, he gave his Order the form of life that would continue his own mission. The "sign of the living God" which was to identify the angel of the sixth seal was a prediction of the wounds that Francis bore after the vision of the seraph. This vision not only confirmed Francis's crossing to contemplative ecstasy but also put divine confirmation on the saint's *imitatio Christi*. The friars, then, were to prepare mankind for the approaching denouement of history by serving as examples of evangelical perfection; moreover, their conformity to the life of Jesus and his apostles was to be both physical and spiritual. They were to lead lives of penitence by poverty, chastity and obedience. Bonaventure saw the Franciscan mission always in terms of reform—perfection, decline, and finally, renewal.

Fr. John Pecham (1232/36-1292) was a student of Bonaventure who later went back to his native England, becoming archbishop of Canterbury in 1279. Beginning in 1270 he wrote a series of treatises in which he defended and expounded on the Franciscan life.[34] One of these, the *Canticum pauperis pro dilecto*, is cast in the form of a dialogue between the author and an unidentified *senior* or elder.[35] The author declares that as a youth he had searched for something to love and believe in, turning first to philosophy or the *artes*. Finding these unsatisfactory, he discovered himself in the company of men who "horribly crucify the flesh, condemn the whole of the earth and call themselves Friars minor as an indication that they subject themselves to the entire human race."[36] The author then raises a series of questions which the *senior* answers satisfactorily.

Had the Order been preceded by visions? Yes, St. Francis had seen a vision of the seraph by whom he received the stigmata. The vision confirmed Francis's conformity to the evangelical life that had been expressly commended to the apostles.

The elder goes on to describe Francis as "the man of the sixth day, made in the image of God . . . the angel of the sixth seal who brings the sign of God to mortal men." Within this last period of history, God had sent Francis as the example of the way by which all men might be redeemed. Francis fulfilled his mission by his conversion and by his subsequent zeal to live according to the form of the gospel as the apostles had done. He is compared to the dog that tried to follow Tobias when he left home and ran joyfully to greet him upon his return. For the Order would continue apostolic preaching as Francis had instituted it until the end of time when it would run joyfully to greet the returning Christ.[37]

The *Canticum* concludes with the image of the New Jerusalem whose gates are the twelve chapters of the *Regula bullata*, saying: "Because I have seen a city built in the shape of a square which with its citizens cannot be changed and of which the lamb is the light, ... I have sought one petition from the Lord and this I ask, that I may dwell in it all the days of my life."[38]

The *Meditatio pauperis in solitudine* is the fullest expression of the christological character of Franciscan eschatology. Although the author of the *Meditatio* remains uncertain, internal evidence indicates that the work was written in 1282 or 1283.[39]

The *Meditatio* begins by demonstrating that Francis had conformed himself perfectly to the supreme poverty, love, and humility that Christ had shown in His passion. St. Francis thus received the stigmata as confirmation and became the angel of the sixth seal.[40] The *Meditatio* equates the sixth seal with the Augustinian sixth age of the world. Just as God created man and woman on the sixth day, so He had become incarnate in Jesus of Nazareth at the beginning of this last age.[41] Then in the *hora nouissima* God had made St. Francis into the image of the crucified Christ and given him St. Clare, as Adam had been given Eve. St. Francis was that servant whom the Lord sent out to invite men to his banquet while the shadows of the evening slowly darkened the world.[42]

And just as St. Francis had imitated Christ, so his friars were to strive toward perfect poverty, love, and humility. "This religion takes its name from no saint, but instead it is called the *Rule* or *Religion of the Friars Minor*, i.e. those who perfectly imitate the crucified Christ."[43] According to Revelation 7:2-3, the angel of the sixth seal shouts with a loud voice against those four angels whose task it is to harm the earth and the sea. Through his Order St.

Francis had performed his mission to preach to all the peoples in order that the faithful might be converted and gathered together as a protection against the evils about to be unleashed.[44]

The *Meditatio*, like the *Canticum pauperis*, concludes with the exposition of the twelve gates of the New Jerusalem, but the image has now been developed into a carefully articulated scale by which the friar may ascend toward mystical ecstasy. Drawing upon Bonaventure, Pecham, and Richard of St. Victor, the anonymous author leads one from the profession of eternal truth to the sweetness of ecstatic excess.[45]

This element of mysticism was unmistakably prominent in Franciscan eschatology at least from the 1220s. The friars saw themselves as a new community that had renounced the way of the world, converted to the life of the kingdom of heaven, and thus in mutual love and peace could guide men to the interior Jerusalem of the mystic, and the New Jerusalem of the future.

III.

Not Words — but Works

The Franciscans' concept of their mission was the direct outgrowth of their belief that the Order was the divinely inspired *renouatio* of the evangelical life in the last age of the world.

The mission was to be universal.

When Francis was asked by the cardinal-protector, Hugolino, why he had sent his followers as missionaries beyond the seas to endure privation and hardship, the Saint replied: "My lord, do you think or believe that the Lord has sent the friars solely for these provinces? I say to you in truth that the Lord chose and sent the friars for the profit and salvation of the souls of all men in the whole world, and they are to be received not only in the lands of the faithful but also of the infidel."[1] According to Thomas of Celano, St. Francis instructed the companions to pray the prayer recorded in the Testament: "We adore you, O Christ, and all your churches throughout the world. We bless you, because by your holy cross you have redeemed the world."[2] The love of Christ for all men was demonstrated by his passion and renewed daily by the consecration of bread and wine upon the altar. To St. Francis the eucharist was the means by which Christ fulfilled his promise: "lo, I am with you alway, even unto the end of the world" (Mt. 28:20). Such love demanded that the redemption he had gained for them be proclaimed everywhere, to the non-Christians as well as to the faithful. As St. Bonaventure explained, St. Francis sought the conversion of those whom he found in a state of sin, because he grieved that those for whom Christ died should be deprived of redemption.[3]

The mission to the faithful and to the infidel was fundamentally one.

St. Francis, of course, distinguished objectively between believers and non-believers. He recognized—and the Order continued to recognize later—that friars would meet not only a harsher reception from the non-Christians but also that they would find it more difficult to observe the religious life among non-believers than among Catholics. Nevertheless the purpose of mission and the methods remained the same no matter who the audience or where the friar found himself.

The friars' message to all men was the call to conversion and penitence.

St. Francis described his own conversion by saying that God had made him penitent.[4] Thomas of Celano says that Francis had begun to preach penitence to all he met with "simple words but an enlarged heart" before he had a single companion.[5] When the little group had grown to eight brothers, he sent them out two by two in order that they might announce peace and repentance.[6] Pope Innocent III originally licensed the friars to preach penitence, promising to "enlarge their privileges later."[7] St. Francis journeyed from town to town "announcing the kingdom of God, preaching peace, teaching salvation and penitence for the remission of sins."[8] He admonished the friars "[to] employ in their preaching a carefully chosen and chaste style, so that their sermons [would] help and edify the people, describing for them the vices and virtues, punishment and glory, in a brief manner because the Lord abbreviated his word on earth." (Rom. 9:28)[9] Whereas St. Dominic had founded his Order with the aim of winning the heretics back and, therefore, had ample reason to emphasize doctrinal training, St. Francis, called to renew the evangelical life upon earth, preferred that his friars not engage in disputations, but preach simply and briefly, exhorting both the faithful and the non-Christians to repent and believe the gospel.

The medieval distinction between doctrinal and penitential preaching is well known. Doctrinal preaching concerned itself with explaining the faith; penitential preaching was designed to sway people toward a more Christian life. Rather than employing lengthy arguments, preachers of penitence relied on stories to move their audiences. Their sermons had more of an ethical than theological purpose.

St. Francis's attitude toward books is understandable in the light of his concept of mission.[10] Doctrinal preaching and disputation with heretics required books and schools to prepare the friars philosophically and theologically, but simple preaching of penitence demanded only that the preacher himself be a true penitent, able to phrase his brief message in simple, everyday language.

"All brothers, nevertheless, preach by their works."[11]

So wrote Francis in his *Regula prima*. In the sixteenth chapter of this same rule, he instructed his brothers to conduct themselves in two ways among the infidels: They were to refrain from disputes or arguments and subject themselves to all men for the sake of God, confessing themselves to be Christians. Thus they would show the infidels the redeeming love that Christ had manifested on the cross. If however, God gave them an opportunity, they might preach His word, calling on the Saracens or others to believe in the one omnipotent, triune God, creator of all and His Son, the Redeemer, urging them to be baptized and become Christians. But the primary means of conversion envisioned by Francis was example. The only glory permitted the friars was to glory in the cross, and that by deeds. Only when they found the infidels ready were they to instruct them in what to do to become Christians.[12]

The commentaries on the twelfth chapter underline this emphasis on example. Hugh of Digne compared the infidels to a field that must be plowed before it is sown, or to a sick man who must be prepared for the medicine that can heal him.[13]

Accordingly, David of Augsburg counseled that only those friars who were of mature age and skilled in the *scientiae*, whose virtue had been proved, and who possessed discretion and good physical health should be licensed to go as missionaries. Their lives were to be exemplary and they themselves devout, able to pray to God for what they needed, and for the strength to avoid what they ought not to do.[14]

John of Wales, writing before 1279, feared lest mere wanderlust draw the friars to become missionaries. The kingdom of God is within one, he said. Changing locations is profitless unless there is an interior renovation of the affections, denial of the carnal passions, and a separation from the temptations of the world. Perfection of life, truthfulness in doctrine, maturity of conduct, rectitude and zeal for righteousness, experience in effort, solid patience and perseverance were the qualities John sought in a missionary. The missionaries were to teach the infidels by word and example, acting among them obediently, faithfully, and humbly as paupers.[15]

So the Franciscan missionary had first to experience renewal himself, to develop a spiritual life within and an evangelical conduct without, before he could hope to set an example for others or preach to them. Willingness to suffer persecution and death was a necessary step in this ascent to evangelical perfection; the friars believed that their patient, even joyful endurance under suffering or execution was the clearest expression of the redemptive love that the *imitatio Christi* must produce.

The text Matthew 16:24 is the key for understanding Francis's concept of suffering: "Let us look, brothers, to the good shepherd who sustained the passion of the redeeming cross for his sheep. The Lord's sheep have followed him in their tribulation, persecution, shame, hunger, thirst, infirmity, temptation and such like, and on account of these they have received eternal life from their Lord."[16] Those who inflicted sufferings, tribulations, shameful things, injuries, griefs, torments, martyrdom, and death upon the friars were their friends, for by these things, the brothers would attain their reward, coming to hate their bodies' vices and sins.[17] The imitation of Christ included both material and carnal renunciation. The pauper rejoices in loving his enemies and bearing the agonies they inflict on him because in this way he follows his Lord who loved him and died for him.

Francis reminded his brothers in the *Regula prima* that they had given themselves and their bodies to their Lord, and for love of Him ought to expose themselves both to visible and invisible enemies. For Jesus said:

Whoever will lose his soul on account of me, will make it to be saved in eternal life (Luke 9:24).

Blessed are those who suffer persecution for the sake of justice, seeing that the kingdom of the heavens belongs to them (Mt. 5:10).

If they persecuted me, they will persecute you (John 15:20).

Blessed are you, when men hate you and curse you and when they have disjoined you and reproached and thrown out your name as evil, and when they speak all kind of evil lies against you on account of me. Rejoice and be glad on that day, seeing that you will have much reward in heaven (Mt. 5:11-12).

I say, moreover, to you, my friends, that you should not be afraid of them, nor should you let yourselves fear those who kill the body but cannot do more than this (Mt. 10:28).[18]

The friars who went as missionaries were charged to remember that they had taken up their crosses. They had embraced the way of suffering love and must persevere in it even if this meant martyrdom. Francis did not urge them to seek martyrdom. Rather they were to seek to imitate the way of Christ though their search might well lead to death—just as his life had led to the passion.[19]

The sources describe the early Franciscan missionaries as moved by zeal for souls and the desire for martyrdom. The evidence available demonstrates that such a desire was the vital, compelling force that motivated them to go to Spain, North Africa and the Middle East in order to convert Muslims. St. Francis himself was the first Franciscan missionary. According to Thomas of Celano: "The blessed father, Francis, made ardent by divine love, wanted always to put his hand to more difficult tasks, and he desired to attain the summit of perfection, since he was already walking according to the commandments of God, his heart having been enlarged. For in the sixth year after his conversion, burning utterly with the desire of sacred martyrdom, he decided to travel to Syria, in order to preach the Christian faith and penitence to the Saracens and the other infidels."[20] This was in 1212. He sailed from Ancona with a number of his companions, but they were forced to land in Dalmatia, and finding it impossible to obtain passage eastward, they returned to Italy.[21]

The failure of Francis's first effort, however, did not diminish his desire nor did the success of his labors in Italy distract him from his wish to sacrifice himself as a missionary.[22] The following year, Francis and a small group of companions, including Bernard of Quintavalle, journeyed to Burgos, hoping to gain permission from Alfonso VIII of Castile to enter Morocco. From Burgos, Francis went to Santiago de Compostela where he prayed at the shrine of St. James; but an illness forced him to give up his plans and he again returned to Italy.[23]

In 1219, the Chapter General sent a number of parties to Spain, Morocco, Tunis, and Hungary; Francis headed a group bound for Syria and Egypt. He succeeded in meeting the Sultan, al-Malik al-Kamil I, upon whom he made a favorable impression. But unable to convert the Sultan and learning of disturbances in the Order, he returned to Italy in late 1220 or early 1221.[24]

The friars whom the Chapter General had dispatched to Morocco traveled by way of Castile and Portugal to Seville; from there the Muslims sent them to Morocco to be martyred in 1220 because they persisted in trying to preach to the people. Their desire to undergo martyrdom rather than return to Christian territories is apparent from the *passio*.[25] It is reported that Francis, on hearing of their deaths, exclaimed: "Now I can truly say that I have five brothers." Jordan of Giano reported that St. Francis prohibited the reading of the *uita* and the *legenda* of these martyrs because "each friar should glory in his own and not in another's passion."[26]

The most important fruit of these martyrdoms was the conversion of Anthony of Padua to the Order. He had studied at the cathedral school of St. Mary at Lisbon and lived there two years after he joined the Order of Canons Regular of St. Augustine. He spent the next eight years in study and prayer at Coimbra[27] where in 1220 he saw the bodies of the martyred friars. He exclaimed, "Oh, if the most high should deign to make me a sharer of the crown of these holy martyrs! Oh, if the sword of the Lictor should find my exposed neck for the sake of the name of Jesus, while I knelt! Do you think I will see such? Do you think that I will fulfill that time of pleasure?"[28] When some Franciscans came to the convent, Anthony told them: "I would take, dearest brothers, the habit of your order, as my soul desires, if you will promise me that, as soon as I will have entered, you will send me to the land of the Saracens, so that even I should merit with the holy martyrs to obtain participation in the crown of martyrdom."[29] Anthony's zeal for the faith grew stonger after his entrance into the Order and his thirst for martyrdom gave him no rest. He received a license to go to Morocco, but once there a serious illness prevented him from fulfilling his desire.[30]

Brother Giles of Assisi was in charge of the group that the Chapter General had dispatched to Tunis. The Longer Life says that: "inspired by the spirit of God and inflamed by divine fire, they desired exceedingly to die for the faith."[31] But once there the friars encountered strong opposition from the Muslims, and the frightened Tunisian Christians compelled them to leave.[32] After St. Francis's death, Giles became a recluse and devoted himself entirely to contemplation. In fact, when confronted by a friar with Francis's injunction that "a servant of God ought always to desire to die and to end by the death of a martyr," Giles replied that he was unwilling to die any death better than that of contemplation. He had gone to the Muslims because his love of Christ had made him desire martyrdom, but believed now that "I should not have wished for a martyr's death then."[33] The *Dicta* sheds further light on Giles's attitude towards martyrdom after 1226. For Giles wrote, "The religious today find themselves in a situation similar to that in the primitive church, when men were converted to the faith who were ardent in bearing martyrdom; but after martyrdom had ceased, they became frigid. So it is today concerning the religious. We are those who in the beginning of our vocation and conversion fervently made fruitful and bitter penitence, but after some time, we have become frigid and tepid."[34] And again, "we are able to be martyrs without steel and the shedding of blood. . . . From holy devotion, joy and happiness a man may deserve to gain the merit and crown of a martyr."[35]

For Giles the desire for martyrdom was part of penitence and in the early days of the Order, he had wanted to suffer in order to mortify himself. After he became a recluse, he desired only to know God by interior experience and this, he felt, was a higher death than martyrdom.[36]

The Chapter General of 1219 also dispatched an expedition to Germany, but it failed because none of its members knew enough German to make their identity and purposes understood. They were mistaken for heretics and badly treated. As a result of this fiasco, the friars came to regard the Germans as so cruel that none would dare to go there unless the desire for martyrdom moved him. Consequently no further effort was made until the Chapter General of 1221.[37] The incident is telling. The meeting was nearly finished when St. Francis, speaking through Brother Elias, brought up the subject of another expedition to Germany. Because of the mistreatment of the first party, Francis did not wish to compel anyone to go: "But to those who, inspired by zeal for God and souls, volunteered, he desired to give the same or, indeed, a greater obedience, than that given to those wishing to go beyond the sea. If there were any who wanted to go, let them rise and stand together." Immediately some ninety friars stood up.

A curious footnote to this story is provided by the experience of the chronicler, Brother Jordan. Although he himself feared martyrdom and had not volunteered, he decided to learn the names of the friars who had, since some of them were certain to be martyred on the mission. But while trying to circulate among them, he was mistaken for one of them and ultimately did go to Germany.[38]

In 1227 Brother Elias licensed seven friars from the region of Tuscany. They went to Ceuta, and after a period of preparation, began to preach openly to the Muslims. They were arrested, imprisoned, and finally martyred. The *passio* describes them as men devoted to God, fervent in spirit, thirsting with all their energies for the salvation of the Muslims, each ready to expose himself to death if only he could offer God the best fruit from among the unbelievers.[39] Part of a letter survives which they apparently wrote from prison to one Hugo, a priest of Genoa. It indicates clearly that they viewed their sufferings as imitation of the agonies of Christ:

> Blessed be the God and Father of our Lord Jesus Christ, the father of mercies and the God of all consolation, who consoled us in all our tribulation; who prepared a sacrificial victim for the patriarch, Abraham; who likewise went out from his own land at the command of God, not knowing, by what way he should go, and this was reputed to him as righteousness and he was called a friend of God. Thus, therefore, he who is wise, should become foolish, so that he may be wise, because the wisdom of this world is foolishness before God. Let it, there-

fore be known to you, that the Lord Jesus Christ, who has suffered for us said: "Go, preach the gospel to every creature." "The servant is not greater than his lord." "If they have persecuted me, they will also persecute you." He directs our steps in his paths for his praise, for the salvation of the faithful, the honor of Christians, and the death and damnation of the infidels. . . . Therefore, the name of Christ has been proclaimed before the king and we confessed that there is no other way to salvation and proved this by living reasons, using an interpreter, before his wise men.[40]

The ruler of Morocco offered them an opportunity to save their lives by renouncing Christ and accepting Islam. But the friars steadfastly confessed their faith and their willingness to be martyred. The Muslims, angered by their stubbornness, finally executed them.[41]

John of Perugia and Peter of Sassoferrato were sent to Aragon by St. Francis. In 1228 they went to Valencia which was under Muslim rule because they were "burning with zeal for the faith and inflamed by the desire of martyrdom, and wanted to preach the word of God to the infidels." Choosing a public place, they proclaimed the Christian faith and attacked the law of Mohammed as false. They were arrested, imprisoned, and when they refused to convert to Islam were martyred.[42]

Robert I. Burns describes the tactics of the early Franciscan missionaries in terms of outright confrontation: "Outrageous, consciously ineffective, yet designed to engage the forces of heaven at some mystical level, it seized the imagination of contemporary Christendom."[43] Even in the thirteenth and fourteenth centuries, the desire for martyrdom was the subject of theological debate, since it was accepted that one ought not to provoke his own execution.[44] It is possible to view the early Franciscans as inspired by heroic fervor to imitate the martyrs of the pre-Constantinian church, but this seems to imply that the desire of martyrdom was not an essential part of the Franciscan *religio*. We can more properly view the desire for martyrdom as an external expression of Franciscan spirituality encouraged by St. Francis's emphasis on example, in imitation of Christ's own life and passion. Tactically speaking, martyrdom was the supreme example since better than any other act it signified the friars' love for their persecutors.

The Franciscan life demanded not only exterior imitation of Christ through poverty, mortification and the endurance of suffering, but also interior conformity through self-denial, obedience, humility, and love.

The temptation to devote as much time as possible to prayer, meditation, and contemplation was strong. Brother Giles of Assisi was by no means the only friar who forsook preaching in order to concentrate exclusively on the search for mystical unity with God.[45] Nevertheless, most friars tried, as did St. Francis, to combine mysticism and mission in some proportion. Although some tension may have existed within individual brothers between their desire to progress spiritually and their calling to proclaim repentance to all men, the Order as a whole maintained a balanced combination of the *uita contemplatiua* and mission.

Thomas of Celano, one of Francis's early biographers, saw the significant elements of the Saint's life—Francis's instructions to his brothers, his desire for martyrdom, his striving by contemplation to understand and fulfill the will of God, his reception of the stigmata, and the sufferings of the last two years of his life—as successive points in a continuum held together by the imitation of the passion of Christ. Introducing his chapter on Francis's first attempt to go to Syria in 1212, Thomas stated that because of his fervent love for God, Francis constantly sought to advance himself toward the summit of perfection. The desire for martyrdom motivating him to undertake the journey to Syria was a further understanding of and step toward the perfection Francis sought.[46]

Despite his failure to reach Syria or Morocco, Francis continued to pursue his desire.[47] His third journey enabled him to attempt personally to convert the Sultan of Egypt but did not gain him martyrdom. "In all of these acts, the Lord did not fulfill his desire, reserving him for a uniquely gracious privilege."[48] This "praerogatiua ... singularis" was the stigmata, clearly conceived as the divine fulfillment of Francis's desire for martyrdom and his efforts to achieve that desire as a missionary.

Francis's "*summa ... philosophia*," his "*summum desiderium*" was to understand the way by which he could more perfectly cleave (*adhaerere*) to God. He was prepared "to suffer all the agonies of the soul and all the torments of the body, if only he were given the opportunity to have God's will completed in him." As Thomas describes the incident, one day after prostrating himself in prayer and making the sign of the cross, St. Francis took a copy of the gospel from the altar and opened it. In so doing, his eyes fell upon a place where the passion was predicted by Jesus. He opened the book twice more, and each time found similar passages. "[He] then understood that to enter the kingdom of God, he would have to pass through many tribulations, hardships and struggles." Immediately after this, according to Thomas, he saw the six-winged seraph and received the stigmata.[49]

Until 1244 Thomas's *Vita prima* was the principal life of St. Francis. The *Vita sancti Francisci* by Fr. Julianus of Spira, composed between 1232 and 1235, followed Thomas of Celano almost literally.[50] Julianus, however, made explicit in some passages the implied meaning of Thomas. Where Thomas had explained Francis's failure to achieve actual martyrdom by saying that God had reserved him for a "unique prerogative," Julianus states directly that this special reward was to be the stigmata. Discussing the tension in Francis between his desire to lead the contemplative life and his sense of his mission to men, Julianus asserted that after Francis had tasted the delights of contemplation, he strove with all his faculties to discover by what actions he might make himself a more acceptable sacrifice to God. In his account of the reception of the stigmata, Julianus explained them as the culmination of Francis's desire for martyrdom and his willingness to suffer all for the sake of Christ.[51] Although Julianus did not add any new material to the *Vita prima*, he corroborated and clarified the portrait of Francis which he discerned there.

The Chapter General of 1244 recognized the inadequacy of the *Vita prima*, and wished to have it supplemented by a more complete life while some of the friars who had known Francis himself were still alive. It ordered the Minister General Crescentius to command all friars who knew stories about Francis or sayings of his to commit them to writing and to send them to Assisi so that Thomas could use them in the composition of his *Vita secunda*.[52]

One purpose, therefore, of the *Vita secunda* was to bring together materials about Francis which had been unknown to Thomas when he wrote the *Vita prima*. The most important of these additions for the present topic is the account of the vision in the church of St. Damian. Thomas reported that while Francis was praying prostrate before the crucifix, a voice spoke to him as if the image itself were addressing him, saying: "Francis, . . . go, repair my house, which, as you see, has been totally ruined." As a result of this experience, compassion and devotion to the crucified Christ took root in Francis. From that time on, his heart and soul were imprinted with the stigmata, although his body did not receive them until later.[53] He was unable to restrain himself from grief when he thought about the wounds of Christ which, henceforth, often occupied his mind.

Taking the *Vita prima* and *Vita secunda* together, as Thomas undoubtedly meant to be done, the pattern is clear. At one pole is the vision at St. Damian from which Francis conceived his ardent devotion to the passion. At the other is the physical symbol of this devotion, the stigmata. Between these two are Francis's division of his life between contemplation—itself centered on the crucified Jesus—and work on behalf of others, or mission. Particularly, there are the journeys to Syria and Morocco made because of his desire for martyrdom as well as his desire to win converts. The unifying element is that of self-denial and assumption of the cross. Self-denial is both internal, directed toward the spiritual conformity of Francis with Christ, and external, expressed by his willingness to suffer in order to persuade nonbelievers to accept the faith. Understood within this pattern, the desire for martyrdom is clearly a desire for conformity with the passion of Christ.

The pattern that Thomas of Celano constructed was developed and interpreted by Bonaventure. The latter made explicit the interior meaning of this construct which Celano had left implicit. In his *Legenda maior*, Bonaventure borrowed his account of the crucified Christ appearing to Francis and its effect on him from the *Vita secunda*, but he went further by asserting that henceforth Francis knew that the words of Matthew 16:24 had been spoken to him. Moreover, from this experience had issued his "spirit of poverty, his sense of humility and the warmth of intimate piety." Thereafter Francis attentively practiced the mortification of his body so that the cross of Christ which he carried in his heart should appear externally in his body.[54] There can be no doubt that Bonaventure saw in this vision of the crucified Christ a critical point in the interior and exterior development of the "poverello."

Bonaventure recounted how Bernard of Quintavalle decided to join himself with Francis—that Francis had opened the gospel three times, his eyes falling upon the familiar texts of Matthew 19:21, Luke 9:3, and Matthew 16:24:[55]

> Jesus said unto him, If thou wilt be perfect, go and sell that thou hast, and give to the poor, and thou shalt have treasure in heaven: and come and follow me.

> And he said unto them, Take nothing for your journey, neither staves nor scrip, neither bread, neither money; neither have two coats apiece.

> Then said Jesus unto his disciples, If any man will come after me, let him deny himself, and take up his cross and follow me.

Repeatedly Bonaventure stresses the friars' willingness to suffer privation and want.[56] He emphasizes the dominance of the cross in their discussions and meditations.[57]

Bonaventure believed that Francis desired to die a martyr's death both as a recompense for the passion and as a means of stimulating others to love of God, but was reserved by God from martyrdom so that he might receive the stigmata.[58]

In recounting the reception of the stigmata, Bonaventure followed Thomas of Celano, but he indicated more clearly than his source that the stigmata were a spiritual and physical martyrdom, a sharing in the suffering of the passion. He stated that Francis saw in the thrice repeated opening of the gospel to the passion of the Lord indication that he must imitate Christ in his activities and be conformed to him by the afflictions and griefs of the passion; this led him to desire martyrdom intensely. Then the vision of the seraph implanted in his flesh the stigmata, so that Francis was martyred not by execution but by the transformation of his ardent self into a similitude of the crucified Christ. The stigmata were the fulfillment of that first vision he had seen before his conversion and subsequent visions of Christ on the cross that occurred at intervals during his life.[59]

Bonaventure portrayed Francis as a passionate lover of Jesus crucified who in his spiritual development and active career manifested above all else that love by which he was conformed to Christ while he sought to draw others to the Lord. His desire for martyrdom, motivating him to undertake missionary journeys to the Saracens, flowed from his devotion to and his longing to imitate the passion of Christ.[60]

St. Francis had suggested in his own writings that the friars were obligated to undergo sufferings as imitators of Christ, and Francis's biographers saw his desire to conform himself to Christ, his longing for martyrdom as a missionary, and the stigmata as a central pattern in his life. But it was Bonaventure whose writings accomplished the transformation of Francis's interior life into the more formal concept of Franciscan spirituality.

St. Bonaventure saw the desire for martyrdom as a step in the mystical ascent toward union with God. In the Prologue of his *De triplici uia*, he posited three modes of ascent: the purgative, the illuminative, and the perfective—producing, respectively, peace, truth, and love. Accordingly, he cited three forms of exercise which would achieve these steps: reading and meditation, praying, and contemplating. In his *De triplici uia*, Bonaventure treated each of these three types of exercise in terms of their correct practice.[61] They were not to be employed consecutively, but simultaneously, as different routes that ultimately converged.

Bonaventure's discussion of prayer clearly reveals his belief that the desire for martyrdom was a necessary part of the mystical quest. Bonaventure saw the goal of prayer as love. The cross was the manifestation of the love of God for the *uiatores*. In response, the *uiatores* would first love God in gratitude, then as an obligation, finally as both. They would come to reject the world and hence to be rejected by it, but ultimately to be crucified for the sake of the world. It is here that the desire of martyrdom becomes a step in the development of love, representing love both of God and of neighbor, and a longing to die in order that other men may come to share this love. According to Bonaventure, this is the state and level of perfect love. No *uiator*, before reaching it, should think himself perfect; for perfection comes only when a man finds his heart not merely willing, but intensely longing, to die for his neighbor's salvation.

Love for God progresses through six stages, the first three being sensitivity, avidity, and satiety. The fourth is ebriety, a state in which the love for God is so overwhelming that, rather than wanting to be consoled, the searcher loves and seeks the cross. He experiences joy from undergoing torment, abuse, or punishment. Such love expels fear and the *uiator* who experiences it is certain that nothing can separate him from God. Thus he attains the fifth stage, security, which leads the heart to the final stage, tranquillity.[62]

Bonaventure described the exercise of contemplation in terms of a triune goal: the eternal possession of supreme peace, the clear vision of supreme truth, and the full enjoyment of the supreme goodness of love.[63] Each of these three were composed of seven steps. The eternal possession of supreme peace was the purgative aspect of contemplation: when the *uiator* achieved the sixth step, ardor, he conceived "a fourfold desire of martyrdom: for the sake of perfect remission of sin, perfect cleansing of blemishes, perfect fulfillment of the penalty, and perfect sanctification in grace."[64] The desire for martyrdom is thus the desire to be completely purged of sin and reformed by grace as well as an expression of love for God and for neighbor.

Describing the seven steps by which the clear vision of supreme truth could be reached, Bonaventure wrote that as the fifth step the seeker should put on Christ by trying to resemble him; and as the sixth step, he should embrace the cross in an access of desire for suffering. It was then that the light of truth would fall on him. For "the illuminative way of contemplation is centered around the cross which is the key, the door, the way, and the splendor of truth. He who is willing to take up the cross and follow its way, as Christ explained, 'does not walk in the darkness, but will have the light of life' " (Jn. 8:12).[65]

For Bonaventure, imitation of, fervent meditation on, ardent prayer about, and contemplation of the cross were the steps that alone could lead the spiritual man to his ultimate goal of union with God. The spiritual life had to produce in him the desire for martyrdom in order that, fired by this longing for death, he might pass over into peace. The willingness to sacrifice one's life for the sake of Jesus Christ as he gave his for men, is the goal that a friar had to attain before he could reach his desired end.

St. Bonaventure emphasized the *desire* for martyrdom rather than martyrdom itself. In his view, this desire was a spiritual state, formed by prayer and contemplation, and directed toward imitation of the cross. It not only looked beyond itself to union with Christ but also outside itself to those neighbors who did not yet love God or share in the faith.

In 1251, two decades of tension between the secular masters at the University of Paris and the friars became open controversy. William of Saint-Amour's attack on Fr. Gerard of Borgo San Donnino's *Liber introductorius ad euangelium eternum* (1254) began a series of *apologiae* by leading figures on both sides of the dispute. When Thomas of York, a Franciscan, wrote his *Manus quae contra omnipotentem tenditur,* it drew a reply from the secular master, Gerard of Abbeville, in 1269.[66] In turn, Bonaventure countered Gerard by writing the *Apologia pauperum.*[67] This work provides us with a good illustration of the role that Bonaventure believed the desire for martyrdom played in the attainment of evangelical perfection.

Thomas of York had attempted to prove that the status of those who renounced the world and retained nothing worldly was more perfect than the status of those who retained worldly goods. He then replied to the objections against that view, with particular reference to the purse that Jesus and his disciples carried with them. He argued that Jesus did some things in order to instruct and to give example to the weaker Christians. To do the contrary of these things was, therefore, praiseworthy, not wrong. He cited as an example the flight of Jesus into hiding (Jn. 8:59; 11:54); this was not due to any defect in the power of Christ, he said, but was done as an example to those not able to face martyrdom.[68]

In reply, Gerard took up this example of the flight of Jesus and argued that Christ did not intend to give an example to the weak but that in certain cases the perfect ought to flee. To flee because of some perversity or malice of the mind, on account of ignorance or mental weakness, or even out of natural fear would be incompatible with perfection; but even a saint might flee because of humility or where prudent circumspection and an abundance of mercy made such a course wise.[69]

Replying to Gerard, Bonaventure defined perfection essentially as

love. He distinguished three grades of love: observing the commandments of the law (doing what is necessary), fulfilling the counsels
(voluntary obedience), and enjoying the eternal delights (reward for
obedience). Evangelical perfection was the second or intermediate
grade—voluntary obedience.[70] It comprised the avoidance of evil,
the pursuit of good and the bearing of adversity.[71] This last had to
include a strong desire for suffering and the experience of joy in
bearing agony.[72] Thus, the desire for martyrdom was perfect as
such, and flight from it imperfect as such. One does not flee—for
evangelical perfection is provided with its own defense: the longing
to be martyred for the sake of Christ; the desire to die and be with
Christ shows perfect love for him. So for Bonaventure, to desire
death for the sake of Christ, to expose oneself to death for him, and
to rejoice in the agony of dying are acts of perfect love. To flee from
death is an imperfect act in itself unless the motive for flight is to
ensure a more glorious victory later on or to provide consolation for
the weak when they might face the threat of death; in that case,
fleeing is a part of perfection.[73]

Perfect love was as much a part of evangelical perfection for St.
Bonaventure as was poverty or obedience. The true friar had to be a
mystic as well as a pauper. Bonaventure viewed mystical love as
directly opposed to self-love; the desire for martyrdom had to be a
part of this love, because it expressed total willingness to deny self
and to obey Christ, simultaneously uniting the lover to Christ,
transforming him into his beloved.

The abundant mystical literature produced by the Franciscans in
the later thirteenth century was invariably dependent on St. Bonaventure's spirituality. Both the *Stimulus amoris* of James of Milan
and the *Meditatio pauperis in solitudine* focused their attention on
imitation of the passion and emphasized the necessity of a desire for
martyrdom within this conformity to the cross.[74]

Hugh of Digne recognized the theological dangers inherent in a
precipitate desire of martyrdom but he also maintained that a
prudent longing was an integral element in the Franciscan missionaries' imitation of Christ.[75] The *Expositio super regulam* attributed
to St. Bonaventure placed even more emphasis on the desire for
martyrdom as the missionaries' motivation.[76]

Among the Franciscans mysticism and mission were closely

IV.

Intellectual Conversion

Two alternative concepts of mission that were developed during the High Middle Ages subjected the Franciscan *religio* to the pressures of influence and attempted merger; indeed, they were held and championed by men within the Order itself; but throughout this period of time the Order's ideals underwent little change, and the three remained parallel movements.

The scholarly world is most familiar with Roger Bacon as a proponent of the *scientia experimentalis*, but Bacon was also a linguist and proponent of the philosophical approach to mission. He believed that missionaries should study languages, particularly Hebrew, Arabic, and Greek, not only to facilitate communication with the non-Christian, but to establish a common ground of scientific and philosophical knowledge for rational disputation with him. He directed his arguments to the papacy rather than to the Order; yet clearly he must be recognized as representative of the philosophical approach among the Franciscans.[1]

Much of Roger Bacon's life remains obscure. His family had some wealth and may have belonged to the lower rank of the nobility. He entered the Arts Faculty at Oxford probably about 1227, studied there until after 1235, and by the 1240s he was lecturing in the Arts Faculty at Paris. Since he had come there from a similar post at Oxford, he apparently did not proceed to the study of theology.[2]

At this point in Bacon's career one must deal with his relationship to the two English scholars Robert Grosseteste (1175-1253) and Adam Marsh (died 1257), since it was certainly their influence that prompted Bacon to enter into the Order of Friars minor. Grosseteste studied and then taught at Oxford, becoming chancellor in 1221. In 1229 he was appointed lector at Oxford's newly founded Franciscan convent and continued to lecture on theology to the friars until 1235 when he was elected to the bishopric of Lincoln—a position he held until his death.

Our knowledge of Adam Marsh is less certain. His date of birth is unknown but tradition asserts that he came from Somerset and possessed wealth and position. He studied the arts and probably theology at Oxford, possibly under Grosseteste. At the urging of Adam of Exonia he joined the Order of Friars minor in 1232. When the Chapter of Definitors of 1241 requested that friars elected from each province annotate *dubitabilia* in the *Regula bullata*, he was one of the friars elected to respond.[3] (The response of the English friars was that the Rule should be allowed to stand as St. Francis had received it from Christ himself by the dictation of the Holy Spirit.) Adam Marsh was lector at Oxford until about 1250. He was nominated in 1256 for the then disputed bishopric of Ely but failed to obtain it.[4] He died in 1258.[5]

Roger Bacon's judgments on his contemporaries tended to be largely unfavorable, but he spoke of both Robert Grosseteste and Adam Marsh with unqualified praise, describing them as models of truly wise men and examples to be followed.[6] He calls himself their disciple, but this is not literally possible. Grosseteste gave up teaching in 1235 after six years of lecturing to the friars at Oxford—a six-year period during which Roger Bacon must have been an Arts student and was definitely not a friar. But although Bacon could never have formally studied under the bishop of Lincoln, upon his return to England between 1247 and 1250, he may well have become one of Grosseteste's friends. There is no doubt that he had studied the bishop's writings and was acquainted with Grosseteste's students. If Adam Marsh was teaching until 1250, Bacon could have been his student, but this relationship too might have been personal rather than formal.[7]

Bacon almost certainly made his decision to become a Franciscan after he left Paris and before returning there again in 1257, but the date cannot be made any more precise than that.[8] His motives for joining the Order, other than the esteem in which the Franciscans were held by Robert Grosseteste and Adam Marsh, are open to conjecture.[9] Bacon nowhere manifests an understanding of or the zeal for the imitation of Christ or for poverty. Inspired as he was by

Grosseteste and Marsh, perhaps he believed that the Order would support his studies in the *scientiae*. If he was already convinced that reforms were needed, he may have hoped that the Order would take up and promote his program. In any case, his motives were surely more scholarly than religious.

If Bacon did expect the support of his fellow friars he was surely disappointed. In fact, between his return to Paris in 1257 and his departure for Oxford in 1268, some form of restriction may have been placed upon him.[10] After the publication of the *Euangelium eternum* by Gerard of Borgo San Donnino (1254), the Order had forbidden the brothers to publish books without prior approval by the ministers; but of course this restriction applied to all Franciscans, not only to Bacon.[11] The thesis that Bacon was a member of the group of Joachite Spirituals to which Gerard belonged is unfounded.[12] Bacon did clearly feel some constraint, however; he was obviously contemptuous of the Parisian theologians and this could have contributed to his problems.

Bacon was acquainted with some of the translations from Arabic that had been made in Spain in the twelfth and thirteenth centuries, but there is no evidence to indicate that he was aware of the activities of Fr. Ramon de Penyafort and the Dominican missionary colleges. Bacon himself suggests that Robert Grosseteste and Adam Marsh were the inspiration of his program regarding language studies and their usefulness as instruments for converting non-Christians. Bacon believed that God had revealed both the law and philosophy first to the Hebrews; the Greeks had learned philosophy from them, and in turn transmitted it to the Muslims. Thus the original sources had been translated from Hebrew to Greek to Arabic. The Latins had never fully assimilated philosophy because the existing translations were faulty. A skilled translator not only needed to know both languages involved, he had also to be familiar with philosophy. According to Bacon, Robert Grosseteste knew the *scientiae* and Boethius the languages. Few of Bacon's contemporaries knew even the rudiments of Hebrew, Arabic, or Greek. Moreover, Bacon contended that relatively few Greeks or Jews were really conversant with the grammar of their own languages and none knew the *scientiae*.[13] Bacon states that Grosseteste, Thomas of Wales, and Adam Marsh sought to learn languages, but Grosseteste himself did not become familiar with Greek until near the end of his life when he brought some Greeks to England and with their help assembled some Greek grammars.[14]

Grosseteste's linguistic interests were responsible for some translations from Greek and possibly from Hebrew. One Nicolaus Graecus aided him in translating, or perhaps translated for him, the *Testament of the Twelve Patriarchs*.[15] In a letter written during the early years of his career as a bishop, Grosseteste informed the abbot and monks of Peterborough about some observations that he had gleaned from a Greek work on the monastic life. This would seem to indicate that he was interested in and could read some Greek by this time.[16] Grosseteste himself is credited with translations of the whole of Aristotle's *Nicomachean Ethics*, the works of Pseudo-Dionysius and the *De fide orthodoxa* of St. John of Damascus.[17]

Grosseteste's linguistic efforts were motivated chiefly by his scientific, philosophical, and theological interests, but in the case of the *Testament of the Twelve Patriarchs* his purpose was clearly apologetical. Matthew of Paris states that the translation was made in 1242 "ad maiorem Iudaeorum confusionem."[18] The *Testament* attracted Grosseteste because of its prophetic references to Jesus Christ; he believed that they might serve as proof that the old law had been superseded by the law of grace.[19]

Grosseteste's interest in the conversion of the Jews dates at least from the period when he was lecturing to the Franciscans. His *De cessatione legalium*, written in 1231, was primarily intended to supply arguments for use in disputing with Jews and refuting their belief in the permanence of the Mosaic law.[20] In that same year he outlined his attitude toward the Jews in a letter written to Lady Margaret de Quinci, the widow of the Count of Winchester. Some lords, including the Lord of Leicester, wanted to expel Jews from their lands in order to force them into homes for converts and to protect Christians from usury. Lady Margaret desired to settle some of these Jews on her estates as laborers. Grosseteste stated that Jews were not to be killed, since God had reserved them for conversion at the end of time, but instead they were to be punished as Cain had been, by being scattered over the world. Christian rulers should not favor the Jews and especially ought not to permit them to prosper by means of usury. Jews, however, ought to enjoy protection and should be used as labor for the sustenance of rulers and themselves.[21] There was no persecution of the Jews in Lincoln during Grosseteste's episcopate and he was able until his death to restrain Simon de Montfort from mistreating the Jews. Grosseteste's influence may have led the Franciscans to intercede for the Jews of Lincoln in 1255 and later in 1290 to rescue Hebrew books when the Jews were banished from England.[22]

Adam Marsh interceded for the Jews with Henry III.[23] He shared Grosseteste's concern for reform of the church and his belief in the approach of antichrist.[24] In 1250 he wrote a letter to Pope Innocent IV on behalf of Henry III who had just taken the cross. He spoke of the pope's position at the head of the ecclesiastical hierarchy and urged him to concern himself with the welfare of the church. Yes, the church possessed both spiritual and material swords, but only soldiers and kings were to use weapons in the service of the church. The sword of churchmen was preaching and until the *plenitudo gentium* had entered the faith, they were to exercise it diligently. They should not hesitate to risk death at the hands of the infidels. Adam did not reject the validity of the Crusade but his primary concern was to persuade the pope to promote preaching to the non-Christians.[25]

Robert Grosseteste and Adam Marsh both exercised a formative role in the development of Bacon's concept of mission. His concern for language study as a necessity for adequate missionary preparation; his emphasis on preaching and condemnation of crusading; his belief that philosophy could serve as a common basis for persuading infidels to accept the truth; his overall preoccupation with reform; and his frequent references to the imminence of antichrist could all stem from ideas and concerns absorbed from Grosseteste and Grosseteste's Franciscan disciple. Neither Grosseteste nor Marsh had developed a philosophy of mission. This was Bacon's work, as was a broadly conceived plan for reform.

By the middle of the 1260s, Bacon had come to believe that the church was seriously endangered and that he must urge on the papacy immediate efforts to ameliorate the evils. Initially he proposed to write a work embodying his views for Cardinal Guy de Foulquois (or Foulques). The Cardinal encouraged him but urged that Roger work secretly in view of the Order's restrictions upon publication. After Guy became Pope Clement IV, Bacon again made his proposal, and the pope replied (June 1266) with a letter commanding Bacon to send his writings, constitutions of the Order notwithstanding. Bacon sent him the *Opus maius* and *Opus minus.*[26]

The purpose of these works was to make the pope aware of the need for reform and to guide him in achieving it. According to Bacon, his program would improve the government of the church and the regulation of the commonwealth of the faithful. It would also promote the conversion of unbelievers and strengthen the defenses of Christianity against those who remained infidels. Bacon was confident that the Pope had the ability to implement the reforms if he wished to do so.

Bacon began by exposing the four chief causes of error: the acceptance of faulty authority, reliance on custom, dependence on the weight of common opinion, and the fact that men who were ignorant because of the first three tried to conceal it by showing off what little knowledge they did possess.[27] Bacon's reform was one of studies. He distinguished six *scientiae*: philosophy, languages, mathematics (which included astronomy, astrology, and geography), optics, the *scientia experimentalis,* and moral philosophy. Deficiencies in these six disciplines were to blame for the limited number of Christians and the comparative multitude of infidels. The reigning philosophers and theologians at the University of Paris were perpetrating errors because they lacked true knowledge of these *scientiae.*[28] The threat of the imminent antichrist was added reason for correcting the situation.[29]

If Clement IV actually intended to act on these proposals, his death in 1268 prevented him from doing so. After Tedaldus Visconti was elected Pope Gregory X in 1271, Bacon wrote his *Compendium studii philosophiae.* It is not addressed to the pope, however, and Bacon may not have published it.[30] Bacon's program remained unchanged in this work, but his tone is quite different. Whereas earlier he had expressed confidence in Pope Clement IV's ability to accomplish reform and apparently felt that Clement was genuinely interested in his program, now he was unsure about who would be the agent of reform. Perhaps an "angel" pope would renew the church and the world; perhaps an *optimus princeps* would cooperate with the pope in reforming the church. However, Bacon feared that renewal might have to come through the persecution of Christendom by antichrist or some tribulation such as discord between Christian rulers that would allow the Tartars or the Saracens to ravage Europe. Bacon was more pessimistic in 1272 than he had been in 1267: the eschatological threat loomed ever more ominously. His criticism of abuses is harsher: the popes' assumption of imperial rights and functions had corrupted them. Christians were tending away from Christ when the sacrament of the eucharist should have been making them more Christlike. He vehemently castigates the Parisian philosophers and theologians.[31]

In his justification of the program he proposed, Bacon formulated a coherent philosophy of mission. Christians were few, non-Christians many. Nonbelievers were to be won to the faith by preaching, not crusading. Many infidels would be converted if missionaries were trained according to Bacon's proposals. Study of languages would provide them with the necessary skills to acquire knowledge and to communicate with non-Christians. Mathematics would equip them with knowledge of the countries, peoples, and sects with which they had to deal. Astrology and moral philosophy would offer them proofs of the validity of the Christian faith.

Bacon's concept of mission recognized the philosophical assumptions on which it rests: All truth is one and derives from the same source, Jesus Christ. All wise men seek truth and as rational beings will accept truth voluntarily. Linguistic, geographical, and cultural training are necessary for the missionaries to work effectively.

Bacon was acutely conscious of the minority status of Christians. The Tartar and Muslim territories and populations seemed to be enormously larger than those of the Christian, and Bacon feared that one people or the other would attack Europe. Reform was urgently necessary because it would blunt that threat in two ways: First, if non-Christians converted in sizable numbers, then the imbalance between believers and nonbelievers would be relieved. Second, the *scientiae* would enable Christendom to defend itself more effectively against those who resisted conversion. (For example, the science of perspective would make it possible to construct a giant mirror which could be used to focus sunlight in such a way as to set fires among the enemy forces.)[32]

Bacon was optimistic about the possibility of converting infidels,

even Muslims. He believed that missionaries had been only margin-
ally successful because they were not properly trained in languages
or philosophy. Furthermore, Christian wars against the non-Christians had made the infidels bitter enemies of Christendom before the
preachers even arrived. Roger Bacon's arguments are similar to the
criticisms of the Crusade which Humbert of Romans sought to
refute in his *Opus tripartitum*. According to Bacon, the Crusades had
often led to military disasters such as the defeat of St. Louis IX at
Damietta. Even when Christians occupied lands beyond the seas,
they lacked the manpower to defend them. Moreover, Crusades did
not convert unbelievers but killed them and condemned them to
hell. In consequence, the surviving infidels became embittered and
more hostile to Christianity than they were before. Bacon singled
out the Teutonic Order for particular criticism. He asserted that its
aim had been to enslave the Prussians and the other Baltic peoples
rather than convert them. The repeated aggression of the Knights
had so antagonized the pagans that peoples who would otherwise
have accepted Christianity long before were now stubbornly resisting
conversion.

Bacon was not opposed to war; he was opposed to continuing the
Crusade because he believed it hindered the mission to the infidels.
The original expansion of the faith had been accomplished by
preaching, not force. Missionaries had won converts despite the fact
that their ignorance of languages compelled them to rely on interpreters. He warned that the Latin church might have to account some
day for its neglect of preaching, when there were so few believers
and so many non-Christians.[33]

Bacon wanted the resources which were then being used for
crusading to be employed instead for the support of missionaries;
missionaries had to be properly trained and Bacon urged the pope to
provide the facilities for such instruction. His program of studies
offered the key to the necessary curriculum.

The foundation of Bacon's philosophy of mission was his belief
that there was one perfect wisdom wholly contained in Scripture
and explicated in philosophy and canon law. Bacon supported this
notion of a single body of truth by his argument that the *intellectus
agens* was God *principaliter* and the illumining angels *secundario*.
Men possessed *intellectus possibiles,* capable of being enlightened by

the divine source of knowledge. Jesus Christ was truth and, there-fore, even the truth which the infidel philosophers knew came to them from him, albeit indirectly. Since God had revealed the whole of wisdom to the Hebrews from whom *philosophia* came to the Greeks and later to the Arabs, in order to acquire the truth of philosophy, the Christians had to study Greek and Muslim philo-sophical and scientific works.[34]

The aim of philosophy was to know the creator through the creature in order that mankind might honor God by worship, right conduct, useful laws and thus live in peace and justice. Philosophy "should be raised to the state of Christian law" that is, be directed toward theology and the church; toward the government of the *respublica fidelium*; toward the conversion of the infidels; and to-ward the reprobation of those who would not be converted.[35] It was useless to argue from Scripture in disputes with nonbelievers since they denied the validity of the Bible—just as Christians refused to accept the authority of the non-Christians' sacred books. Yet people had to be persuaded to accept the faith voluntarily. Bacon believed that this persuasion could be accomplished only by proofs drawn either from miracles or from philosophy. Philosophy was the common ground between believers and non-Christians by means of which the Christian could demonstrate the principles of theology.[36]

Bacon himself spent much effort in learning Hebrew and Greek, although he apparently never studied Arabic. He believed that it was impossible to interpret the Old and New Testaments properly with-out Hebrew and Greek. Even if an accurate text of the Vulgate were established—Bacon contended that the version currently used at Paris was corrupt—still one would need to know the original lan-guages for a literal understanding without which spiritual under-standing could not be developed. Bacon blamed the deficiencies of his contemporaries' philosophical and scientific studies on the fact that they did not know Greek and Arabic and were compelled to rely on corrupt translations. He stated that important works still remained untranslated. In many instances Arabic or Greek words that were left in the Latin versions made them largely unintelligible. Scholars skilled only in Latin had corrupted the few good transla-tions.[37] The *scientia linguarum* had to be mastered, therefore, in order for the Latins to obtain full possession of wisdom. Christ, the one truth, could only be completely acquired when there were men capable of reading, translating, and interpreting the Bible and the corpus of scientific, philosophical, and theological writings.

Another science necessary to the missionary was mathematics, and Bacon believed astrology to be the most important branch of it. He was aware of the strictures against astrology but he met them by distinguishing philosophical mathematics from magical beliefs, condemning the latter as fatalistic.[38] Although they exerted a determining influence terrestrially, celestial bodies did not infringe on the will's freedom.[39]

Bacon subsumed geography under astrology because he believed that celestial influence was responsible for climate, topography, and differences in the nature and customs of peoples.[40] If papal or royal envoys sent to negotiate treaties were properly to advance the interests of Christianity, they had to have a thorough knowledge of the best seasons for travel, the regions they were to penetrate, and the religions of the peoples to whom they were dispatched. Bacon had read enthusiastically the report that William of Rubruk, a Franciscan, wrote about his journey to the Mongols in 1253 as a representative of St. Louis IX. He also talked personally with William and others who had traveled in the Middle East and Central Asia.[41]

Mathematical geography was especially useful, in Bacon's view, because of the information it could provide about the apocalyptic peoples of Gog and Magog whose coming would combine with the advent of antichrist. Since tradition held that Alexander the Great had shut them outside the Caspian Gates, knowledge of the peoples who lived beyond this region would help the church prepare for these invaders.[42]

Just as astrology was the better part of mathematics, so moral philosophy was the chief branch of philosophy. The teleology of knowledge directed all the *scientiae* toward moral philosophy. This discipline taught people to formulate laws and rules for living, showed them why they were to be accepted and obeyed, and motivated them to conduct themselves in accordance with those precepts. It regulated the obligations of persons toward God, toward one another, and to themselves. Its principles were derived from the other branches of philosophy and the sciences, particularly from metaphysics. Among the principles that Bacon established by reason and by citations from pagan authorities were the trinity, the incarnation, the coming of antichrist, the future judgment, the creation of the universe, mankind and angels, the immortality of the soul, the resurrection of the body, and the future happiness of good and misery of evil. Hence philosophy, rightly treated, drew the philosopher toward revealed theology.[43] Even non-Christian philosophers were seeking Christianity in their search for wisdom.[44]

Bacon distinguished six principal sects, excluding that of antichrist,[45] relating them through astrology to the conjunctions of the planets. According to Bacon, astrological study proved that Christianity was only one of the principal sects, but philosophical comparison proved that Christianity was the true faith that all men should accept.[46] In fact, Bacon said, according to his studies, the duration of the sect of Mohammed had been set at the 693rd year after its foundation; since Bacon was writing in the 665th, the destruction of the Muslim faith must be expected soon, to be followed by the appearance of the sect of antichrist.[47] Bacon believed that his arguments could be used with the non-Christian philosophers to persuade them to accept Christianity. Their conversion would then draw others to accept the truth of the faith as well.

The last two decades of Bacon's life are obscure. According to the *Chronica 24 generalium*—whose accuracy on this period is suspect— Hieronymus de Ascoli, the Minister General (1274-1279), condemned and reprobated the teaching of Roger Bacon (the chronicle describes him as *sacrae theologiae magister*) because his teachings contained "aliquas nouitates suspectas." Roger was imprisoned and the friars were commanded to avoid his opinions. Hieronymus is also said to have written to Pope Nicholas III in order to solicit a papal condemnation of Bacon, but no record of any papal action has survived.[48] A late tradition asserts that Raymond Gaufridi, Minister General between 1289 and 1295, freed Bacon from prison. While most scholars have accepted the statement that Bacon was subjected to some form of confinement, they have not agreed on the reasons for this punishment. According to tradition, Bacon died on June 11, 1292 while he was writing his *Compendium studii theologiae*. Nothing in this last work suggests either that he was still in prison or that he had recently been released from it.[49]

There is considerable difference between Roger Bacon's philosophy of mission and the Franciscan mission as treated by St. Bonaventure. St. Bonaventure moved from evangelical *renouatio* to develop a spirituality proclaimed primarily by example. Bacon began with the assumption that reform meant an overhaul of the existing state of philosophy and the *scientiae*. The sources are silent about the ultimate influence of Bacon on his Order and its missionaries; but it would seem that his program did not exert enough influence on the Friars minor to deflect the purpose and approach given them by their founder.

While Bacon was writing his *Opus maius* for Pope Clement IV, another man was striving to equip himself to undertake the mission to the Muslims on the island of Majorca. Ramon Llull has often been made to appear as a kind of exotic—if not quixotic—figure. It is possible, however, to place him within the context of the Franciscan approach to mission and the scholastic or philosophical mission developed by the Spanish Dominicans. I would like to discuss his concept of mission in terms of an attempt on his part to merge these differing ideologies into a single, coherent program which he hoped the friars or the papacy would implement.

The biographer of Llull is unusually fortunate because the *Vita beati Raimundi Lulli* which describes his career from his conversion until the eve of the Council of Vienne (1311) is a contemporary account written by someone who knew Llull intimately and derived much of his information at firsthand.[50]

Llull's father, also named Ramon, and his mother, N'Elisabet, were both from noble families. The elder Llull had served in the army that conquered Majorca for Jaime I of Aragon, and in consequence he received considerable lands on the island in the *repartimiento* of 1230. His son was probably born two years later. Ramon was educated for a career at the royal court where he became a page about 1246 and companion to the two young princes, Pedro and Jaime. He served Jaime as seneschal and majordomo and their close attachment to one another became a lifelong friendship.[51] Ramon's education was evidently minimal in Latin and the liberal arts, but he became an accomplished poet, writing verse in Catalan on the model of the troubadors.[52] He married Blanca Picany, herself of a noble family, about 1256 or 1257, and they had a son, Dominic, and a daughter, Magdalena,[53] The *Vita* tells us that both before and after his marriage, Llull courted many ladies. One night while he was composing a song in Catalan for one of them, he glanced to his right and saw a vision of Jesus hanging on the cross. Terrified, he immediately sought safety in bed. The next morning he shrugged off the vision and resumed work on his song, but a week later, when he was again engaged in writing it, the vision reappeared at the same hour and place. Llull, more frightened than before, swiftly sought sleep again. The following morning he resumed his composition, but the vision occurred three more times.

After the fifth of these visions, Llull lay awake the entire night, pondering what they meant. He decided that Christ wanted him to leave the world for his service, but Llull's conscience made him feel guilty and unworthy. Alternately remembering his sins and praying for mercy, he could not resolve his doubts until at dawn he considered Christ's clemency, patience, and mercy.

He decided that one could best serve God by giving his life for His love and honor seeking to convert the Saracens; but he lacked the necessary knowledge for such work. Perhaps he could write a book against the errors of the infidels. He could not imagine what form or mode such a book should have, but the more he thought about it, the more strongly this aim took hold of him. Still he knew that even if he could write such a book, it would accomplish little or nothing, because he was ignorant of Arabic. He resolved, therefore, that he would go to the pope and to Christian kings and princes in order to urge them to establish monasteries in diverse places where suitable religious and other persons could be instructed in Arabic and the other languages of the non-Christians. These then were the three goals which dominated the remainder of Llull's life: to be martyred as a missionary; to write a book against the errors of the infidels; and to urge the establishment of missionary colleges.

For the next three months Llull prosecuted his intentions only tepidly. Then, on the feast of St. Francis, he happened to hear a Franciscan bishop preaching on the manner in which Francis had decided to leave the world and devote himself to the service of Christ. Inspired by Francis's example, Llull sold all of his possessions, except what was necessary to sustain his wife and children, and set out on a pilgrimage.[54] Thus the *Vita* implies that Llull believed himself to be in a situation similar to the one in which Francis had been at the time of his conversion, and decided to act as Francis had.

Llull was now about thirty or thirty-one.[55] He spent the next two years as a pilgrim. He wanted to go to Paris to study, but his parents, friends, and particularly Fr. Ramon de Penyafort persuaded him to return to Majorca.[56] Undoubtedly his friendship with this advocate of the Dominican missionary colleges went back to the days when Llull had been a page at the court of Jaime I, for Penyafort had been the king's confessor. If Llull found in St. Francis a model for his spirituality, he discovered in the Catalan Dominican a guide for his plans to refute the errors of the infidels and for the establishment of missionary colleges.[57]

He began to wear a habit of coarse cloth. In order to learn Arabic, he bought a Muslim slave, but after working with him for nine years, Llull had occasion to slap him for blaspheming the name of Christ. Angered, the Muslim attacked him with a sword—and subsequently hanged himself in prison. Although none of the Arabic versions of his works survive, Llull apparently learned not only to speak the language but also to read and write in it. The *Vita* says of his Latin studies merely that he learned something of grammar, but he must have also read in theology and philosophy.[58] Throughout his life he was on intimate terms with the Cistercian monks of Nostra Doña de la Real, situated just outside of Parma, and, since it already maintained a school, the monks probably guided his reading and allowed him to audit their classes. His later works indicate that he was well acquainted with Cistercian spirituality.[59] While he was engaged in his studies, he began writing his *Llibre de contemplacio de deu*, first composing it in Arabic, then translating it into Catalan.[60]

After his slave's suicide, Llull retired briefly to Mount Randa where the *Vita* states that God revealed to him the form and mode of his *Ars*. Returning to Nostra Doña, he wrote his *Ars magna*, later known as his *Ars generalis*.[61]

About 1274 or 1275, Jaime, now King of Majorca, summoned Llull to Montpellier asking a Friar minor, Bertrand Berenguer, to examine Llull's writings, especially the *Llibre de contemplacio* which Berenguer admired.[62] His reception undoubtedly encouraged Llull to ask Jaime to establish a monastery in Majorca sufficiently equipped to allow thirteen Friars minor to study Arabic there. When the original thirteen were sufficiently prepared to go as missionaries, others would replace them.[63] On October 15, 1276, Jaime granted Nostra Doña a farm at Deya in return for another named Miramar, also at Deya. Here he permitted Llull to found his monastery. Pope John XXI confirmed the new foundation in a bull dated from Viterbo on October 17, 1276.[64] Miramar apparently flourished, winning the support of Alphonso III and Jaime II of Aragon while they controlled the kingdom of Majorca. In 1292, however, some unknown disaster ended its brief career and it was never refounded. No record of its students or their activities as missionaries survives.[65] Llull's doings and whereabouts are unclear between 1277 and 1282. In 1282 he traveled to Perpignan to meet again with Jaime of Majorca and the next year he was present at a Dominican Chapter General at Montpellier. Apparently he sought to promote his *Ars* and his program of missionary colleges, but he received only a lukewarm reception.[66]

Several years later Llull decided to go to the papal curia in order to persuade Pope Honorius IV and the cardinals to establish colleges, but upon arrival, he discovered that Honorius had recently died (April 3, 1287). So Llull went to Paris. Bertoldus of Saint-Denis had just been elected chancellor of the University (Dec. 1288), and he permitted Llull to lecture on his *Ars generalis.* Llull also presented his *Libre de les besties* to Philip IV at this time. The *Vita* adds enigmatically that, having observed the mode of the schools, Llull went back to Montpellier where he resumed lecturing. Possibly the reception of his *Ars* at Paris was less favorable than he hoped it would be. At Montpellier he wrote his *Ars ueritatis inuentiua*, reducing the number of diagrammatic figures to four, because he had realized in Paris that the capacity of the human mind is limited.[67]

On October 26, 1290, the Minister General of the Franciscans, Raymond Gaufridi, gave Llull letters of introduction, instructing the friars in Italy to welcome Llull kindly as a former benefactor of the Order, to give him a suitable place for teaching, and to license those friars interested in his *Ars* to hear him lecture.[68] Llull traveled by way of Genoa to Rome, but because of the *impedimenta curie*, he accomplished little of what he intended. Therefore, he returned to Genoa, intending to go to the Muslims alone to see what he could do by himself if he employed his *Ars* in discussions with their schol-ars.[69] There is no indication that Llull used his letters from Ray-mond Gaufridi to lecture at any of the Franciscan convents in Italy. Possibly he wanted them to attract friars to Miramar or his proposed college; more likely he hoped to use them to gain the hearing of Pope Nicholas IV. Llull's ties with the Aragonese royal house could only have made matters more difficult for him, since Nicholas strongly supported the Angevin claims to Sicily; but Nicholas was also a Franciscan who was likely to receive a benefactor of the Order favorably.

Llull prepared to embark from Genoa for Tunis but, when the ship was ready to sail, his courage deserted him. Remorse induced illness and Llull began to seek membership in the mendicant orders. He approached the Dominicans but was refused admission on the ground that the prior was absent. The Franciscans told him that they would accept him only when he was closer to death. According to the *Vita,* Llull believed that he must join the Friars preacher if he was to be saved, but since the Franciscans had proved favorable to his *Ars* and the Dominicans had not, he was drawn to the former, even though he risked damnation by joining them. Finally, when he heard that another ship was sailing to Tunis, Llull had himself carried aboard and as he sailed toward North Africa, he gradually recovered his health. In Tunis he was able to engage in discussions with some Muslims who were skilled in the Koran, but someone reported his activities and Llull was imprisoned and deported. He returned to Naples and lectured on his *Ars* until he heard that the aged hermit, Peter Morrone, had been elected Pope as Celestine V (1294). Llull went to Rome and, after Celestine's resignation, tried to persuade Boniface VIII to implement his plans, but to no avail.[70]

During the next fifteen years Llull divided his energies between promoting his *Ars* and his missionary colleges, and the missionary activities which took him to Majorca, Tunis, and the eastern Mediter-ranean.[71] When he heard that Pope Clement V had convoked a general council to meet at Vienne in October 1311, he decided to attend in order to promote three proposals: the establishment of missionary colleges, the combination of the military orders into one order, and the suppression of the opinions of the "Averroists."[72] The council adopted the first of Llull's proposals in its decree, establishing colleges of languages at the Universities of Rome, Salamanca, Bologna, Paris and Oxford.[73] It also summoned another Crusade and entrusted it to Philip IV.

After the closing of the council in March 1312, Llull returned to Majorca by way of Montpellier. Then he traveled to Messina where with the protection of King Frederick of Sicily, he sought to convert the Jews and Muslims. In August of 1314 he sailed from Majorca to Tunis from where he wrote to Jaime II of Aragon and asked for the help of his disciple, Fr. Simon de Puigcerda, as a Latin translator. Llull was still in Tunis in December 1315.[74] One late tradition declares that he was stoned, probably at Bugia, and taken back to Majorca where he died. Another claims that he died on Majorca early in 1316.[75] As a member of the third order of the Franciscans, he was buried in the church of St. Francis in Palma.[76]

Llull's relationship to the Franciscan Order needs to be clearly defined. Peers argues that Llull was originally drawn to the Dominican Order, received a cool reception from them, and then turned to the Franciscans about 1287; this led to his decision to become a tertiary about 1294 or 1295. However, Peers has not taken into account the role of the bishop's sermon about St. Francis nor of Miramar, which was founded specifically to train Friars minor. The *Vita* notes the friendship between Ramon de Penyafort and Llull and Penyafort's role in persuading Llull to seek his education in Majorca. It later states that God promised Llull salvation if he joined the Friars preacher, but that the Friars preacher did not receive his *Ars* favorably. His *Ars* had been sympathetically received by the Franciscans, possibly at meetings of the Chapter General, and certainly by Raymond Gaufridi; this ultimately led Llull to seek membership in the Friars minor at the risk of damnation. The *Vita* says nothing of his decision to become a tertiary and this cannot be precisely dated. It is more appropriate, therefore, to see Llull's relationship to the Franciscans in terms of divine confirmation of his aims and work. The example of St. Francis served to validate in Llull's mind his own conversion, as well as to indicate the direction his postconversion life should take. Similarly the favorable reception of his *Ars* confirmed its divine origin for him. The *Vita* emphasizes this role of validation with regard to the Franciscans more than any influence they may have exerted upon Llull.

Llull's ultimate decision to become a tertiary rather than a friar of either order may be explained by various reasons but one seems to be fairly obvious. Since his conversion included adoption of a tripartite aim that was henceforth to dominate his life, his course was, in fact, inner-directed. If he had become a friar, he would have had to subject himself to the direction of his superiors within his chosen order. While Llull sought validation of his aims and possibly guidance, he would not have taken the vow of absolute obedience unless he were willing to forsake his own chosen goals were such a command issued him. At that moment in Genoa when his confidence in his own mission was drastically shaken, Llull seemed ready to place himself under the authority of one or the other of the orders, but he was refused and wisely turned down. As a tertiary, Llull could obtain support without having to vow obedience. His decision to become a Franciscan tertiary reflects Llull's feeling that a bond existed between him and the Friars minor. He sensed in the Friars minor not only sympathy but a degree of resemblance in their respective approaches to mission.

The resemblance between Llull's desire to find martyrdom as a missionary to the infidels and the ideology of the Franciscans is at once superficially apparent. Both Llull and the Franciscans derived their desire to suffer for Christ from a mystical spirituality, but herein lies the difference: Franciscan spirituality flowed from evangelical *renouatio* and the *imitatio Christi*. Llull developed his spirituality primarily from courtly love. Love draws the lover to his beloved for whom he weeps, sighs, and fears; it gives the lover the endurance to suffer scorn, contempt, pain, torment, and even death for the beloved. The lover naturally wants to be drawn upward toward his beloved but after letting him taste the delights of contemplation, his beloved thrusts him down once more into the world so that he may contemplate him amid tribulations and sorrows. Believing that all men ought to love and honor his beloved, the lover devotes himself to awakening that love in those who do not possess it. He becomes, in effect, a missionary for his beloved. There is a resemblance between Llull and the Franciscans, but not kinship.[77]

Although his *Ars* differed sharply from the philosophical apologetics of St. Thomas's *Summa contra gentiles* or Ramon Martí's *Pugio fidei*, there can be no doubt that the example of Ramon de

Penyafort and the Dominican colleges for the study of Hebrew and Arabic influenced Llull's program. Undoubtedly Llull found it difficult to understand the indifference of the preaching friars to his *Ars*; he believed his emphasis on the necessity of a logical and philosophical common ground between missionaries and non-Christians and his insistence on language study to be akin to their program.

Llull's program differs from both the Franciscan and the Dominican programs, but Llull combined key elements of each in his approach toward mission. Both Miramar and the letters he requested from Fr. Raymond Gaufridi indicate that Llull made some effort to attract the Franciscans to his program.

Miramar was not carried on by the Franciscan Order, however, nor did the Order found any other missionary colleges. No evidence indicates that Llull made any impression on the friars. And yet, the friars were certainly aware of the problem that faced the missionary who was ignorant of the languages of the people he intended to convert. William of Rubruck indicated that he had tried to preach to the Mongols through an interpreter until he learned enough of their language to realize that for lack of theological training, the interpreter was completely distorting his sermons.[78]

Information scattered in the sources demonstrates that the Franciscans dealt with the problem of languages in varied ways. Many groups of friars tried to include one or more brothers who were either bilingual or whose native languages could be understood by the non-Christians. These men probably served as reliable interpreters, but they must have been difficult to find, especially outside of East Europe and the Balkans. In some cases indigenous non-Christians who possessed the necessary languages became friars and could be instructed in the Catholic faith. Some friars attempted to learn the languages of the nonbelievers after they had arrived in their intended country. Fr. Paschalis spent a year in Sarai for this purpose; and if the letter of Peregrinus is genuine, his lament about his inability to master the languages used in China shows that this approach often proved difficult.

Outside of Aragon, Dominican colleges were rare and those founded by Ramon de Penyafort and his Spanish brothers scarcely survived the thirteenth century. Possibly the absence of enough qualified instructors was an important factor in undermining the existing colleges or restricting the establishment of any new ones.

No elaborate explanation appears to be necessary to account for the lack of such institutions among the Franciscans. The Friars generally adhered to the approach of their founder, emphasizing spirituality and the desire for martyrdom. In fact, the model of St. Francis proved to be surprisingly tenacious.

BIBLIOGRAPHICAL ESSAY

Despite its date, the biography by Emile A. Charles, *Roger Bacon* (Paris, 1861) is still valuable as is J. M. Bridges, *The Life and Work of Roger Bacon* (London, 1914). See also A. G. Little, "On Roger Bacon's Life and Works," *Roger Bacon Essays* (Oxford, 1914):1-31; Edward Lutz, *Roger Bacon's Contribution to Knowledge* (N.Y., 1936); and Albert Garreau, *Roger Bacon, frère mineur* (Paris, 1942). Stewart C. Easton, *Roger Bacon and his Search for a Universal Science* (N.Y., 1952) is the most recent biography, but Mr. Easton's hypotheses about Bacon's Joachitism and his adherence to the Spiritual Franciscans are unfounded (see E. R. Daniel, "Roger Bacon and the *De seminibus scripturarum*," *Mediaeval Studies* 34[1972]: 462-67). Raoul Carton, *L'expérience mystique de l'illumination intérieure chêz Roger Bacon* (Paris, 1924); idem, *La synthèse doctrinale de Roger Bacon*, (Paris, 1924); Theodore Crowley, *Roger Bacon, the Problem of the Soul in his Philosophical Commentaries* (Louvain, 1950); and D. E. Sharp, *Franciscan Philosophy*, BSFS 16(Oxford, 1930) are still valuable.

On Robert Grosseteste, see Francis S. Stevenson, *Robert Grosseteste: Bishop of Lincoln* (London, 1899); D. Callus, ed., *Robert Grosseteste: Scholar and Bishop* (Oxford, 1955); S. Harrison Thomson, *The Writings of Robert Grosseteste, Bishop of Lincoln, 1235-1253* (Cambridge, Eng., 1940); and Sharp, *Franciscan Philosophy*, pp. 9-46. See also Servus Gieben, "Bibliographia universa Roberti Grosseteste ab an. 1473 ad an. 1969," *Collectanea franciscana* 39(1969):362-418; and idem, "Robert Grosseteste at the Papal Curia, Lyons 1250, editions of the documents," ibid., 41(1971):340-93.

A. G. Little, *The Grey Friars at Oxford* (Oxford, 1892), pp. 134-39; and E. d'Alencon, "Adam de Marisco," *DTC* 1, pt. 1:387, treat the life of Adam Marsh. These accounts are based on Thomas of Eccleston, *Tractatus de aduentu fratrum minorum in Angliam*, ed A.G. Little (Manchester, 1951). Only Adam's letters have survived, ed. J. S. Brewer, *Monumenta franciscana, RS* 4, pt. 1:77-489.

On Ramon Llull's life and his missionary theory, see P. Otto Keicher, *Raymundus Lull und seine Stellung zur arabischen Philosophie*, Beiträge zur Geschichte der Philosophie und Theologie des Mittelalters, 7, pts. 4-5(Münster, 1909); Adam Gottron, *Ramon Lulls Kreuzzugsideen* (Berlin & Leipzig, 1912); Gundisalvo Valls, "L'ideale missionario del b. Raimondo Lullo, terziario francescano martire a Pugia (Africa) 1315," S.F. n.s. 12(23)(1926):117-28; J. W. Probst, "Lull, mystique pour l'action," in *Miscellanea lulliana, Estudis franciscans* 47(1935):436-45; E. Allison Peers, *Ramon Lull: A Biography* (London, 1929); Ramon Sugranyes de Franch, "Ramon Llull, docteur des missions," *Studia monographica et recensiores* 5(1951):3-44; idem, "Els projectes de creuada enla doctrina missional de Ramon Llull," *Estudios lulianos* 4(1960): 275-90; Armand Llinares, *Raymond Lulle: philosophe de l'action* (Paris, 1963); J. N. Hillgarth, *Ramon Lull and Lullism in Fourteenth-Century France* (Oxford, 1971); and Robert I. Burns, *Christian-Islamic Confrontation*, pp. 1398-400.

The most complete exposition of Llull's mysticism is contained in his *Llibre de contemplacio*, the Catalan version edited in *Obres de Ramon Llull*, 7 vols. (Barcelona, 1906-14), the Latin version in the *Beati Raymundi Lulli . . . opera*, ed. Ivo Salzinger, 8 vols. (Mainz, (1721-42). The *Llibre* is analyzed by Peers, *Ramon Lull*, pp. 43-81 and by Llinares, *Raymond Lulle*, pp. 368-92. On the relationship between Llull's mysticism and his desire to convert the infidels see Sugranyes de Franch, *Ramon Lull* pp. 7-12, 29.

Llull outlined his program in a number of treatises, among which are his *Epistola*, addressed to the Univerity of Paris, in H. Denifle and A. Chatelain, eds. *Chartularium uniuersitatis parisiensis*, 2, pt. 1 (Paris, 1891):83-84.

V.

Apocalyptic Conversion

From the publication of Fr. Gerard of Borgo San Donnino's *Liber introductorius in euangelium eternum* (1254) until the condemnation of Fr. Peter John Olivi's *Lectura super apocalipsim* (1322), the adherence of some of the Franciscans to Abbot Joachim's Apocalypticism was a source of controversy within and outside the Order.

The term *Joachite* was first employed by the chronicler, Fr. Salimbene of Parma to designate those individuals who accepted and developed Joachim's three-*status* historical scheme. This definition must be retained.[1] While men like Roger Bacon and St. Bonaventure may have been influenced by Joachim's thought, they cannot properly be called Joachites.

The expectation of the final conversion of the Jews after the entrance of the fullness of the Gentiles into the faith existed independently of Joachitism—it was a tradition that went back to St. Paul himself. Thus, where the Joachite program as a whole might not find acceptance, the expectation of apocalyptic conversion might well be current. For example, about 1204-05, an anonymous monk of Bamberg wrote the *De seminibus scripturarum* in which he explained the development of history in terms of the Hebrew, Greek and Latin alphabets, alloting a century to each letter. Associating the first letter of the Latin alphabet with the foundation of Rome and proceeding from there, he placed his own century under the letter "x"; during this period of time, he believed, Christ would reform the church. In the following century, designated by "y," the achievement of the *plenitudo gentium* and the conversion of all Israel would result in universal peace before the onslaught of antichrist and the end of the world.[2]

St. Bonaventure's reference to the final conversion of Israel in his *Collationes in Hexaëmeron* appears to be traditional.³ And while Robert Grosseteste did have some acquaintance with Joachim's writings, his belief in the final conversion of the Jews was apparently not influenced by them. In a letter to Innocent IV, Adam Marsh wrote that missionary preaching must be continued until the *plenitudo gentium* be converted; yet his only interest in Joachim was as a prophet of the imminent appearance of antichrist.⁴ In the fourteenth century, Fr. Paschalis de Victoria referred to Jesus' promise that the consummation of the age would only come when the gospel had been preached throughout the entire world (Mt. 24:14). No evidence connects him with the Joachites.⁵

The Joachite program made ample use of traditional beliefs, lending them fresh vitality and significance. The expectation of apocalyptic conversion of non-Christians took on a sense of imminence for those who accepted Joachim's interpretation of history.

Between 1248 and 1250, Alexander of Bremen, a Franciscan, wrote a commentary on Revelation in which he employed a twofold *concordia*, resembling that of Joachim's two ages. He was familiar with the pseudo-Joachim commentary on Jeremiah and quoted a series of texts from it which he regarded as prophecies of the appearance of the Franciscan and Dominican orders. This would suggest that the *Expositio super Hieremiam* stimulated Franciscan interest in Joachim by relating the two transitional orders of *uiri spirituales* to the mendicants.⁶ Alexander cannot be classified as an Early Franciscan Joachite, however, since he ignored the three-*status* scheme.

The most prominent member of the Early Franciscan Joachites was Fr. John of Parma, Minister General from 1247 through 1257. Fr. Hugh of Digne, who had taken an important role in the development of the Order in the early 1240s, was also a member. Our source of information about these Joachites is Fr. Salimbene of Parma. He too was a Joachite, well acquainted with both John and Hugh, and he devoted considerable space to them in his Chronicle. The black sheep of the group was Gerard of Borgo San Donnino whose *Liber introductorius* only managed to attract notoriety for himself, John of Parma, and Joachim himself. Also included in this group were Bartolomaeus Guiscolus, a *socius* of Gerard, and Rudolph of Saxony, a lector at Pisa, but neither of them is much more than a name.[7]

One is obliged at this point to ask how and where John of Parma, Hugh of Digne, and Gerard of Borgo San Donnino were introduced to Joachitism. Salimbene recounts his own introduction to Joachim's writings during Salimbene's stay at Pisa (1243-1247). An abbot of a Florensian Monastery fearing that the Emperor Frederick II would destroy the monastery, gathered up all the copies of Joachim's writings in his possession and deposited them in the Franciscan convent at Pisa. Rudolph of Saxony, a lector at this convent, subsequently became immersed in studying them. This has been cited as the start of Franciscan Joachitism, but Salimbene's account suggests that he was speaking only of his own career. Rudolph is otherwise unknown and none of the other Joachites had known links with Pisa.[8]

There is a significant amount of circumstantial evidence, however, pointing to Southern Italy and Sicily as a more likely area for the development of Franciscan Joachitism, particularly the vicinity of Naples. Gerard was en route from his native Sicily to study in Paris when Salimbene first encountered him in 1248. Gerard had been sent by that province to Paris in company with Bartolomaeus Guiscolus, apparently a former guardian at the convent in Capua. Salimbene tells us that they had with them the *Expositio super Hieremiam* and tried to persuade him to accept their interpretation of Joachim.[9] At Hyères in 1248, Salimbene met two more Joachites from the convent at Naples who had come to visit Hugh of Digne. At this same time, two Dominicans came to Hyères and entered into a discussion with Hugh about Joachim—they had read his writings in Naples.[10] John of Parma had been a lector in Naples for some years prior to 1245 when he was summoned to Paris after the deaths of Alexander of Hales and John de la Rochelle, the holders of the Franciscan chairs in theology. He was chosen Minister General in 1247. He was certainly a Joachite by 1248. It is, of course, possible that his introduction to Joachim occurred at Paris, but in light of our other information, it is more probable that it did in fact take place in Naples.[11]

Salimbene apparently first met Hugh of Digne in Siena in 1242 or 1243, but in his Chronicle he says only that Hugh discussed the glory of paradise and contempt of the world. Hugh's *Expositio super regulam,* written in 1240 or 1241, contains no evidence of Joachitism.[12] Yet, by 1248 Hugh's cell was a well-known center for the discussion of Joachim's writings. Hugh apparently became a Joachite sometime after 1243, but how this occurred cannot be ascertained.[13] Hugh's *Expositio* is purely Franciscan in its commentary on chapter twelve of the *Regula bullata,* but since the work probably antedates his adoption of Joachitism, he may well have altered his views later.

Gerard's *Liber introductorius* is lost but excerpts survive, as do some of his glosses on Joachim's writings. Gerard interpreted Joachim radically, arguing that his writings were themselves the *euangelium eternum* and that Joachim was the angel "indutus . . . lineis" (Dan. 12:7). The Holy Spirit had given this eternal gospel to the angel of the sixth seal, St. Francis, whose friars would be the monks of the third *status.* The New Testament and the clergy would be supplanted by this gospel and its bearers. Gerard's interpretation of Matthew 24:14 was unique. According to him the *euangelium Christi* had already been preached to all the nations but the consummation of the world had not yet come. He concluded, therefore, that the *euangelium regni* was the eternal gospel, not the New Testament.[14]

Gerard also adopted the hostility of the *Super Hieremiam* toward the Crusade. Salimbene declares that when he met Gerard and Bartolomaeus in Provence in 1248 they employed the *Super Hieremiam* to ridicule the expedition that was about to depart and to forecast its failure—even the capture of Louis IX at Damietta in 1250. Since Salimbene does not state which passages were cited by Gerard, it is impossible to determine precisely the reasons for their prophecy.[15]

Like Gerard, Salimbene believed firmly that Joachim had prophesied the appearance of the Franciscan and Dominican orders. Furthermore, he was convinced that Joachim had understood God's plan in history. While he did become more cautious when Frederick II died before he had accomplished the deeds that the *Super Hieremiam* ascribed to him, he was obviously very strongly influenced by this commentary. His interpretation of Joachim is far more moderate than was Gerard's, however. Salimbene believed that God had called St. Francis to reform the church and that the *uita franciscana* was the penitent life according to the model established by Christ and his apostles. The friars were the scriptural *paruuli*, the humble whom God would use to demonstrate the foolishness of worldly wisdom. Whereas Gerard substituted the *status* of the Holy Spirit and its eternal gospel for the *status* of the Petrine church and the New Testament, Salimbene adhered firmly to a christocentric understanding of Joachim.[16]

Salimbene does not say what he thought about Gerard's prediction that St. Louis's Crusade would fail. But his own attitude toward the Crusade was clearly derived from Joachim: the Crusade was opposed to God's plan because the year 1260 had already passed. It was now time for the Greeks to be reunited to the Latin church, for the Gentiles to be converted, and for the Jews to become Christian. He compared Gregory X to Josiah, the King of Judah, a holy ruler taken by death in mid-reign. In bringing the Greeks to the Second Council of Lyons (1274) and there achieving an end to the schism, Gregory had succeeded because the time was right; but because his imperial and crusading plans were contrary to God's will, his death in 1276 left them frustrated.

Salimbene cites Joachim as the source for his use of the year 1260 and as his authority for certain texts that supported his belief in the imminent healing of the schism and the conversion of the Gentiles and the Jews. The pseudo-Joachite *Super Hieremiam* was the authority for his belief that the *imperium* had been abolished. As far as Salimbene was concerned, the time of the third *status* had already begun, possibly with the flagellant movements that appeared in 1260. The Crusade was past. Greeks, Jews, and Gentiles were to be brought together in the one faith in order to achieve the unity characteristic of the third *status*.[17]

Although Salimbene was a Franciscan, he did not fuse his Joachitism with the ideology of his Order. In fact, he did not even assign the Franciscans a role in the realization of the unity and peace of the third *status*. It is possible that the first steps in this direction were taken by John of Parma and Hugh of Digne, but lack of evidence makes this unprovable. Gerard on the other hand clearly saw the Franciscans as the agents of the third *status*, but his notoriety makes it unlikely that he was influential.

According to Salimbene, it was John of Parma's Joachitism that induced him to resign as Minister General in 1257. Angelo Clareno says that John was later tried before his successor, St. Bonaventure, and saved from imprisonment only by the intervention of Cardinal Ottobonus Fliscus (later Pope Hadrian V). However, Angelo's account cannot be taken without question.

In the last quarter of the thirteenth century, two rather loosely organized parties emerged among the friars in Provence and Italy, usually known as the Spirituals and the Conventuals. They were divided on the issue of poverty. The Order's convents, clothing, food, and other "belongings" were legally owned by the papacy; the friars simply used them. This device enabled the friars to make use of their various necessities without having to claim ownership of them. The Conventuals seem to have relied on this legal fiction as a sufficient fulfillment of the vow of poverty and the commands of the Rule, and they were flexible in admitting the use of property or goods. The Spirituals insisted on the *usus pauper*. Legal renunciation was insufficient unless the friars also restricted their use to those things which were truly necessary. Whatever seemed to be too luxurious or abundant was, accordingly, a violation of the Rule.

There were three separate groups of Spirituals, one located in Provence, another in Tuscany, and a third in the March of Ancona.[18] The leader of the Provençal Spirituals was Peter John Olivi (1248/49-1298). The Tuscans' spokesman was Ubertino da Casale, a disciple of Olivi and link between the two groups. The March of Ancona Spirituals were led by Peter of Macerata (known as Liberato) and the chronicler Peter Fossembrone, better known by his later name of Angelo Clareno. Angelo's obvious hostility toward St. Bonaventure, derived from a tradition current in the Spirituals of the March of Ancona, distorted a hearing at which John cleared himself of some accusations regarding Joachitism in such a fashion that it became a full-fledged trial. The hearing seems to have been, therefore, simply an attempt to clear John, so that he could continue to serve the Order. Finally, John retired to a hermitage at Greccio, lived there until 1288 or 1289, then set out for Greece, and died en route. Angelo's account has been one reason for the accepted view that St. Bonaventure was moderate Conventual, but there is considerable evidence to show that Hugh of Digne, John of Parma, and St. Bonaventure shared similar views on learning and poverty. Since Bonaventure adapted Joachim's schemes of double seven, it is apparent that he had an interest in Joachim, although he cannot be called a Joachite as Hugh and John apparently were. History has tended to link the Spiritual point of view with John and Hugh, and the Conventual with St. Bonaventure; but if our perspective on Bonaventure's position vis-à-vis his predecessor as Minister General is altered, then we must necessarily reevaluate his role in the succeeding struggle.[19] Bonaventure attempted with considerable success to continue John's policies as Minister General. Peter John Olivi was in some measure a disciple of St. Bonaventure. To describe Bonaventure as a Spiritual would be fallacious, but until further studies clarify his position, he must be viewed with an open mind.

The origins of the controversy in Provence are obscure. Until 1292 the dispute centered around Olivi himself and appears to have involved neither poverty nor Joachitism but theological issues. Olivi had studied at Paris under John Pecham and Matthew of Aquasparta and had heard St. Bonaventure himself. In 1279 he participated in the discussions prior to the issuing of Pope Nicholas III's bull "Exit Qui seminat." At papal suggestion, Matthew of Aquasparta assigned Olivi as lector to Florence (1287-1289) and Raymond Gaufridi sent him to Montpellier. By the time of his death, Olivi had a considerable following among the friars and the Béguins in Provence and evidence indicates that some of them were punished for accepting his views. Olivi himself satisfied the Chapter General of Paris by his agreement to "Exit" and by his statements, but after his death controversy broke out again, culminating in the condemnation of his commentary on Revelation (1326). Ubertino argued that it was Olivi's zeal for the *usus pauper* that really motivated his opponents though they did not dare to attack it openly. But the posthumous attacks on Olivi were undoubtedly aimed at his disciples who until 1316 were treating his tomb as a shrine.

Olivi created a genuine fusion between Franciscan eschatology and the *Geschichtestheologie* of Joachim. He described the period between the incarnation of Christ and the end of the world as the *tempus ecclesie*, dividing it into seven *status ecclesie*, or ages of the church. The second of Joachim's three *status* began with the incarnation and coincided with the first five *status ecclesie*; Joachim's third and last *status* was to coincide with the six and seventh *status ecclesie*. In his commentary on Revelation Olivi placed most of his emphasis on these seven *status ecclesie*, possibly because of their exegetical correspondence to the sevens in Revelation, more likely because they served his understanding of history better than Joachim's *status generales*. The latter's trinitarian thrust had in fact lent itself to radical interpretation in Gerard's hands. Gerard had believed that the church of the christological *status* would be superceded by the new order of the *status* of the Holy Spirit. Olivi, however, firmly maintained the preeminence of Christ throughout the sixth and seventh *status*.[20]

In each of the stages of the church's history, Olivi saw a pattern of persecution leading to the triumph of the faithful over their tormentors. He designated the fifth *status* as a period of *condescensiua*. It had begun with Charlemagne and during its course the church permitted mitigation of the evangelical life for the sake of those Christians who could not attain the strict life of Christ and his apostles. The result was laxity among the religious and the clerics. Heresy reappeared in the Cathari (called Manichaeans by Olivi) and the Waldensians. In the thirteenth century, the introduction of philosophical paganism among the doctors at Paris added another element to the emerging carnal church, the rise of which would culminate in the mystical and great antichrists. Their downfall would bring an end to the fifth *status*.[21] When Olivi wrote his *Postilla super Apocalypsim* in 1297, neither of the antichrists had appeared—at least not openly—but he believed that the sixth *status* had already begun, thus overlapping the fifth. Although Olivi admitted that the *status euangelice renouationis* had had varied initial points— Joachim as its prophet, the conversion of St. Francis, and the persecution of the Spiritual Franciscans by the Conventuals to name three—he placed his emphasis on Francis's conversion in 1206. As the angel of the sixth seal, Francis was not only an Elijah but also the embodiment of the mystical advent of Christ, particularly of the crucified Christ, as confirmed by the stigmata. By founding the Order and by giving it his *Regula*, Francis had initiated that *euangelicus ordo* or *ecclesia spiritualis* which by 1297 had already begun to renew the evangelical life in its perfect form. Although Olivi did not place much emphasis on St. Dominic, it should be noted that he and the *Odro fratrum predicatorum* were also part of this *reunouatio*.²² At the end of the thirteenth century, the members of the evangelical order were still few in number and were being subjected to increasing persecution by the carnal church. Olivi saw this persecution in the attacks by the secular doctors and clergy on the mendicants occurring at Paris and elsewhere, and the efforts of the Conventuals to repress the Spirituals and relax the observance of the Rule.²³ Yet, despite its sufferings the evangelical order had won support among the laymen and begun to preach the gospel to the infidels and the Jews—often incurring martyrdom but converting some unbelievers. Eschatologically, the mendicant missions were moving toward the entrance of the *plenitudo gentium* into the faith.

> [St. Francis] . . . placed his right foot upon the sea (see Rev. 10:2), because moved by intense desire and fervor, he sought to go to the Saracens, in order to convert them and to receive martyrdom at their hands. As the angel of the sixth seal (Rev. 7:2), he set out in the sixth year after his conversion [1212], signifying thus that the Saracens would be converted in the sixth *status* of the church by means of his *ordo*. [He went] again in the thirteenth year from his conversion [1219] as a sign that in the thirteenth century after the passion and resurrection of Christ, the Saracens and other infidels would begin to be converted by his *ordo*, many of the members of which would be martyred.²⁴

Olivi, following the apostle Paul's argument in Romans, designated the whole of the first *status ecclesie* as the *tempus plenitudinis gentium*—or as the second *status generalis*. The conversion of most of the infidels, however, would take place only after the fall of the great antichrist and the carnal church. The entrance of the *plenitudo gentium* would be followed by the salvation of the Jews, so that the *euangelicus ordo* would achieve virtual universality at the threshold of the seventh *status ecclesie*.²⁵

This "apotheosis of history" would be an age of peace, fulfilling Isaiah's promise that "they shall beat their swords into plowshares and their spears into pruning hooks" (Isa. 2:4). The principal characteristic, however, in Olivi's view was interior peace.

For as in the first time God the father had revealed himself as terrible and fearsome, so that fear of him appeared, thus in the second [time] God the son had shown himself as teacher, revealer and as the expressed word of the wisdom of his father. In the third time, therefore, the Holy Spirit will show himself as flame and as a furnace of divine love, a wine-cellar of spiritual inebriation ... a pharmacist of divine aromatics, spiritual ointments and salves and a tripod of spiritual jubilation and joys, by whom the entire truth of the wisdom of the word of God incarnate and the might of God the father will be seen not only through understanding alone but also through tastable and palpable experience.[26]

This period would see the faithful ascend to that "excess of contemplation in which the mind, separated and resting in God, tastes his ineffable sweetness and peace which obliterates all sense awareness."[27]

The mystical attainment of the seventh *status* would be anticipated in the sixth when the members of the *euangelicus ordo* would be given the *spiritualis intelligentia;* this would enable them to understand the secrets of the Scriptures, to preach them so that they would penetrate the hearts of their listeners, and to open the unbelievers' hearts that they might believe in Christ and fulfill his law. The conversion of the *plenitudo gentium* and of all Israel would be a consequence of the renewal of evangelical perfection and the gift of the Holy Spirit.[28]

Thus, Olivi's concept of mission was at once Franciscan and Joachite. He insisted upon the christological and evangelical character of the *renouatio ecclesie* but saw this renewal of the perfection of the primitive church as the initial stage of a final *status* of universal peace and mystical contemplation. Martyrdom, conformity to the passion of Christ, and spiritual understanding were to characterize the spiritual church.

Olivi saw the incipient apocalyptic conversion of non-Christians as a motivation of the Franciscan missionaries. Commenting on the beginning of the twelfth chapter of the *Regula bullata*, Olivi stated that this section showed the "superabundant and supererogative fruit and end for which ... this order is erected higher than all the other orders of the church of God. This end is the drawing not only of the faithful but also of the *uniuersitas* of the infidels to Christ. On this account the friars ought to offer and expose themselves among unbelievers to every martyrdom and pilgrimage." When Francis wrote that "quincumque fratrum . . . uoluerint ire inter Saracenos et alios infideles," Olivi commented that this was written not only "concessiue, set etiam consultiue seu indicatiue aut etiam prophetice," for just as the apostles had been sent first to the Jews and then to the Gentiles, so the Franciscan Order in the sixth *status* had been sent, first to the Latins, and then to the nations of the unbelievers so that the *plenitudo gentium* might enter and all Israel be converted.[29] Olivi believed that the friars' first concern should be the conversion of the Muslims and other non-Christians; this was the means by which the friars could perform their role in the renewal of evangelical perfection and the consummation of history. Olivi reminded them that the sixth *status* was not some distant, future age but had already begun with St. Francis. The struggle with the carnal church and the achievement of universal peace were imminent.

In effect, Olivi formulated a second recension of Joachim's concept of apocalyptic conversion. Rather than the monastic orders which the Calabrian abbot had envisioned, the agents would be the members of the *euangelicus ordo.* This shift was clearly the result of Olivi's recasting Joachitism within a Franciscan framework; his combination of *renouatio* and the historical movement from the second to the third *status generalis* emphasized the *imitatio Christi,* poverty, and humility as the means by which the *euangelicus ordo* would convert the great mass of infidels and Jews in order to realize the final age of outer peace and inner contemplation.

Olivi's personal influence was widespread in the last decade of the thirteenth century and in the first quarter of the fourteenth. It penetrated the courts of the Aragonese crown, especially the circle of Philip of Majorca.[30] In Provence and Catalonia the lay Béguins regarded him as a saint and were profoundly influenced by his teachings. His *Postilla super apocalypsim* was regarded as the authoritative key to the understanding of scripture and history. An anonymous disciple of Olivi, writing c. 1315 to 1318, composed a treatise which he entitled *De statibus ecclesie secundum expositionem apocalypsis.* It was a collection of extracts from the *Postilla* translated into Catalan so that the Béguins could read it. The *De statibus* is known to us through the articles abstracted from it between 1318 and 1321 at the order of Pope John XXII. According to article 24, the *De statibus* asserted that the "Saracens and other infidels ought to be converted by the spiritual Friars minor in this sixth time, namely in the thirteenth century, computing this from the passion of Christ, which rightly will be within fifteen years."[3] [1]

The influence of Olivi extended, at least briefly, to Greater Armenia in conjunction with the Spiritual-Conventual controversy. In 1274, a rumor had circulated that Pope Gregory X was going to decree that the mendicant orders would have to hold property just as the monastic orders did. The rumor was false; but some of the friars in the March of Ancona protested and as a result of the ensuing debate, Thomas of Tolentino, Liberato, and Traymundus were deprived of their habits and detained in hermitages. Later, they were imprisoned along with Angelo Clareno, perpetually, without the sacraments or books. They were released only in 1289 when Raymond Gaufridi examined their case and sent them as missionaries in response to a request from King Het'um II of Armenia. They worked successfully with the king, and he later became a Franciscan; but their opponents pursued them from Syria and the friars returned to Italy in 1294. At this time, Pope Celestine V freed them from their obedience to the Order and allowed them to assume the name "The Poor Hermits of Pope Celestine." When he abdicated at the end of that year to resume an eremetic life, they feared a hostile reception from Pope Boniface VIII and fled to the island of Trixonia in the Gulf of Corinth. Boniface was told that they maintained the view that Celestine was still pope and took action against them; but they succeeded in getting to Thessaly. They again returned to Italy to 1304 and 1305 to seek out Pope Clement V, and he agreed to protect them until the issue could be decided.

In 1309 Clement established a commission to examine the controversy; Ubertino da Casale successfully represented the Spirituals, and the pope used the Council of Vienne to settle the issue of Olivi's theology—by stating the church's stand on certain points without mentioning Olivi at all. He took up the *usus pauper* and the dispute over observance of the Rule in his Bull "Exivi de paradiso," issued on November 20, 1312. This the Spirituals regarded as a statement of their position. However, upon Clement's death, the controversy reopened. Pope John XXII enforced obedience to the Order on the Spirituals in Provence and had some of them put to death. Nevertheless, Ubertino and Angelo were allowed to separate from the Order.

Almost immediately another dispute was touched off. At issue was the poverty of Christ and the apostles, a doctrine that formed the biblical foundation of Franciscan poverty. And this time the Conventuals were forced to defend themselves against the pope and the Dominicans. When John XXII ruled against the Franciscan position in 1326, the Minister General, Michael of Cesena, opposed the pope and fled to the protection of the Emperor Lewis of Bavaria, who was himself locked in conflict with John. Fr. Geraldus Odo was chosen to replace Michael in 1329 by the majority of the Order who remained obedient to the pope.[32] Three years later, Geraldus answered a request from Archbishop Zacharias, an Armenian uniate, by sending a party of friars to that area. Guilelmus Saurati and his companions settled at the monastery of Zorsor late in 1332 and won the archbishop's favor. By July of 1333, Guilelmus was lecturing on *The Gospel According to St. Matthew,* following closely the commentary on that book by Peter John Olivi. At this time he wrote a letter to Fr. Rainerius di Firenze, vicar of the Vice-Custody of Tabriz, requesting that Rainerius send him a copy of Olivi's *Postilla super apocalypsim.*

From the letter written by Fr. Giorgio di Adria in response to Guilelmus's request, we learn that there were disagreements among the followers of Peter John Olivi in Tabriz. Giorgio himself was inclined to side with Michael of Cesena and to see in Pope John the antichrist or one of the heads of the dragon. But there was another friar in this group who believed that the Order would be divided into three parts and that the true disciples of St. Francis would gather in the East in order to work for the conversion of the Muslims. These friars came into conflict over property with the Dominicans in Tabriz who instituted a process against them at Avignon in 1334.

Another Tabriz friar, Giovanni di Firenze, wrote to Guilelmus about the same time that Fr. Giorgio dispatched his letter. He mentioned news from France about a rumored alliance between the kings of France, England, Bohemia, the Emperor Lewis, and the anti-pope—a Franciscan named Pietro di Corbara—and revealed intense concern about the imminence of the appearance of antichrist. "There are not a few nor unimportant matters about which I should ask concerning these last times, which appear to have begun already." He then asked a series of questions about antichrist and suggested that this figure might be Pietro di Corbara, the dragon, and the Emperor Lewis, the beast. He spoke of his fears about the false Friars minor, a greater danger in his opinion even than antichrist. He thought that, according to Olivi, the final conversion of the schismatic Greeks and Saracens ought to begin in 1333 but, while Olivi had predicted that the Franciscans would be the agents, the Dominicans seemed to be accomplishing more than the Friars minor. He wondered why the conversion of the Greeks and Muslims should occur simultaneously with the appearance of antichrist. Was it to occur so that the converts would be perverted by his errors?[33]

Since our sources are extremely scanty, it is difficult to know how many Spirituals there were or what views they held, but certainly Olivi's commentaries had created excitement and tension in this small group in Armenia and Persia. With mixed hopes and fears, they waited for news from the West about the struggle between Pope John XXII, the Emperor, the anti-pope, and Michael of Cesena.

Although the Béguins seem to have been suppressed and, apart from the brief glimpse in the records of 1332-1334, Guilelmus and the Spirituals are unknown, Olivi's writings and his recension of the Joachite tradition of apocalyptic conversion remained influential. St. Bernardino of Siena, the Observant theologian of the fifteenth century, read widely in the works of Peter John, including the *Postilla super apocalypsim,* and frequently quoted from them, without, however, using Olivi's name.[34]

Perhaps the most important propagator of Olivi was his defender at the curia, Ubertino da Casale. Between 1287 and 1289 he had attended the lectures of Peter John at Santa Croce in Florence. In 1304, his superiors sent him into retirement in the solitude of Mount Alverna where he wrote his *Arbor uitae crucifixae Iesu,* completed on September 22, 1305. It became one of the most important mystical and devotional books produced by the Franciscans. Its intensity of feeling is in some passages almost poetic. Dante paraphrased parts of it in the *Divine Comedy.*[35] The first four books are an exposition based on the life of Jesus Christ from his eternal origin as the Son to his ascension. Book Five covers the history of the church as the realization of Christ's mystical body, culminating in the *renouatio* of the sixth *status ecclesie* and the felicity of the millennial seventh *status,* both of which Ubertino, like Olivi, equated with the third *status generalis.* Much of this book is a summary, often by literal borrowing, from Olivi's commentary on Revelation and the disciple follows his master faithfully.[36] Ubertino believed that a prominent part of the work of the *euangelicus ordo* would be the apocalyptic conversion of non-Christians. The time for missionary work was the present. The conversion of the *plenitudo gentium* had to be consummated so that all Israel might be saved.[37] Because of its moving mystical devotion, the *Arbor uitae* was widely read in the fourteenth, fifteenth, and sixteenth centuries. Surviving manuscripts are especially numerous in Spain and the Low Countries. A manuscript preserved at the University of Valencia formerly belonged to Ferdinand of Aragon, Duke of Calabria. Another manuscript now at Salamanca contains a translation of the *Arbor uitae* into Castilian which was made by Alonso Ortiz on the order of Queen Isabella the Catholic. In 1404 Martin of Aragon requested that Benedict XIII send a copy of it to Valencia for translation into Catalan. In the Low Countries manuscripts survive in Latin and parts of the work are preserved in Flemish translations.[38] St. Bernardino of Siena was well read in the *Arbor uitae* and it was popular among the Observants. Ubertino's work was published at Venice in 1485.[39] One copy, now in the Library of Congress, was read and extensively annotated in Segovia in the sixteenth century.[40]

The relationship of Angelo Clareno, who ultimately became the leader and spokesman for the Spirituals from the March of Ancona, to Peter John Olivi is not clear. They agreed fully on the strict observance of the *Regula* regarding poverty, but on eschatology there appears to have been a considerable difference between them. Despite his division of the history of the Franciscan Order into seven tribulations, Angelo's *Historia septem tribulationum* treated St. Francis within the context of a *renouatio,* which is Franciscan, not Joachite. And while his commentary on the twelfth chapter of the *Regula bullata* is genuinely Franciscan, he abruptly introduces the crucial Joachite text from Olivi's *Expositio super regulam,* quoting it in full. His commentary on this text is, to say the least, enigmatic.

He refers to Joachim's own *Expositio* on the angel of the sixth seal, rightly pointing out that Joachim interpreted this angel as a *pontifex* or pope under whom the church would be restored (*innouare*); time would be given for preaching to the Gentiles and Jews; and all the elect would be marked on their faces with the sign of the living God. Angelo next asserts that the promises made to St. Francis would be fulfilled in the elect, but that only those who truly belonged to the Spiritual Israel would be saved. Angelo seems to be suggesting that Olivi's commentary might lead some to believe otherwise.[41]

Herbert Grundmann's hypothesis that Angelo was the author of the series of papal prophecies which circulated under the name of Anselm of Marsico, if correct, would posit another difference between Olivi and Angelo. The papal prophecies end with a series of angelic popes who were to reform the church and initiate the final *status*. If Angelo was the author of these prophecies, then he had replaced the *euangelicus ordo* with these holy popes. Grundmann's attribution, however, rests principally on the fact that Angelo knew Greek and had done translations from Greek into Latin, and the papal prophecies were principally Latin versions of the Byzantine Leo-oracles. Angelo could have been the author or translator, but his genuine works offer no proof that he was, since nowhere in them does he look for the coming of such angelic popes.[42] It is necessary, therefore, to distinguish Angelo from Olivi and Ubertino and, although he was conversant with Olivi's Joachitism, to classify him among those who maintained the Franciscan understanding of mission.

Whether Angelo did or did not play a role in the introduction of the notion of a series of angelic popes, these figures came to play an important role in Joachitism during the last decade of the thirteenth century and the first decade of the fourteenth. Of course, this period included the resignation of Pope Celestine V and his succession by Pope Boniface VIII, a controversial affair further complicated by Boniface's revocation of his predecessor's acts. Thus placed in the position of being schismatics, some of the Spirituals of the March were led to denounce Boniface as uncanonical. So the sudden popularity of prophecies regarding angelic popes needs little explanation. The dispute between Pope Boniface and King Philip IV of France merely introduced politics into a situation where the papacy had become prominent in the minds of those who sought to under-stand their times apocalyptically.

The first unmistakable appearance of the angelic pope is in the works of Roger Bacon. In his *Opus tertium* Bacon cited an anony-mous prophet who predicted that an angelic pope would reform the church, reunite the Greeks with the Latin Christians, convert the Tartars, and destroy the power of the Saracens.[43] In his *Compen-dium studii philosophiae,* Bacon stated that such a pope might renew the whole world so that the *plenitudo gentium* would enter the faith and the Jews be converted.[44] The *Oraculum angelicum Cyrilli,* written by an anonymous Joachite between 1280 and 1300, spoke of a future pope, described as an "ursus mirabilis," who would, among other things, rebuke the corrupt religious orders.[45]

The development of a series of such popes, however, was the work of the Catalan Joachite, Arnau de Vilanova (1238-1311). Like his contemporary, Ramon Llull, Arnau was a layman, but he had studied in a Dominican *studium,* learning Hebrew under the friar, Ramon Martí. Arnau was educated in medicine at the University of Montpellier and served both Jaime II of Aragon and his father as physician. He later taught at that university between 1289 and 1299. In 1289 Peter John Olivi became a *lector* at the Franciscan *studium* in Montpellier; it was probably he who introduced Arnau to the Spiritual Franciscans' concept of the evangelical life and to Joachit-ism. Arnau's earliest theological works date from 1292 and indicate that he had been strongly influenced by the *De seminibus scriptur-arum,* a work which he believed to have been written by Joachim himself.[46] In 1299 Jaime II sent Arnau to Paris on a diplomatic mission to the court of Philip IV. Arnau took the opportunity to present his *Tractatus de tempore de aduentu antichristi,* the first part of which he had composed in 1297, to the theologians of the University of Paris. The *Tractatus* stirred up a controversy that lasted into the second decade of the fourteenth century.[47] When his work was condemned, Arnau turned to Pope Boniface VIII, winning his favor by his medical skills. During the remainder of his life, Arnau journeyed between the courts of Jaime II and Frederick III of Sicily (Jaime's younger brother) and to Avignon, where he secured the favor of Pope Clement V. Arnau's diplomacy persuaded Jaime II, Frederick III, and King Robert of Naples to intercede with Pope

Clement V on behalf of the Spirituals in 1309.[48] He also wrote a series of treatises for the Béguins in Catalan and some of his works have survived in Italian translations.[49]

Arnau believed that the universe was in its old age and the medicine which had served the ancient Greek physicians was, therefore, inadequate to heal a decayed humanity. A new medicine was urgently needed in order to restore mankind to its youthfulness just as a reformation of the church and of the universe itself was to be expected.[50] Arnau, like Olivi, combined the three *status generales* with the seven *status ecclesie*. The thousand years during which Satan would be bound and the church free had begun in the time of the Emperor Constantine and would come to an end in the fourteenth century with the final struggle against antichrist. Arnau differed from Olivi in believing that the sixth *status* of the church had not yet begun, but was imminent. It would see the greatest ruin of the church, tribulations of the faithful culminating in the coming of antichrist, and the reformation of the church to the evangelical life and truth of the apostolic *status* by a series of evangelical popes. Arnau, influenced by the *De seminibus scripturarum*, expected all this to be consummated during the fourteenth century. He believed that, after the defeat and death of antichrist, the seventh *status* of rest and peace for the reformed church would ensue in a renewed world.[51]

Arnau viewed the mendicant friars and especially the Spirituals and their disciples, the Béguins, as examples of that evangelical life to which the church needed to be recalled, but he looked to a series of five popes to accomplish this, the fifth being the angelic pope himself under whom the reformation of the church would be completed and antichrist overcome.

Arnau combined elements derived from Ramon Martí and the Dominican program of philosophic conversion, especially its concern for the study of languages, with the Joachite tradition of apocalyptic conversion. He expected one part of the seventh *status* to be the realization of the full number of the elect. The fourteenth century was to be the time of the conversion of the *plenitudo gentium*. Thus, Arnau tried to persuade his royal patrons and Clement V to establish schools in which the evangelical life and diverse missionary languages would be taught.[52] His *Informació espiritual*, written for and partly implemented by Frederick III, included plans for the conversion of the Saracens in Sicily.[53]

The reunion of the Greek and Latin churches was one of the signs of the coming of antichrist that remained to be fulfilled.[54] In his *Informació espiritual* he urged that the Greeks in Sicily be treated favorably in order to facilitate this reunion.[55] In 1308 Jaime II wrote from Valencia to Arnau granting the latter's request that the Aragonese soldiers do no harm to the monks of Mt. Athos. Arnau translated nine of his works into Greek, perhaps for these same monks.[56]

Arnau believed that some of the Jews would be converted during the sixth *status*, but it is not clear that he expected the conversion of all Israel. He encouraged Frederick III to intensify efforts to convert the Jews in Sicily but to follow also the example of the kings of England and France and to expel those who refused to be converted.[57]

Frederick III, who combined the Swabian imperialism of the Hohenstaufen dynasty with a receptivity to Joachitism and Spiritual Franciscanism, protected the Spirituals who took refuge in Sicily. On October 15, 1310, he issued a series of constitutions which sought to facilitate the conversion of the Saracens, especially Muslim serfs, and commended more favorable treatment of those Greek serfs who accepted the Roman faith. It laid various restrictions on the Jews of Sicily but did not provide for their expulsion.[58]

During the interval between the death of Pope Boniface VIII in 1303 and the accession of Pope Clement V in 1305 two significant treatises on the advent of the angelic popes appeared. The *Vaticinia de summis pontificibus* or papal prophecies was originally a reworking in Latin of the Greek Leo-Oracles. The anonymous redactor transformed the emperors into popes and added captions which applied the prophecies to the popes from Nicholas III through Benedict XI. The remaining prophecies were adapted to the future reforming pontiff and his successors.

The *Liber de flore* was written during the same period as the *Vaticinia,* although the commentary, attributed to "Rabanus," must be later than the election of Clement V since it speaks of two popes between Boniface VIII and the first angelic pastor. Interestingly, it refers to Arnau de Vilanova as the anointed one (*unctus*) who marked the beginning of the reformation of the church. According to the *Liber de flore*, there would be four angelic popes. The first would reunite the Greek and Latin churches, cooperate with an Angevin King of Sicily who would recover the Kingdom of Jerusalem by means of a Crusade, become a Franciscan, purify the cities of Italy, restore peace, and finally, leave his realm to his descendants. During the reign of the second pope, the Germans and French would be united and the *imperium* dissolved. The third would reform the Order of the Friars minor, reduce the number of cardinals to twelve, and take away all the wealth of the prelates, leaving them only what was necessary for living. During his pontificate the Jews and Saracens would be converted. The last pope would go to the East through Greece and Palestine and be met by two barbarian peoples, perhaps Gog and Magog. They would greet him with palm branches and song and thus the whole world would be united under Christian domination. Only then would the devil be loosed and the last great antichrist appear.[59]

In the middle of the fourteenth century, the ideas of Jean de Roquetaillade, a Franciscan, dominated the Joachite program. Born at Marcolès, near Aurillac, he had been a student at the University of Toulouse for five years when he became a friar. Between 1340 and 1344 he was living in the convent at Aurillac, but in December 1344 was imprisoned by his superiors in the convent at Figeac. He was released in 1346 but was confined twice again during the following decade, the second time on the order of Pope Innocent VI. He did not die in prison, however, but in the Franciscan convent at Avignon, possibly in 1365.

Jean believed that the mystical antichrist had already come in the person of the Emperor Lewis of Bavaria. The great or imminent antichrist would appear in 1365. In his earlier works, Jean believed that this would be Louis, the son of Frederick III of Sicily, aided by the Aragonese king. The approach of an infidel army from the East and the flight of the curia from Avignon would be signs of the approach of two Franciscans, the mystical Elijah and Enoch. In the *Liber secretorum euentuum* Jean had predicted that four popes would follow Clement VI; the great antichrist would appear under the last. In the *Liber Ostensor*, Jean foresaw a series of four *reparatores,* strongly reminiscent of the angelic popes of the *Liber de flore*. A fifth *reparator* would succeed the oriental antichrist and, after his advent, the Jews would be converted.[60]

In the *Vade mecum in tribulatione*, Jean described the mystical Elijah and Enoch as a pope and a cardinal, wearing sacks, who would come in the same year as the great antichrist, i.e., 1365. Then in 1367 a *reparator* would appear. The Jews, Saracens, Turks, and Greeks who had followed antichrist would be converted during the *recuperatio orbis* to begin in 1370 and last into the first quarter of the fifteenth century. The central figure in this universal reformation would be the angelic pope—aided by a holy emperor in ending the schism of the Greek church—and by a king of Sicily in recovering the Holy Land. The Franciscan Order, purified from all its false brethren, would endure. When the conversion of all the elect from the Greeks, Jews, Saracens, Turks, and Mongols had been accomplished, the millennium would begin and endure a thousand years, although signs of decay would appear in the later centuries, presaging the ultimate tribulations before the second advent of Jesus Christ and the end of the world.[61]

Jean's interest in the conversion of non-Christians was intense. He states that he once prayed in prison with tears for the conversion of the Jews and infidels and felt himself transported into paradise.[62] He argued in the *Vade mecum* that the entire church must be led back to the evangelical mode of living because it was impossible for the nonbelievers to be converted unless the most spiritual men preach to them, not so much with words as with works, a clear echo of St. Francis's own missionary theory.[63] It would be the task of the reforming popes to prepare the church for its task of converting the world so that, when completed, the millennium would begin.

During most of the fourteenth century, Avignon had been the seat of the papacy. Although the city was located in the Empire and was ceded to the papacy, its proximity to France had resulted in the growth of French influence. The Italians had never assented to the removal of the papacy from Rome and in 1377 Pope Gregory XI finally moved the curia back to the banks of the Tiber. Unfortunately he died in the following year and his successor, Urban VI, tactlessly offended the majority of the cardinals who were French. Withdrawing from Rome, they declared Urban's election invalid on the ground that it had been held under coercion from the Roman people and elected a Frenchman as Clement VII. The Great Schism, which began with the return of the cardinals to Avignon, lasted until 1417 and divided the Latin church. While there had been anti-popes before, none had endured so long nor had the choice between the two claimants to the See of Peter ever been so difficult.

The Great Schism motivated the last major Joachite, a Calabrian hermit and priest named Telesphorus to compile his *De magnis tribulationibus et statu ecclesie*, a work finished in 1386 although he may have begun to collect his materials as early as 1356.[64] Telesphorus believed that he was living at the end of the fifth *status*, and the mystical antichrist was soon to appear: a German Emperor and his pseudo-pope. Together with the infidels they would persecute the church until the angel pope, aided by a French Emperor, a king of England and the Venetians would overcome them. The *angelicus pastor* and emperor would then reform the church. Under the succeeding three angelic popes the clergy would be led back to poverty and the orders combined into one new order. The infidels, crushed by the king of England and the Venetians, would be converted and the *plenitudo gentium* achieved. The great antichrist, a bastard from the tribe of Dan, would come and be received by the Jews as their Messiah. Confronted by Elijah and Enoch, he would martyr them but after his death, the Jews would be converted to Christ. The sixth *status* would, however, still have to undergo the persecution of Gog and Magog whose defeat at the hands of the Archangel Michael would introduce the seventh *status* of universal concord and peace, preceding the Second Coming of Christ and the Last Judgment.[65]

Telesphorus used a considerable range of sources, the Sibyls, Pseudo-Methodius, Joachim, Ubertino, Jean, and a number of pseudo-Joachite texts including the *Oraculum Cyrilli* and the *Liber de flore*. His own *De magnis tribulationibus* and the *Vade mecum* of Jean de Roquetaillade were two of the most popular of all the Joachite works during the fifteenth century.[66]

During the thirteenth and fourteenth centuries there was a proliferation of Joachite texts. Many of these were either written by the Spiritual Franciscans or related to their struggle to observe the *Regula* strictly. Peter John Olivi had succeeded in fusing the Joachite expectation of an imminent *status* of universal conversion and peace with the Franciscan concept of mission and among his disciples some at least carried out missionary efforts among the Armenians. Nevertheless, it cannot be said that apocalyptic conversion in its Joachite form became widespread in the Order. Few missionaries were Joachites, and the fifteenth century produced no Joachite of the stature of Peter John Olivi or Arnau. More typical was Luke of San Gemignano who between 1442 and 1494 carried a notebook in which he copied prophecies, trying thus to understand his own time and to penetrate the mysteries of the future.[67]

As Professor Marjorie Reeves has demonstrated, people in the last century of the Middle Ages and the Renaissance were fascinated by any prophecy which seemed to cast some light on their troubled world. In this ferment the Joachite vision of a world in which all of mankind had become one in Christ and had melted their swords into ploughshares attracted wide attention. It has been suggested that it exercised considerable influence on the missionaries of the sixteenth century, but this period lies beyond the scope of the present study.

BIBLIOGRAPHICAL NOTE

The chief sources for the history of the Spirituals from the March of Ancona and the controversy there are Angelo of Clareno's *Historia* (see chap. 5, n.40), tribs. 5-6, pp. 127-53, 287-327; idem, *Apologia pro uita sua,* ed. P. V. Doucet, "Angelus Clarenus, 'Apologia pro uita sua,'" *AFH* 39(1946):63-200. In addition to Decima L. Douie, *The Nature and Effect of the Heresy of the Fraticelli* (Manchester, 1932), pp. 49-69, A. Frugoni, *Celestiniana* (Rome, 1954), pp. 125-67, and Lydia von Auw, *Angelo Clareno et les spirituels franciscains* (Lausanne, 1952), are the most useful studies. The principal source for the life of Ubertino da Casale is his *Arbor uitae crucifixae Iesu* (Venice, 1485; repr. with intro. by Charles Davis, Turin, 1961), prol. primus, 3-7.

The fundamental studies on Peter John Olivi are F. Ehrle, "Petrus Iohannis Olivi, sein Leben und seine Schriften," *ALKG* 3(1887):409-552; Ernst Benz, *Ecclesia spiritualis* (Stuttgart, 1934; repr. Stuttgart, 1964), pp. 256-332; Raoul Manselli, *La 'Lectura super apocalipsim' di Pietro Giovanni Olivi,* Studi storici, fasc. 19-21 (Rome, 1955); Carter Partee, "Peter John Olivi: Historical and

Apocalyptic Conversion / 99

Doctrinal Study," *Fran. Studies* 20 (1960):215-60; Servus Gieben, "Bibliographia Oliviana," *Collectanea franciscana* 38 (1968):167-96; David Burr, "Petrus Ioannis Olivi and the Philosophers," *Fran. Studies* 31 (1971):41-71; idem, "Olivi on Marriage: The Conservative as Prophet," *Journal of Medieval and Renaissance Studies* 2 (1972):183-204; idem, "The Apocalyptic Element in Olivi's Critique of Aristotle," *CH* 40 (1971):15-29; Raoul Manselli, "Une grande figure serignaise: Pierre de Jean Olivi," *Études franciscaines* 61 (1972):69-83. P. Dionysius Pacetti compiled the most complete list of Olivi's works in his introduction to his edition of Olivi's *Quaestiones quatuor de domina, BFAMA* 8:15-29. Douie, *Nature and Effect*, pp. 82-91, and Partee, pp. 215-40, are the best biographical sketches.

The groundwork for the study of Arnau as a theologian was done by B. Haureau, "Arnauld de Villeneuva," *Histoire littéraire de la France*, 28 (Paris, 1881):26-126; M. Menendez y Pelayo, *Historia de los heterodoxos españoles*, 2d ed. Obras completas, 8 (Madrid, 1918), 3:179-225, xlix-cxxix; Finke, *Aus den Tagen Bonifaz VIII: Funde und Forschungen*, 2 vols. (Münster, 1902); idem, *Acta aragonensia*, 3 vols. (Berlin and Leipzig, 1908-1922; rep.); P. Diepgen, *Arnald von Villanova als Politiker und Laientheologe* (Berlin, 1909); Ramon de Alos-Moner, "Colleccio de documents relatius a Arnau de Vilanova," *Estudis universitaris catalans* 3, 4, 6 (1910-1912); Marti de Barcelona, "Regesta de documents arnaldians coneguts," *Estudis franciscans* 47 (1935):261-300; Juan Antonio Pangiagua, *Estudios y notas sobre Arnau de Vilanova* (Madrid, 1963); René Verrier, *Études sur Arnaud de Villeneuve, v. 1240-1311* (Leiden, 1947); and Manuel de Montoliu, *Ramon Llull i Arnau de Vilanova*, Les grans personalitats de la literatura catalana, 2 (Barcelona, 1958):127-60. J. Carreras i Artau and M. Batllori, "La patria y la familia de Arnau de Vilanova," *AST* 20 (1947):5-75; M. Batllori, "La documentacion de Marsella sobre Arnau de Vilanova y Joan Blasi," *AST* 21 (1948), pp. 75-119; J. Carreras y Artua, *Relaciones de Arnau de Vilanova con los reyes de la casa de Aragon* (Barcelona, 1955); Marti de Barcelona, "Nous documents per a la biografia d'Arnau de Vilanova," *AST* 11 (1935):35-127; J. Carreras y Artau, "La polemica gerundense sobre el anticristo entre Arnau de Vilanova y los dominicos," *Anales del instituto des estudios Gerundenses* (Gerona, 1950); Arnau de Vilanova, *Obres catalanes*, ed. M. Batllori and J. Carreras i Artau, 2 vols. (Barcelona, 1947), 1:12-33, treat the career of Arnau.

The standard list of the theological works of Arnau is J. Carreras i Artau, "Les obres theologiques d'Arnau de Vilanova," *AST* 12 (1936):217-31, although other manuscripts have been discovered and editions published subsequent to that list. "The first volume of the *Obres catalanes* includes all of Arnau's theological works and letters which survive in Catalan and supersedes the previous editions. On Arnau and alchemy see Lynn Thorndike, *A History of Magic and Experimental Science,* vols. 2 and 3 (N.Y., 1923, 1934), 2:841-61; 3:654-78.

The best study of the life of Jean de Roquetaillade is J. Bignami-Odier. *Études sur Jean de Roquetaillade* (Paris, 1952). See also E. F. Jacobs, "John of Roquetaillade," *Bulletin of the John Rylands Library,* 39 (1956-1957):75-96; Thorndike, *History of Magic,* 3:347-69.

M. J. Reeves, *The Influence of Prophecy in the Later Middle Ages: A Study in Joachimism* (Oxford, 1969) is the only adequate overview of the influence of Joachite apocalypticism and prophecy in the 15th through the 17th centuries. Various aspects of 14th and 15th century apocalypticism are treated in the *L'attesa.* Norman Cohn, *The Pursuit of the Millenium,* 2d ed., rev. (N.Y., 1970) traces the influence of Joachim and millennialism. Sylvia Thrupp, *Millennial Dreams in Action: Essays in Comparative Study* (The Hague, 1962) contains articles by Cohn, Howard Kaminsky, and Donald Weinstein.

VI.

The Measure of the Rule

Both the philosophical approach to mission and the Joachite vision of an "apotheosis" of history in which Gentiles and Jews would all be converted during the inaugural phase of the ultimate *status* of universal peace had made some impact on the Franciscan Order during the second half of the thirteenth century. But despite the efforts of Roger Bacon and Ramon Llull to obtain missionary colleges, or the fascination of Joachitism for Peter John Olivi and his followers, neither of the alternative traditions was able to dislodge or even significantly modify the Franciscan missionaries' adherence to their Order's ideal during the fourteenth century. With surprising uniformity, both missionaries and those who discussed the Franciscan mission looked to Saints Francis and Bonaventure, to an eschatology of renewal, and to a spirituality of conformity to the passion of Christ. I say surprising because the continuity of this ideology seriously challenges the accepted view of the history of the Franciscan Order during the late thirteenth and fourteenth centuries. Since the studies by Paul Sabatier, historians within and outside the Order have portrayed its development as an evolution in which the ideal of St. Francis was gradually modified and distorted. Depending on the historian's particular bias, this evolution has been either justified or lamented, but always a foregone conclusion.[1]

Furthermore, there is general agreement among historians that the transformation or, as some would put it, betrayal of the ideal of St. Francis was the all but inevitable result of the clericalization of the Order. The growing number of learned friars in the Order who had been clerically trained demanded that the ideal be recast so that a worldwide apostolate could be carried out in the service of the church. Priests needed proper education for which *studia* were required. Teaching necessitated suitable convent buildings as well as books. By distinguishing *dominium* from *usus,* that is ownership from possession and use, poverty remained, but its substance was drastically altered. A legal fiction justified or covered the radical deformation of the evangelical goal as St. Francis himself had sought it. And although the Companions, especially Leo, and later the Spirituals fought to preserve the pristine ideal from this tendency toward modification, they themselves modified it in part.[2]

Historians, therefore, have not interpreted the history of the Franciscan Order in terms of the usual pattern of primitive fervor, gradual corruption, and subsequent reform of practices. Instead, they have tried to explain how and why the friars altered the ideal of St. Francis. If this view is correct, the change should be reflected in the subsequent understanding and ideology of the Franciscan mission. The tradition of mission was an integral part of the eschatology of renewal and the spirituality of St. Francis. It is difficult to see how that eschatology and spirituality could be radically changed without the ideology of mission being correspondingly modified. At the very least the clericalization of the Order and its alleged results should have weighted the balance toward learning and away from example. Certainly not all of the missionaries or even a majority of them were Spirituals and they could hardly have existed in a vacuum unaffected by such fundamental alterations in the ideal of the Order. The evidence at hand, however, indicates that continuity, not deviation, marked the concept of mission during the later thirteenth, fourteenth, and early fifteenth centuries. Perhaps the failure of many friars to adhere to the evangelical life as the Rule taught it has been taken as evidence of a transformation of the ideal of the Order. But this is an entirely different phenomenon. Corruption and mitigation are one thing, a new set of goals and aims is quite another. The missionaries of the later thirteenth and fourteenth centuries have left us valuable evidence in their accounts and letters. Their testimony clearly indicates that they conceived of their journeys and activities within the framework of Franciscan eschatology and spirituality. This testimony, moreover, serves to reinforce the evidence found in the various biographies of St. Francis.

The controversies within the Franciscan Order generated a succession of lives of St. Francis (and of other holy brothers) among the

Companions and later generations of friars. One of the most important, though least datable, is the curious *Legenda trium sociorum,* a fragment of a biography which is nevertheless the best account extant of St. Francis's early life and conversion. The *Legenda* summarized its eschatology in a brief speech attributed to the bishop of Assisi when he asked Pope Innocent III to confirm the primitive rule drawn up by St. Francis in 1209: "I have found some most perfect men who want to live according to the form of the Holy Gospel and to observe evangelical perfection in all things. Through them, I believe, the Lord wants to renew the holy church throughout the world."[3]

The *Legenda*'s lengthy account of St. Francis's conversion describes a gradual reversal of basic values and desires. Francis could have pursued knighthood; instead, he adopted the evangelical life, desiring to conform himself to Christ's life and death. His dislike for lepers gave way to love in serving and touching their diseased bodies. Originally he wanted wealth; now he took true *religio* as his bride and shared her poverty. While he was praying at St. Damian church, the voice he heard from the crucifix so melted his heart by memories of the passion that he bore the stigmata in his heart from that moment on; later those wounds would appear openly in his body.[4] After this experience Francis practiced constant mortification of his body, rejoicing in the taunts and hardships he endured from his father and his former friends who now thought him mad. In this manner, according to the *Legenda,* Francis began to be conformed to the cross through poverty and the endurance of suffering.

The *Legenda* maintains that Francis first lived as a hermit, but upon hearing the gospel in which Christ commanded his disciples to go and preach, taking with them neither gold nor silver nor two tunics, he realized that this was the life he desired to adopt himself. When Bernard of Quintavalle and Peter announced that they wanted to join him, the three of them went to the church of St. Nicholas; there they had the gospel book opened three times, and three times in succession it yielded the texts:

If thou wilt be perfect, go and sell that thou hast. (Mt. 19:21)

Take nothing for your journey. (Lk. 9:3)

> If any man will come after me, let him deny himself, and take
> up his cross, and follow me. (Mt. 16:24)

Francis exclaimed: "Brothers, this is our life and rule and the life
and rule of all who wish to join our group. Go, therefore, and do as
you have heard." This, the unknown author of the *Legenda* contended, meant that a friar ought to desire to live according to the
form of the gospel.[5]

In his account of the conversion of St. Francis and the founding
of the Order, the author of the *Legenda* went to considerable length
to explain precisely what renewal of the evangelical life meant; in his
view the mission of the Order originated from and was defined by
this *renouatio*. He offers the example of Brother Silvester, who had
been a priest. Brother Silvester had sold Francis a number of stones,
and one day demanded that the saint pay him what he owed. A few
days later he dreamed that an immense cross issued from Francis's
mouth, its top touching the sky and its arms extending from one
side of the world to the other. Realizing that his dream meant that
Francis was indeed a friend of God and that his *religio* would spread
throughout the entire world, he became a friar.[6]

Making the same point, the *Legenda* tells us that St. Francis one
day assembled his six followers in the woods near St. Mary of the
Portiuncula and told them that God had called them not only for
their own salvation, but for the salvation of many. The friars were to
go through the world exhorting all men and women by example and
words to repent and keep the divine commandments. According to
the *Legenda*, Francis told them not to fear because they were so few
but to preach repentance simply, trusting that God would speak and
work through them. Some of the faithful would joyfully receive
their words and many infidels would resist them, but they must
learn to tolerate all types of response patiently and humbly.[7]

The *Legenda* emphasized the fact that the friars were to arouse
men to repent and prepare for the coming judgment by example
more than by preaching. It tells us that St. Francis urged his brothers
to conduct themselves among the peoples in such a way that whoever saw or heard them would glorify and praise God. They were
especially to set an example of peace.[8]

In the tradition of Franciscan spirituality the passion occupied a central position. The *Legenda* underlined the devotion of the early friars to churches and crosses, attributing this to their belief that through the passion Christ had redeemed the world. It recorded that Francis admonished his friars to exhibit reverence always to priests and to the sacramental elements.[9]

The *Legenda* omitted any mention of the missionary journeys of St. Francis, but this was probably due to the abbreviated nature of its account after the initial confirmation of the Order by Innocent III in 1209. Still, it is clear that the anonymous author understood the role of love and the desire for martyrdom in the Franciscan ideology of mission. He noted that love burned so ardently in the early friars that it seemed easy to them to hand their bodies over to death, not only for love of Christ but also for the salvation of the souls and bodies of their brethren. The stigmata had their role in this context. After Francis's death, the *Legenda* declares, one of his friars saw his soul ascending directly to heaven, shining like a star the size of the moon but brighter than the sun. Thus Francis was rewarded for his fasting, praying, keeping of vigils, traveling, preaching, caring compassionately for his neighbors, denying himself, and always, from his conversion until his death, assiduously remembering, vocally praising, and glorifying Christ. Because he had constantly borne the yoke of Christ in his heart, God conferred on him this unique privilege, the stigmata. The *Legenda* did maintain, however, that Francis's love of the crucified had already lifted him above into God when he went to Mount Alverna. The vision of the seraph only impressed in his flesh the wounds he already felt inside himself.[10]

In 1318 when Pope John XXII was harshly settling the question of the Spirituals and the Order was faced with the task of defending itself and its doctrine of the poverty of Christ and the apostles, a Spiritual whose identity is unknown compiled the work known as the *Speculum perfectionis*.[11] The *Speculum* revealed its polemical purpose in its opening chapter when it recounted the effort of the ministers and Brother Elias to prevent Francis from composing another Rule; the author tells us that the attempt was frustrated by Christ himself—He proclaimed that the Rule was not the work of Francis but His own and should be obeyed literally without glosses.[12] The *Speculum* gave poverty first place in its portrait of Francis, but retained the Franciscan eschatology of renewal: the

Order had been established by Christ himself in this last hour of the world to observe the form of the gospel. It was, therefore, to maintain the strictest poverty in dress, houses, and books if it was to fulfill its function as an example to both Christians and non-Christians. The *Speculum* combined poverty and humility as two of the chief characteristics of the Friars minor. This, in fact, was the reason Francis called them *minores*.

In its charge that the thirst for knowledge was one of the chief factors that corrupted the Order by bringing into it men who desired to vaunt their own learning, the *Speculum* showed the influence of Spiritual Franciscan eschatology. Even so, it adhered to the primitive concept of mission. It emphasized Francis's love by stories of his compassion for his brothers and the poor. It repeatedly states that Francis had tried to be an example to his friars and that he expected them to live as examples to other men. The *Speculum* particularly emphasized obedience in its portrait of the character of St. Francis; it tells us that Francis compared perfect obedience to the behavior of a corpse—for when it is handled, it allows itself to be moved with absolutely no will of its own. Supreme obedience, according to the *Speculum*, is the willingness to go among the infidels by divine inspiration either to save their souls or to gain martyrdom.[14]

The *Speculum* focused attention on the centrality of the passion in Franciscan meditation by a series of chapters on Francis's devotion to the crucifixion. It tells us that shortly after his conversion he was observed trudging along a road, bewailing Christ's sufferings in a loud voice; it also states that in the last two years of his life, Francis's infirmities were a source of consolation to him because of his love for the passion. The *Speculum* mentioned too Francis's zeal for the divine office, prayer, and meditation. Friars might attain a spiritual martyrdom if, deprived of necessities, they bore their penury patiently out of love for God. The author of the *Speculum* firmly believed that God had chosen and sent the Franciscans so that by their example and preaching of repentance, the souls of Christians and infidels might be perfected and saved. Poverty, humility, obedience, and love—all of which can create a desire for martyrdom—were vital aspects of the imitation of Christ, and the Order had to preserve them if it was to perform its mission of renewal.

Between 1322 and 1328 a Spiritual compiled a work called the *Actus beati Francisci*. It is a collection of stories, some of which are about Francis and his companions, others about friars in the March of Ancona in the latter years of the thirteenth century. Later it was translated into Italian with the title of *Fioretti di San Francesco*. In this version it became one of the best known and most delightful versions of the life of *il poverello*.[16]

The *Fioretti* emphasized the conformity of Francis and the companions to Jesus and the apostles. Francis was an *alter Christus* given to the world. He imitated Christ by sending his disciples out into the world to preach two by two and, after the model of Jesus, he went himself as an example to his brothers. Because he followed Christ so obediently, Christ worked miracles through him.[17]

According to the *Fioretti*, Francis and his brothers focused particularly on the crucified Jesus. Observers saw the friars as crucified men in their manner of dress, their eating habits, and their joyous endurance of suffering. The friars desired the scorn and insults of the world rather than its deceptive and vain blandishments. They traveled as pilgrims, taking only Christ with them, and, therefore, won many souls.[18]

The *Fioretti* expressed its conception of the friars' attitude most clearly in the dialogue it records between St. Francis and Brother Leo on perfect joy. It describes a winter's day when the two were walking together from Perugia toward the Portiuncula; along the way, Francis told Leo that even if God granted that the friars might give a good example of holiness in every corner of the earth, perfect joy would not be attained. A little later, he added that even if the friars could work all types of miracles, still perfect joy would not be attained. Nor would there be perfect joy if the friars received the knowledge possessed by angels. Even if a Friar minor could preach so well that he could convert all the infidels to the faith, perfect joy would still be lacking. Finally Leo asked Francis to tell him where perfect joy was to be found. Francis answered that if they arrived at St. Mary of the Angels, frozen, hungry, and muddy, and asked as friars to be admitted, but were turned away harshly by the doorkeeper as deceivers; if they had to spend the night outside, but did not murmur against the doorkeeper; if they believed that God had told the doorkeeper who they were and had made him turn them away; and, if the next day they were again refused admittance, but bore a beating patiently and cheerfully, thinking of Christ's own sufferings, then they would find perfect joy. The friars ought not to glory in any gift except in the cross of tribulation and affliction, for that was theirs; the other gifts are God's. The *Fioretti* says further that when Brother Pietro was before a scene that portrayed Christ on the cross and the Apostle John and the Virgin Mary at its foot, he wondered which of the three—the Virgin, the apostle, or Francis—suffered the most agony over the passion. The Virgin and John then appeared to him and told him that they had suffered the most but after them, Francis had grieved most over Christ's death.[19]

The third of the five *Considerazioni,* which this author also wrote, stated that it was Francis's intense desire to feel in his own flesh the agonies that Christ had suffered on the cross and to experience personally the love that had led Jesus to offer himself for men that caused God to confer the stigmata.[20]

A friar had two alternatives according to the *Fioretti*; he might share in Christ's agony and suffering through contemplation or he might participate in it by going as his disciple among men. The *Fioretti* emphasized the contemplatives, among whom it named Bernard of Quintavalle and Giovanni of Alverna. It described Francis himself as torn between his desire to devote himself completely to prayer and his sense of obligation to serve his neighbors, whether believers or unbelievers. Both Brother Silvester and Saint Clare prayed for an answer to Francis's dilemma and were told that Christ had not called Francis for himself alone but also for the salvation of others. The *Fioretti* followed this with its account of the sermon to the swallows; after the sermon, the birds flew away in four groups to the north, south, east, and west, as a sign that the preaching of the cross of Christ would spread throughout all the earth by the efforts of Francis and his brothers. For the author of the *Fioretti,* the universality of the Franciscan mission was the most striking proof that God himself had founded the Order.[21] Conformity to Christ's passion expressed in contemplation and in mission was, therefore, the chief characteristic of the Friars minor.

The authors of the *Speculum perfectionis*, the *Actus,* and the *Fioretti* were all Spirituals whose adherence to Franciscan eschatology and the Order's ideology of mission reflected their conscious effort to achieve reform of the Order. However, the ideology of the Franciscan mission remained as important to the moderate Conventuals of the later fourteenth century as it did to the Spirituals. Bartholomew of Pisa began his *De conformitate uitae beati francisci ad uitam domini Iesu* in 1385 and presented it to the Chapter General at Assisi in 1399. He divided his work into forty *conformitates;* in each, he described some aspect of Jesus' life and ministry and then showed how Francis had imitated Christ.[22] He drew his materials from a wide range of sources including not only the *Vita secunda* of Thomas of Celano and the *Legenda maior* of St. Bonaventure but also the *Actus* and a wide range of historical works.[23] Bartholomew was a man of the schools who aimed at demonstrating his thesis by bringing together an overwhelming mass of evidence, much of it quoted directly from his sources; consequently, the *De conformitate* lacks the charm and intimacy of the *Fioretti.*

Bartholomew saw Francis as the *renouator mundi,* prophesied by Joachim of Fiore among others, who had been sent to renew the light of the gospel in the senescent, dark, and cold world. Francis had imitated Christ by gathering together twelve companions in order to send them out two by two, and by founding the Order of Friars minor which spread throughout the entire world in order to bring the gospel to men through their example and preaching.

Bartholomew quoted the dialogue from the *Actus* between Fr. Leo and Francis on perfect joy, pointing out that Francis believed suffering for God was the true happiness of a Friar minor. He noted the devotion of Francis to the passion. "For he preached, knew, meditated and urged the brothers assiduously to meditate and speculate about nothing except the passion of the Lord."[24]

Bartholomew repeatedly referred to the three journeys that Francis attempted or made to the Saracens, describing the saint as drawn by his zeal for the souls of the infidels and his longing for martyrdom.[25] Bartholomew also cited a number of the friars who had shared this desire to die for Christ as missionaries.[26] He believed that the stigmata were the martyrdom that Francis had sought, the fruit of his total dedication to the passion and the zeal of Francis's mystical conformity to Jesus.[27]

The various biographies, written by both Spirituals and Conventuals, are supplemented by the writings and communications left

us by the missionaries. The early missions of the Order were principally directed toward the Muslims of North Africa and the Middle
East. Then the rise of the Mongol Empire, which was opening up
central Asia and the Orient to the Italian merchants, opened these
areas to the friars as well. The first friars to venture east of the
Caspian Sea were emissaries rather than missionaries, although they
sought to use the opportunity to convert the pagans and the Nestor-
ians. The disappearance of the last crusading states on the mainland
hampered the friars' effort in the near East but the Franciscans
continued to work among the peoples of the interior.

The accounts written by John of Plano Carpini, Benedict the
Pole, and William of Rubruck are well known.[28] But these works
were written primarily to acquaint their readers with the history and
mores of the Mongols, the geography of central and oriental Asia,
and to recount the journeys of their respective authors. More valuable than the travel accounts are the letters sent by the missionaries
from their posts to their friends and superiors. Fr. John of Monte
Corvino was able to establish a mission to China that persisted
throughout the first half of the fourteenth century. He wrote three
letters, reporting his activities and urging that more friars be sent to
aid him.[29]

John was a devout imitator of St. Francis, rigorous and severe
with himself, and a fervent teacher and preacher.[30] He believed that
many converts could be won in India if brothers would go there, but
that only the most solid men should be sent.[31] They had to be
willing to give themselves as examples rather than seek their own
glory.[32] The men chosen as bishops for China were to be good
Friars minor, born to the virtues, approved by experience, and
learned in the scriptures.[33]

Fr. Paschalis de Victoria was born in Spain; about 1333 he
journeyed to Avignon to obtain letters of obedience from Pope John
XXII and the Minister General, Geraldus Odo, and then went to the
region of the Caspian Sea. There he spent a year learning the Cuman
and Uighur languages before continuing his mission farther into
central Asia where in 1339 he and his companions were martyred. In
a letter to the guardian and friars at the convent in Victoria, he
recounted the stages of his journey to Sarai where he stayed to study
while his companion went on. When his fellow missionary decided to

return to Spain, however, Paschalis remained, unwilling to return to his "vomit," and wishing to obtain the grace promised by the Pope. For all friars coming to this region had the same plenary indulgence as those going to Jerusalem, and all those who persevered to the end would receive a crown of life, the martyr's reward. Since he possessed a mandate from his vicar, salutary obedience obligated him to perfect his pilgrimage. From Sarai where Fr. Stephen of Hungary had been martyred shortly before this, Paschalis set out with a caravan of Muslims. War delayed it and this gave him an opportunity to successfully dispute with his escorts. His opponents then sought to bribe him with offers of women, gold, and silver. When he spurned these temptations, they tormented him with stones, burned his face and feet, and insulted him. "God, who is blessed and by whom I, a pauper, rejoice and exult in our Lord Jesus Christ, knows," he wrote, "that by his admirable piety I was worthy to suffer such things for his name." Eventually Paschalis arrived in Amalech where he had been five months, "alone, proclaiming publicly the name of Jesus Christ by work, example and habit," when he wrote his letter. Despite his tribulations, he thanked God because "I expect to suffer greater agonies than these for his name in remission of my sins so that I may securely go to the heavenly kingdom by divine piety." In conclusion he exhorted the friars to pray for him and for those who planned to make such a pilgrimage "because, God helping, this pilgrimage is useful, profitable and fruitful for many souls. You should not want to see me except in these regions or in paradise, where there is rest, consolation and the inheritance left by our Lord Jesus Christ . . . who said: 'When the gospel will have been preached throughout the whole world, the consummation of the age will come.' (Mt. 24:14). Therefore, beloved brothers, it is my duty to preach among diverse nations and to demonstrate their guilt to sinners and to show them the way of salvation, but it is for God to infuse the grace by which they will be converted."[34]

Paschalis saw in his mission an opportunity to convert the nonbelievers while suffering for the sake of Christ. He would not give up his work until he had preached to all the infidels or been martyred in the attempt to persuade them. Yet his tribulations were less an imitation of Christ than a means of penitence and redemption. By voluntarily undergoing the torments and hardships of his obedience, he was assured of the full indulgence granted a Crusader and the martyr's joys of paradise.

Unlike most of the friars, Paschalis learned the languages of the peoples of central Asia but he sought to convert them by example as well as by preaching. The eschatological motif which appears in his concluding exhortation appears to be the traditional interpretation of the conversion of the Gentiles as a sign of the approaching end. There is no evidence of a Joachite apocalypticism in Paschalis. The Order had been sent in the last age of the world to bring sinners to repentance before they had to face the final judgment.

Fr. Hugo Panziera was a mystic as well as a missionary. Although he had received a theological education, he remained a lay brother out of humility. In 1307 he joined a group of friars being sent to work with John of Monte Corvino and five years later wrote a letter back to his brothers at Prato.

Hugo's autobiographical *Cantici spirituali* underline his mystical concept of his mission.[35] In the first poem Hugo describes how the love of Christ displayed on the cross transformed his own intense self-love into love for his Lord. In the second song he describes his union with Christ, which gave him peace. In the third Hugo describes union with the triune God through love of Christ and urges the mystic to make himself an example to the world.[36] In the fourth song he portrays St. Francis as the model lover of the passion, continually praising Christ, tasting his sweetness, and contemplating him in his supernal height, but always concentrating on grievously remembering the crucifixion. Because Francis so much desired to share the agonies of the passion, Jesus embraced him with the stigmata, thus fulfilling his desire to die for love. St. Francis preached—Hugo cites his sermon to the birds—and conformed himself to the evangelical life, founding three orders by whose poverty the world would be converted. Hugo himself had become a friar, mystic, and missionary because of the example of St. Francis.[37]

When Hugo wrote to his brothers at Prato, he reminded them that they were conjoined with him in one spiritual company by supernal love, communicating their oneness by their feelings, their thoughts, and by fervently serving one another. The theme of his letter was the perfect love of Christ for men and the way in which men could respond perfectly to it. The incomprehensible depth of this divine love was revealed by Christ's willingness as supreme Lord to humble himself for the sake of humankind, the vilest serfs, his enemies; to live as a man, totally obedient to love; and to die an agonizing death on the cross. Men could not doubt his love for them, but they could not be certain about their love for him. Qualitatively, their love was to be total, quantitatively to embrace everything they were capable of doing virtuously—that is, living like apostles, crucified to the world. This love appeared in their bodies when they suffered torments, and in their minds when they simultaneously sorrowed for Christ and followed him. The aim of this love was to make the creature who, according to his own deserts should suffer, eternally glorious. Sin had corrupted the human natures of the *uiatores,* and grace was the remedy, but men had to want to receive God first if they wished to become like him. Knowing that grace would aid them, they had to renounce all the vices they had loved and deny the sensuous will which would incite them to want pleasures. With as much virtuous grief and physical agony as possible, they had to live penitently, day by day, week by week, month by month, year by year, thus taking up their crosses and following their Lord.

Hugo distinguished between the physical virtues and the mental virtues. Though physical virtues could effect the true salvation of one's neighbor and be a source of suffering and fervent love for the *uiator,* they were not sufficient by themselves to attain to excellence. The mental virtues most concerned Hugo, for they could raise the mind to perfection.[38] Certain circumstances facilitated their development, but one had to observe all conditions perfectly, for each contained the possibility of impediment. Just one impediment was sufficient by itself to hinder perfection even if a man observed all the other conditions.

In order to elucidate the circumstances necessary to develop the mental virtues, Hugo employed the analogy of a musician playing a stringed instrument. First he had to strum it, that is, concentrate physically and mentally on the passible body of the son of God. Perfection would be impeded if one entertained other subjects for meditation, even if these thoughts were also spiritual. Second, the musician had to play his instrument worthily, that is, remember the inconceivable sorrows that afflicted Christ's mind. Perfection would be impeded if one remembered the physical sufferings of Jesus, but not his wounded soul. Third, the musician was not to multiply dances; that is, he was not to allow his thoughts to be distracted from meditating on the passion. Because the liturgical day covered the period between the Last Supper and the entombment, the hours served to fasten the contemplative's thoughts upon the crucifixion and the events that preceded and followed it. Fourth, he was to play for a long time, grieving over the passion and remembering how much time he had in this present life in order that he might learn to say of himself: "My soul is exceedingly sorrowful unto death" (Mk. 14:34). Fifth, he was to sound his instrument continually, that is, focus mentally on the passion without any wavering. Sixth, he was to play lovingly. He had not only to grieve over the crucifixion, but also to love him for whom he sorrowed. Meditation without loving was comparable to the arid ideas of the philosophers discussing the courses and influences of the celestial bodies. Finally, the musician was to remember that he played unworthily and blindly, because he did not deserve such a gift as remembrance of the passion, nor could he fully comprehend it.[39] Hugo's emphasis on the passion as the focus of meditation and his insistence on penitent imitation of Christ demonstrate the Franciscan character of his spirituality. He does not refer to the desire for martyrdom but it is clearly implicit in his mysticism. Although he was an active missionary when he wrote his letter, he concentrated his attention on remembering what Christ had suffered for him. Only insofar as a life of penitence, virtue, and contemplation might provide a model and stimulus to others did Hugo look outward to the infidels. Thus, one can conclude that Hugo believed example more than words would convert non-Christians. The rigorous exactitude of the life of contemplation he demanded would have left little room for other types of approach.

Even where motivations differed, eschatology and concept of mission remained true to the original Franciscan ideal. Angelo Clareno, leader of the Spirituals in the March of Ancona after the death of Fr. Liberato, was a zealous exponent of Franciscan eschatology, spirituality, and mission, both in his life and in his writings.⁴⁰ He became a missionary when the Minister General, Raymond Gaufridi, freed him and his fellow Spirituals from prison and sent them to Armenia where King Het'um II had requested help.⁴¹ Certainly, in this case, motivation devolved upon the fact that Armenia offered Angelo and the Spirituals of the March an opportunity to observe the Rule as they desired. But even though Angelo's Spiritual allegiance is obvious from his emphasis on adherence to the Rule and to poverty, he did not share Peter John Olivi's Joachitism.

In the life of St. Francis with which he began his *Historia septem tribulationum*, Angelo carefully described the *religio* of the friars as he believed their founder had intended it to be. The world had now arrived at its last hour and the final judgment was near. Men, even Christians, had diverged from the love of God into frigid selfishness. In order to bring men to repentance and to renew the evangelical life among them, Christ had obtained permission from the Father to make St. Francis and his friars followers of the gospel. The Rule which Jesus gave to Francis embodied fully the evangelical life, and Francis observed it faithfully. Its cardinal characteristics were poverty and humility, and for Angelo, these included chastity, obedience, and love. By adhering strictly to this Rule, Francis and his true companions were united with Christ as Christ was with His Father.⁴² They were imitators of the Son of God, spurning the world and its ways. The sufferings they endured from mortification, poverty, or by martyrdom at the hands of the infidel, were occasions of joy, since by these agonies they shared in the afflictions and passion of Christ. By example and by word the friars showed the world the path to repentance and true salvation, thus fulfilling their eschatological function.⁴³

Satan, however, strove against the Order and succeeded in including within it many friars who lived by human wisdom and prudence rather than the simplicity and foolishness of the gospel. Trusting in their own learning, they sought to modify and gloss the Rule, claiming that their concern was to bring salvation to men. They persecuted those who remained faithful to the evangelical life, hindering them from the pure observance of the Rule.⁴⁴ St. Francis, anticipating Satan, had sought to provide in the Rule permission for the genuine friars to live unmolested within the Order but Hugolino

(Pope Gregory IX) fearing schism, had altered Francis's words. As a result seven persecutions had occurred, beginning while Francis was in Egypt and culminating in the persecution of the followers of Peter John Olivi by Pope John XXII.[45]

Angelo's zeal for poverty is obvious, but for him poverty represented only one part of the Franciscan ideal. He repeatedly describes the *religio* of St. Francis as "conformed to the cross" (*cruciforma*).[46] He habitually combines humility with poverty.[47] The unity of Francis and his true followers with Christ is lyrically, dramatically, and mystically expressed, often by introducing Christ himself into the narrative, speaking to Francis or to the assembled brothers.[48] The simplicity and foolishness of the gospel were opposed to reliance on human wisdom just as poverty was opposed to possession of things. The mission to the infidel was a part of the Order's function to renew repentance and lead men to salvation in preparation for the end. Zeal for the faith and the desire for martyrdom were the motives that propelled Francis and his followers to go to the Muslims.[49]

In his commentary on the twelfth chapter of the Rule, Angelo declares that those who have attained true purity of heart and body by means of evangelical poverty, humility, and obedience, may perceive the breadth, height, and depth of God's love and thus come to desire to imitate the death of Christ. St. Francis himself, inflamed by this perfect love, had placed this chapter at the end of the Rule. He had desired martyrdom in order that he might participate not only in the life of Jesus but also in his death. He had proposed to his friars that they should choose this desire because it seemed to him to be the summit of all perfection. Francis knew that when perfect love inspired his friars to long for martyrdom, morality and grace would multiply in the world; for this desire would motivate them to go among the Saracens and other infidels, proclaiming by their lives, words, and blood the gospel of eternal salvation.

In order to confirm by Francis's own words his interpretation of the Rule, Angelo quotes the entire text of the sixteenth chapter of the *Regula prima.* Here St. Francis had taught those who desired to imitate the life of Christ that they should be zealous for the souls of all men; by prayer, the example of holy lives, preaching, and spontaneous submission to death, should that become necessary, they should seek to convert both Christians and non-Christians. Francis warned that not all friars should be licensed to go as missionaries, but only those who were inspired by the spirit of Christ and were suitably prepared and motivated for such a task. Those who were suitable, however, should not be forbidden to go.[50]

Angelo's exposition of the twelfth chapter is more detailed than any other commentary from the medieval period. This undoubtedly reflects his experience as a missionary but it also emphasizes the importance he attached to the Franciscan ideology of mission. Despite the controversies over poverty in which he participated, he never lost sight of the primitive *religio* or of the missionary function of the Order.

When primary sources attribute motivation to a missionary friar in the thirteenth or fourteenth centuries, they employ the same recurrent phrases. Friars journeyed to the infidels because they were "inflamed by love for Christ" or they "burned with desire for martyrdom." They are described as motivated by "zeal for the faith." They went as missionaries "from devotion." The *passiones* continue to employ these standard formulae. Anticipating martyrdom, the friars daunted their judges by asserting: "We, whom you see here, shall soon die for the faith of Christ." They exclaimed that they were "willing to expose themselves to death, so that they . . . [might] possess the optimum reward."[51] The repetition of these phrases and statements in various combinations indicates a common, well-understood ideology of mission.

Thomas of Tolentino was a friar from the March of Ancona who, like Angelo Clareno, had been imprisoned by the provincial chapter. After his release, he set out with Jacobus de Padua, Petrus de Senis, and Demetrius for India, but they were martyred by the Muslims in Thana, near Bombay in 1321. A Dominican friar, Jordanus, accompanied them and, since a part of his narrative is preserved in the *passio*, it is one of the best documented of all the accounts of the Franciscan martyrs. They were put ashore at Thana accidentally. Jordanus was away baptizing some native Christians when the wife and husband with whom the Franciscans were staying quarreled and she revealed the presence of the friars to the authorities. Summoned before the Kadi, the friars repudiated all efforts to convert them to

Islam, maintaining the truth of the Christian faith and declaring the falsity of Mohammed's teachings. Eventually Thomas, Jacobus, and Demetrius were executed, and Petrus, who had stayed at the house to look after their possessions, was captured and killed soon afterward. Jordanus regretted deeply that he had not been present to share their martyrdom.

The brief *passio* that records the martyrdom of Fr. Livinus in Cairo (1345) is unusually informative. According to the account, Livinus was always noted for his humility, his assiduousness in prayer, and his virtuous life. He possessed the capacity for theological study but never wanted to be a *lector*, preferring prayer and contemplation to doctrine. Burning with the desire for martyrdom, he went as a missionary to the Muslims. After he arrived in Cairo, Livinus wondered how he could go about shedding his blood for the honor of God and the Catholic faith. He put his thoughts into the form of a *questio*, which he submitted to the judgment of the church. The question was phrased: "Whether it is licit according to God for a Christian to enter the mosques of the Saracens in order to preach the Catholic faith and attack the law of Mohammed." He summarized the view of those who held that this was not permitted because anyone who did this was immediately seized and, if he did not apostatize, was martyred. Thus his effort was utterly useless and he had in effect committed suicide. Livinus answered the question affirmatively, pointing out that there had been many friars who had preached in the mosques and had not been martyred. But if a friar was martyred because he had preached against Islam, his death should not be construed as suicide because many saints had confessed their faith, knowing that this could lead to martyrdom, and the church regarded their deaths as salutary examples.[53] The *questio* itself is lost, but its very composition indicates that the desire for martyrdom and the means by which this longing could be legitimately satisfied were significant questions among the missionaries of the fourteenth century. This could scarcely have been the case if the desire for martyrdom had not still been the dominant element in the motivation of most of the friars.

The defense of martyrdom was taken up in the fifteenth century by the anonymous author of the *Tractatus de martyrio sanctorum* which survives in the form of an *incunabulum*, probably printed in

Basel about 1492 by Jacobus Wolff de Pforzheim.[54] Although his name is unknown, the author of the *Tractatus* has told us much about himself and the composition of this treatise. He had come from the Latin West about two years before he wrote in order to study Greek at Constantinople. There, in addition to his studies, he enjoyed searching for manuscripts of the Greek fathers and the classical authors. One of his discoveries was a manuscript of Marcus Aurelius's *Meditations* in Greek. Another was a copy of Athenagorus's *Supplication for the Christians*. Apparently he was "a secular clerk of the first tonsure . . . little experienced in the spiritual life." In Constantinople he became a disciple of the Dominican friar, Johannes de Ragusio, who served as a legate to Constantinople from September 24, 1435 through November 2, 1437. According to the author, Johannes one day encountered three Franciscan friars in the church of St. Peter, used by the Latins. They were Petrus de Bethonto, Angelus of Estulo, and Petrus Alemannus de Maguntia. The friars revealed to Johannes that they had decided to go as missionaries to the infidels, hoping thus to find martyrdom. Through Johannes the author of the *Tractatus* was introduced to these three Franciscans and decided to join them on their journey in order to share their martyrdom. With their cooperation and perhaps partly at their instigation, he wrote the treatise on martyrdom in the space of a few days. In fact, he left it in rough form, partly because they were anxious to leave Constantinople for the lands of the infidels and partly because the Friars minor persuaded him that the bare truth deserved to be presented in a simple, unadorned manner. He submitted the *Tractatus* to Albert of Sarteano, an Observant Franciscan and humanist who had been sent on a mission to the Greeks by Pope Eugenius IV in 1435. Albert was probably in Constantinople sometime between September 1436 when he left Venice and the September of 1437 when he returned to Italy.[55]

Thus the *Tractatus* was probably composed about 1437 in Constantinople. It states that four Franciscans had been martyred in Jerusalem about forty years previously. Since this refers to Nicholas de Taveleis and his companions, executed in 1391, it indicates that the date *ante quem* must have been 1439 or 1440. Certainly it was written after the arrival of Johannes de Ragusio in Constantinople in 1435 and probably before his departure in 1437.[56]

In part, the treatise was a justification of the author's decision to devote himself to mission, desiring martyrdom. But there is little doubt that the precarious situation of Constantinople was influential. The Seljuq Turks had thrust into Asia Minor in the second half of the eleventh century and flourished there as the Sultanate of Rūm until internal weaknesses and the Mongol thrust into Persia created confusion in the thirteenth century. About 1300 a Turk named Osman emerged as the successful leader of a number of warriors in northwest Anatolia. Although the Palaeologi had recaptured Constantinople from the Latins in 1261, they were unable to restore the empire to more than a fraction of the strength it had enjoyed before the Fourth Crusade shattered it in 1204. In the second half of the fourteenth century the successors of Osman organized the Ottoman emirate and created a powerful army composed of infantry and cavalry. Thereupon the Ottomans thrust eastward into Asia Minor and westward across the Aegean, making rapid progress from Gallipoli into the Balkans. Despite several Crusades, the resistance of such notable leaders as John Hunyadi of Transylvania and George Castriota from Albania, and the meteoric rise of Timur who briefly smashed the Ottoman army (1402), the Ottomans took the title Sultan and by the 1430s had virtually surrounded Constantinople.

In desperate need of help from the West, the Emperor John VIII Palaeologus negotiated reunion with Rome at the Council of Florence in 1438. The *Tractatus* contains no hint of these negotiations which may be further indication that it was written no later than 1437. Its author, however, knew that both Asia Minor and the Balkans were gradually being absorbed under Ottoman rule. He was acquainted with the Ottoman practice of using Christian boys as infantry and thus converting them to Islam. He felt that great numbers of Christians in the Balkans and Asia Minor would become Muslims if something was not done soon to encourage them to retain their Christianity more firmly and zealously.[57]

As is often true with medieval polemics, it is impossible to know against whom the author of the *Tractatus* was arguing. Even though he sometimes addresses his opponent as if he were a personal acquaintance, it is possible that the adversary was fictitious. Quite possibly the adversary is only made to reflect the general attitudes the author thought he discerned among fifteenth-century Christians.

Many of the arguments are directed against the view that the best response for Christians to make to Turkish rule was to continue living submissively while carrying out their responsibilities as priests, religious, or lay persons. In his opinion there would be a gradual drift toward Islam unless the conquered Christians were stirred to defend the faith by the passive resistance of martyrs.

The prologue of the *Tractatus* asserts that martyrs were the foundation and the cause of the growth of the pre-Constantinian church because they led other men to seek Christ's name and bewail his passion. After the Roman emperors adopted Christianity, the fathers had to contend with the heretics, but when orthodoxy triumphed, the church flourished and the monks in the Egyptian desert became as numerous as "the stars at night." Idleness then induced some Christians to serve God fraudulently, actually desiring the world's pleasures. Christian princes quarreled with one another, and both monks and clerics involved themselves in secular disputes. Hatred, avarice, love of luxury, and impurity became characteristic of Christians. Then Satan sent Mohammed with his new law and by conquest it engulfed a great part of the world. Because love had grown cold among the Christians and none of them wanted to die for the glory of God or for their neighbors, Islam flourished. Christians did not care enough to search for a remedy and could, therefore, justly expect God's judgment.[58]

St. Francis, stirred by love of Christ and thirsting for the salvation of his neighbors, saw that the treachery of Satan could only be confounded by imitation of the passion through martyrdom. For this reason he inserted the twelfth chapter into the *Regula bullata*, urging his friars to undertake journeys to the infidels, sparing no hardship or tribulation and offering themselves as martyrs. He himself went as a missionary but God reserved him from martyrdom in order to make him an example of poverty and love through the transformation of his mind into the similitude of the crucified Christ. Just as the martyrs had enabled the early Christians to convert the pagans of their day, so the renewal of martyrdom and not Crusades would overcome Islam.[59]

According to the *Tractatus*, martyrdom was a passion sustained by someone for the sake of the glory of God and the salvation both of the martyr and his neighbors. Others who suffered death, whether they were merchants in search of profit or soldiers tempted by the spoils of war, were not to be counted as martyrs. The willingness of Christians to risk death for commerce or military advantage and their simultaneous distaste for offering themselves as martyrs amazed the author of the *Tractatus*. Some people said that this was not a time for martyrdom, he noted, but was martyrdom to be avoided when faith had waned, seeing that it was sought when the faith was strong? Suffering was to be undertaken discreetly, however, since precipitate action might be suicide rather than martyrdom. One had to be induced by the spirit of God. Whatever the circumstances which led to death, one could be a true martyr only if he died because God had inspired him to this end.[60] All martyrdoms typified the crucifixion. For this reason the martyrs were called witnesses in Greek. Their deaths testified to Christ's passion. Those who suffered martyrdom for reasons other than to give testimony to their faith were, therefore, not to be called martyrs.[61]

According to the *Tractatus*, martyrdom could take varied forms. A man who possessed an abundance of goods but lived a life of poverty could be called a martyr, or a young man who embraced the strictest chastity. Those who bore their tribulations patiently were martyrs, and those who felt compassion for the sufferings of others. In fact, all struggles that a Christian must undergo in order to lead the true life could be regarded as forms of martyrdom. The ultimate and perfect martyrdom, however, was to expose one's life and blood for the sake of the glory and name of Jesus. Martyrdom was equivalent to baptism since those who executed a Christian were in fact persecuting Christ. The martyr was thus made one with Christ, even if he had never been baptized.[62]

There were three ways in which one could become a martyr: First, by imprinting in one's mind the agonies of the crucified Jesus; second, by developing a spirit so filled with joy that one was undisturbed by the pains and sufferings of the body; or third and most sublime, by suffering both physically and mentally. Christ himself was the prime example of the third, since he endured both physical agony and mental torment on the cross. St. Francis's case was unique. The vision of the six-winged seraph transformed his mind into the similitude of the crucified Christ and imprinted in his body the wounds of the passion. St. Francis's constant meditation on the passion and his ardent desire to imitate the death of Christ made him worthy of the stigmata.[63]

Caritas was the virtue that obliged the Christian who possessed it to suffer martyrdom, for *caritas* was that love by which one loved God more than himself and other men as much as himself. One who was filled with *caritas* would not hesitate to suffer physically or to die, knowing that he would thereby gain the crown of martyrdom—full remission of sin, entrance into eternal life, and the presence of God—and inspire others to seek salvation.[64]

There were four grades of martyrs: those who suffered death involuntarily—for example, children; those who desired to avoid martyrdom but when faced with the choice of denying Christ or dying decided to die; those who could have fled but voluntarily died instead; and those who spontaneously offered themselves as victims because their *caritas* made them desire to imitate Christ. This last, the grade that Francis desired to attain, was perfect martyrdom.[65]

After clarifying the nature, necessary conditions, and ultimate reward of the martyr, the *Tractatus* came to the heart of its problem by taking up popular arguments against martyrdom. These arguments stemmed from the proposition that since Christians were not being persecuted now, they were compelled neither to deny Christ nor suffer death. The spontaneous offering of oneself as a confession of Christ was not justifiable since as soon as a Christian began to attack Mohammed or his law he was given the choice of apostasy or death. Neither preaching nor charitable instruction could precede martyrdom. The Muslims regarded slaying such Christians as meritorious acts which would help them to gain the paradise promised them under Islam. Moreover, martyrdoms did not result in the conversion of Muslims as they had Romans. Instead of seeking to become martyrs, lay Christians did better to live quietly, act justly, and do works of mercy, consoling their parents and keeping their wives and children from being implicated in superstitions. Secular clerics who ruled their churches as good pastors would be accounted martyrs. The religious who loved poverty, maintained chastity, and were joyfully obedient would be martyrs also.[66]

Against these arguments for submission to Islamic rule, the author of the *Tractatus* argued that Christ's passion constituted the foundation of the church, that the church was strengthened by martyrs, and weakened by those who drew back from dying for the sake of Christ. Furthermore, Christians *were* being persecuted physically by the Turks; Christian churches had been closed and public observance of the sacraments forbidden. The Christians who lived under Islamic rule tended to become Muslims, the author asserted, citing the Christian peoples of Asia and Africa as examples. They were attracted by the indulgence of the senses permitted the Muslims. The Ottoman rulers were converting Christian youths to Islam in order to use them as servants.[67] Christians were justified in spontaneously offering themselves as martyrs because their example would strengthen the Christians who lived under Islamic rulers. And despite the difficulty in preaching to the Muslims, the example given by the martyrs could encourage the infidels to seek out the truth concerning the Christian faith and thus lead ultimately to their conversion. In a passionate appeal the author of the *Tractatus* argued that Christians refrained from martyrdom because they desired the riches of this world and because their faith was weak. He himself, he admitted, almost decided not to become a friar and go as a missionary because he did not want to give up the Greek manuscripts he had collected.[68] "Martyrdom is a supreme and difficult act and only those who have been inflamed by the spirit of Christ can bear it fervently." God gave this spirit to some people freely, but others had patiently to invoke the name of Christ again and again in order to receive the strength to undergo suffering.[69]

According to the *Tractatus*, some opponents of martyrdom argued that only those skilled in theology or the scriptures should be permitted to go as missionaries. The author refutes this position by citing the sixteenth chapter of the *Regula prima* where St. Francis states that there are two modes of behavior for those among the infidels: setting an example of Christian humility and submission, or preaching. The *Tractatus* contends that the first mode was suitable even for the layman who had no theological training. If such a man were inflamed with the desire for martyrdom and the zeal for souls, he should be permitted to go to the infidels and even express his faith simply; but he was not to engage in disputation with the Muslims. Those who were sent as bishops, priests, and deacons, however, were to have the proper training. Nevertheless, the Koran forbade Muslims to dispute with Christians and theological skills were less important than the spiritual virtue which would enable the missionaries to convert the infidels by their example.[70]

The *Tractatus* next raises the question of whether the Friars minor were obliged to martyrdom, more so at least than were other religious or clerics. Some people argued that the twelfth chapter of the Rule obliged the Franciscans to go as missionaries, desiring martyrdom, and that it was this obligation that made the Rule of St. Francis excel the Rules of St. Augustine and St. Benedict. Taking the contrary position, the *Tractatus* quotes the twelfth chapter of the *Regula bullata* and part of the sixteenth chapter of the *Regula prima*, in order to show that Francis counseled his friars to seek license to go only if they were divinely inspired to do so. The intent of the Rule was to encourage the friars to live the evangelical life in imitation of Christ and the apostles whom Christ had commanded to go into all the world. Francis intended only to encourage his brothers to undertake complete imitation, which would include going as a missionary. In support of this view he cites Peter John Olivi's commentary on the Rule as well as St. Bonaventure's *Legenda maior*. Francis himself set an example for his brothers by his three journeys, although God reserved him from martyrdom in order to confer on him the stigmata. The *Tractatus* concludes: "His friars are not, therefore, obliged to offer themselves for martyrdom, nor obligated to do so more than others are, if they do not want to fulfill perfectly the great counsels and exhortations of their Rule as he did." The command to observe the gospel did not compel the friars to seek martyrdom because the gospel gives the timid permission to flee. Those friars, however, who did go among the infidels, having vowed their bodies to Christ, were obliged not to flee but to expose themselves boldly to their enemies; in this respect they were more obligated than others to seek martyrdom.[71]

In its final chapter the *Tractatus* attempts to deal with a problem that always troubled medieval missionaries, that is, ignorance of the languages spoken by those to whom they went. Such ignorance, the author states, should not detain a man from going as a missionary if he is ardent for martyrdom and zealous for the souls of the infidels. But missionaries were not to depend on Christian merchants who knew the languages to help them, because most merchants would not want to risk coming into conflict with the infidels. It was also unlikely that the missionaries would find interpreters among the non-Christians who knew sufficient Latin to serve them. The best means of solving the problem was for the missionaries to live for some time among the infidels and learn the language. The author especially recommends this method to those who were sent as bishops, priests, or deacons. A Christian layman, however, who knew neither language nor theology could imitate the Egyptian monk Menne who lived in the time of the emperor Diocletian. Suddenly appearing among the crowd of pagans celebrating the emperor's birthday, he announced: "I am the servant of my Lord Jesus Christ, maker of heaven and earth and all things contained in them." Maintaining his faith in spite of threats, he was martyred. An uneducated layman might use this same brief confession. Learned Christians could follow the example of the early apologists and write a treatise attacking the errors of the infidels and defending the faith, which they could then deliver to a prince or a priest; the *Tractatus* contends, however, that such an apology would be difficult to translate, make tedious reading, and probably have little effect. A brief, apologetic broadside (*carta*) that could be delivered to a local official, prince, or priest would better serve its purpose. Should the Muslims want to hear the faith explained or defended in greater detail, the layman would have to find another, trained Christian to help him. If, however, the Muslims proceeded to threaten him with death and tempt him with promises, he ought to stand firm on his confession and, remembering the rewards of a martyr, undergo patiently and quietly whatever torments are inflicted on him, imitating Jesus himself who neither rebuked nor reviled his tormentors.[72] For the author of the *Tractatus* the early church was a touchstone by which to measure the church of his own day. Citing many instances of martyrs and would-be martyrs on behalf of his argument, the author drew his proofs both from the ancient church and the Franciscan and Dominican orders.[73]

His attitude reflects a fusion of humanist passion and Franciscanism. He was eager to learn Greek at a time when knowledge of and concern for the study of the Greek classics and fathers was beginning to emerge in the humanist circles in Italy. Certainly his interest in the second and third century apologists was linked with his humanism. He refers most often to Cyprian and Jerome among the Latin fathers. He states that Eusebius was the source of much of his knowledge of the early church although he and his three Franciscan companions had also used many lives or *acta* of the early martyrs. He expressly refers to Peter John Olivi's *Expositio super regulam* and to the *Legenda maior* of St. Bonaventure as well as to both the Rule of 1221 and the *Regula bullata*, but here he may have been relying on the friars.[74]

The author believed firmly that martyrdom had been the foundation of the pre-Constantinian church. In his view, the Franciscans were the Order closest to the primitive Christians in the friars' zeal for souls and willingness to suffer death for the sake of Christ and the honor of God. St. Francis and his Order were the *renouatio* of the evangelical life in a world that had grown corrupt, and the heart of this life was the imitation of Christ, especially of the passion, by means of martyrdom. *Caritas*—loving God more than self and one's neighbor as much as oneself—was the chief virtue. Divine inspiration constituted the gift of such love.

He was aware of the language problem faced by the missionary but contended that the example of a devout Christian and especially the testimony of martyrdom were more effective in converting infidels and strengthening the persecuted believers than sermons. He apparently was aware of the tradition that emphasized disputation and preaching but, perhaps because it seemed more congruent with his understanding of the early church, preferred the Franciscan approach. His eschatology was Franciscan and, even though he had read Olivi's *Expositio*, he nowhere alludes to the apocalyptic conversion of unbelievers or to an apotheosis of history. His outlook on history came from Francis and Bonaventure, not from the Joachites.

It may be possible to interpret the evidence of the *Tractatus* from an entirely different perspective, but it appears to crown the cumulative testimony of the fourteenth century biographies of St. Francis and his brothers, the writings of Angelo Clareno, and Hugo Panziera and the missionaries. Taken together they demonstrate that the ideology of the Franciscan mission remained dominant at least into the first third of the fifteenth century. The difficulties presented by the issue of poverty notwithstanding, the goal of the friars continued to be renewal of the evangelical life and Christian witness to faithful and non-Christian alike.

APPENDIX

Hugo Panziera, Cantico 4

(DE BEATO FRANCESCO
E DELLA SUA VITA)*

Ardenti de'amore,
    Li cui cor van danzando,
    San Francesco, il mio amore,
    Sempre gite laudando.
Laundando lo gite
    Quello santo amoroso:
    Gustate, e vedete
    Quanto è dilettoso:
    Francesco gioioso,
    Primo frate minore
    Col caldo d'amore
    Vita già predicando.
Elli predicò vita,
    Poi fece sermone.
    Li uccelli prima invita
    Alla predicazione;
    Francesco loro impone
    Che laudino lo Signore
    Con canti d'amore,
    Per l'aria volando.
Li uccelli volaro,
    Poi che li fu in piacimento;

E Cristo laudaro
Al suo comandamento.
Francesco era attento,
Vide a sè ubbidire;
E lo suo dolce sire
Ne già sempre laudando.
Cristo Gesù laudava,
    Gustando sua dolcezza,
    E lui contemplava
    In superna altezza:
    Francesco d'asprezza
    Affliger si volea;
    E sempre piangea,
    La croce rimembrando.
La croce amorosa
    Nell'anima avea,
    Con forma piatosa
    In lui risplendea.
    Francesco tenea
    Lo corpo sempre afflitto
    Per la morte di Cristo,
    La qual già pensando.

*The text is taken from *I cantici spirituali del beato Ugo Panziera*, Della Miscellanea Pratese di cose inedite or rate, antiche e moderne, 4 (Prato, 1861).

Pensava e piangeva
    Iesu innamorato,
    Che 'n croce vedeva,
    Meditando, chiavato.
    Francesco gustato
    Avea quella morte
    Con crudel pena e forte,
    Alla Vernia orando.
Orando alla Vernia,
    Cristo rimembrava;
    In una caverna,
    Là dov' egli orava.
    Francesco amava
    In croce esser chiavato:
    Cristo l' ha abbracciato,
    Le sue stimate dando.
Le stimate avesti
    Del nostro Redentore,
    Per ciò che volesti
    Morir per amore.
    Francesco el suo cuore
    Teneva innamorato,
    Poi che fu segnato
    A Dio simigliando.
Simile fatto
    A Dio omnipotente,
    In abito e in atto,
    In virtù splendiente:
    Francesco umilemente
    Sè volse sprezzare,
    Per me' predicare
    Virtù operando.

Virtudi operasti
    Sopra natura umana;
    Sulla fede fondasti
    La speranza soprana;
    Francesco, fontana
    Di caritade piena,
    La qual virtudi mena
    In grazia abondando.
Di grazia fu pieno,
    E di virtù ornato:
    Tre ordini almeno
    Nel mondo ha ordinato.
    Francesco beato,
    Tre viti piantasti;
    In povertà andasti
    Sempre evangelizzando.
La vangelica vita
    Di Cristo ha tenuto.
    Ad amare tutti invita
    L'amor non conosciuto.
    Francesco, el tuo aiuto
    Ti volemo domandare;
    Te volemo seguitare,
    Il mondo disprezzando.
Sia il mondo sprezzata
    Per ogni amadore;
    Sia ciascuno infiammato
    Del superno ardore.
    Francesco, il tuo amore
    Per lui trovare m' ha costretto
    Tu se' il mio gran diletto,
    Per cui i' moro amando.

Notes

CHAPTER I

1. Howard Saalman, "Medieval Cities," *Planning and Cities,* ed. George R. Collins (N.Y., 1968), p. 41.

2. On the expansion of the awareness of Latin Christians see R. W. Southern, *The Making of the Middle Ages,* pb. ed. (New Haven, 1965), pp. 15-73.

3. Francis Dvornik, *Byzantium and the Roman Primacy* (N.Y., 1966); Steven Runciman, *A History of the Crusades,* 3 vols., pb. ed. (N.Y. & Evanston, 1964-67), 3:107-31; idem, *The Eastern Schism: A Study of the Papacy and the Eastern Churches during the Eleventh and Twelfth Centuries* (Oxford, 1955) and R. Janin, *"Constantinople," DHGE* 13 (Paris, 1956): 656-754.

4. James Addison Thayer, *The Medieval Missionary: A Study of the Conversion of Northern Europe, A.D. 500-1300* (N.Y. & London, 1936); Jean Leclercq, Francois Vanderbroucke, and Louis Bouyer, *A History of Christian Spirituality,* vol. 2; *The Spirituality of the Middle Ages,* trans. the Benedictines of Holmes Abbey, Carlisle (N.Y., 1968), pp. 34-43, 60-62, 81-83, 110-19.

5. Leclercq, *History of Christian Spirituality,* 2:111-12.

6. Francis Dvornik, *The Slavs: Their Early History and Civilization* (Boston, 1956), pp. 114-15, 258-61.

7. The *passio* of Adalbert, chap. 13, edited in *PL* 137:872, quoted in Leclercq, *History of Christian Spirituality,* 2:117.

8. The *passio* of Adalbert, chap. 25, *PL* 137:883, quoted in Leclercq, *History of Christian Spirituality,* 2:117; Dvornik, *The Slavs,* pp. 266-67.

9. Leclercq, *History of Christian Spirituality,* 2:111.

10. Robert I. Burns, "Christian-Islamic Confrontation in the West: The Thirteenth Century Dream of Conversion," *AHR* 76(1971):1386-434.

11. C. J. Bishko, "Peter the Venerable's Journey to Spain," ed. Giles Constable and James Kritzeck, *Petrus Venerabilis 1156-1956,* Studia Anselmiana, 40(Rome, 1956):163-75; James Kritzeck, *Peter the Venerable and Islam,* Princeton Oriental Studies, 23(Princeton, 1964):10-36; M. Th. D'Alverny, "Deux Traductions latines du Coran au Moyen Age," *Archives d'histoire doctrinale et littéraire du Moyen Age,* 22-23(1947-1948):69-131. Neither Bishko nor Kritzeck thinks that it is possible to determine with certainty whether Peter already had this project in mind before his journey or whether the project was a by-product of his stay at Najera, but Bishko is inclined toward the latter view.

In addition to the Koran, the translations included the *Fabulae Saraceno-*

rum, the *Liber generationis Mahumet et nutritia eius*, the *Epistola Saraceni*, written by the Muslim Al-Hashimi, and the *Rescriptum Christiani*, composed by Al-Kindi.

12. Peter the Venerable, *Liber contra sectam*, ed. James Kritzeck, *Peter the Venerable*, p. 228.

13. Peter wrote the *Liber* several years after the completion of the translations (Kritzeck, *Peter the Venerable*, p. 89).

14. *Liber contra sectam*, ed. Kritzeck, *Peter the Venerable*, pp. 231-32.

15. Ibid., pp. 231-47; also see analysis by Kritzeck, pp. 161-74.

16. Ibid., pp. 247-91, 175-94. Kritzeck believes that Peter did not intend to reject the validity of the Crusade per se, but felt that more conquest or even conquest followed by forcible conversion was unjust. He therefore wanted to combine a Crusade with an effort to obtain the voluntary conversion of the Saracens by persuasion (see ibid., pp. 19-23, 101-62). Virginia Berry, "Peter the Venerable and the Crusades," ed. Constable and Kritzeck, *Petrus Venerabilis*, pp. 141-62, argues that Peter supported the Crusade in its "ideal meaning as an unselfish, sacrificial journey to faraway lands to combat the enemies . . . of the christian faith." She admits, however, that "undoubtedly . . . some disillusionment and modification had crept in."

17. See the anonymous *Vita sancti Raymundi*, ed. Franciscus Balme and Ceslaus Paban, *Raymundiana seu documenta que pertinent ad sancti Raymundi de Pennaforti vitam et scripta*, *MOFPH* 6, fasc. 1 (Rome, 1898):19-37. Ramon's life is summarized by A. Teetaert, "Raymond de Penyafort," *DTC* 13, pt. 2 (Paris, 1937), cols. 1806-23. J. M. Coll, "San Raymundo de Penafort y las misiones del Norte Africano en la edad media," *Missionalia hispanica* 5 (1948):417-57, and Burns, *Christian-Islamic Confrontation*, 1401-1402, describe his work as a promoter of mission.

18. Teetaert, "Raymond de Penyafort," cols. 1806-9. There is a critical edition of the *Decretales Gregorii IX* in A. Friedberg, *Corpus iuris canonici*, 2 vols. (Graz, 1955), 2:1-927.

19. The text is preserved in Gerardus de Fracheto, O.P., *Vitae fratrum ordinis praedicatorum*, ed. Benedictus Maria Reichert, O.P., *MOFPH* 1(Louvain, 1896):309-10.

Miramolin was probably the Hafsid, Abū-Zakariyā Yahyā I (1228-49), although the title of caliph was not adopted by this dynasty until 1253 under Abū-Abdullāh Muhammad I al-Muntasir.

20. *Vita sancti Raymundi*, pp. 31-32; Coll, "San Raymundo," p. 423; C. Douais, *Acta capitulorum prouincialium ordinis fratrum praedicatorum* (Toulouse, 1894), pp. 612-13, 617, 625, 626; Benedictus Maria Reichert, O.P., *Acta capitulorum generalium ab anno 1220 usque ad annum 1303*, *MOFPH* 3(Rome, 1898): 9, 98, 263.

21. Petrus Marsilio, *Cronica*, ed. Balme and Paban, *Raymundiana*, fasc. 1, 12; St. Thomas Aquinas, *Liber de ueritate catholicae fidei contra errores infidelium seu'summa contra gentiles'*, ed. Ceslai Pera, O.P., 3 vols. (Turin, Rome, 1961), bk. 1, chap. 2, sects. 10-11, 2:3-4.

22. *Litterae encyclicae magistrorum generalium ordinis praedicatorum ab anno 1233 usque ad annum 1376*, ed. Benedictus Maria Reichert, O.P., *MOFPH* 5(Rome, 1900):16-20, 38-42.

23. Palmer A. Throop, *Criticism of the Crusade* (Amsterdam, 1940), pp. 11-25, 147-83; E. R. Daniel, "The Medieval Crusade and Vietnam: A Debate about War," *Lexington Theological Quarterly* 6(1971):93-101.

The *Opus tripartitum* was printed by P. Crabbe in his *Concilia omnia tam generalia, quam particularia* (Cologne, 1551), 2:967-1003, and repr. E. Brown, *Fasciculus rerum expetendarum et fugiendarum,* 2 vols. (London, 1690), Appendix, 2:185-228. Brown's text is referred to here. An abbreviated version which differs considerably from the original was published by J. D. Mansi, *Sacrorum conciliorm nova et amplissima collectio,* 53 vols. (Paris, Arnheim and Leipzig, 1901-1927; repr. Graz, 1960-1961), 24:109-32, and by E. Martene and Durand, *Veterum scriptorum collectio,* 9 vols. (Paris, 1724; repr. N.Y., 1968), 7:174-98. See also Fritz Heintke, *Humbert von Romans,* Historische Studien, 222 (Berlin, 1933; repr. Vaduz, 1965):117-44. Humbert also wrote a treatise entitled *De predicatione crucis* which was printed as the *Tractatus solemnis fr. H. de predicatione sanctae crucis* (Nuremburg [?], 1490), and was analyzed by A. Lecoy de la Marche in "La predication de la croisade au treizième siecle," *Revue des questions historiques* 48(1890):1-28.

24. *Opus tripartitum,* pp. 187-90.

25. Ibid., pp. 214-16, 218, 220-21.

26. A. Lukyn Williams, *Adversus Iudeos: A Bird's Eye View of Christian Apologiae until the Renaissance* (Cambridge, Eng., 1935), pp. 248-55; J. M. Coll, "Escuelas de lenguas orientales en los siglos xiii y xiv," *AST* 18(1945):72-75. The *Pugio fidei* was published by J. Voisin (Paris, 1651) and by Carpzov (Leipzig, 1687; rep. Farnsborough, Hants., 1967). Marti's *Explanatio simboli apostolorum ad institutionem fidelium* was partially edited by H. Denifle and Emile Chatelain in "Inventarium codicum manuscriptorum capituli Dertusensis," *Revue des bibliothèques* 6(1896):1-64.

Another student of these schools was the Jewish convert, Pablus Christiani, who in 1263 engaged in a disputation with Rabbi Moses Nachmani (Nachmanides) at Barcelona before King Jaime of Aragon. (See Williams, *Adversus Iudeos,* pp. 244-47; Coll, "Escuelas," 19[1946]:217-24; and Yitshak Baer, *A History of the Jews in Christian Spain,* 2 vols. [Philadelphia, 1959, 1966], 1:152-59.)

27. Reichert, *Acta capitulorum generalium,* p. 9.

28. Berthold Altaner, "Sprachstudien und Sprachkenntnisse am Dienste der Mission des 13. und 14. Jahrhunderts," *ZMW* 21(1931):117-18; R. P. Mortier, O.P., *Histore des maîtres généraux de l'ordre des frères prêcheurs,* t. 1:1170-1263(Paris, 1903), pp. 381-83.

29. *Tractatus de statu Saracenorum et de Mahomete pseudo-propheta et eorum lege et fide,* ed. Hans Prutz, *Kulturgeschichte der Kreuzzüge* (Berlin, 1883; repr. Hildesheim, 1964), pp. 575-98. Throop, *Criticism,* pp. 115-46, has analyzed the work.

30. *Tractatus de statu,* chaps. 26-53, pp. 590-98.

31. Johannes Munck, *Paul and the Salvation of Mankind* (Richmond, Va., 1959), pp. 36-68; idem, *Christ and Israel: An Interpretation of Romans 9-11,* trans. Ingeborg Nixon (Philadelphia, 1967).

32. A more detailed treatment of this tradition is presented in E. R. Daniel, "Joachim of Flora and the Joachite Tradition of Apocalyptic Conversion in the Later Middle Ages" (Ph.D. diss., University of Va., 1966), pp. 67-78. St. Bernard of Clairvaux, writing in 1146, condemned the persecution of the Jews initiated by the monk Rudolph by appealing to the prophecies of their final salvation. See Bernard of Clairvaux *epistolae,* 262, 265, *PL* 182:567-68, 570-571; and Edward A. Synan, *The Popes and the Jews in the Middle Ages,* pb. ed. (N.Y., 1967), pp. 19, 37.

33. St. Augustine, *De ciuitate dei*, bk. 18, chaps. 3; bk. 20, chaps. 7, 9; bk. 22, chap. 30, *CC* 48:652-53, 708-12, 715-19, 757-58; idem, *Epistola* 119, *PL* 33:904-25. Gerhart B. Ladner, *The Idea of Reform*, pb. ed. (N.Y. & Evanston, 1967), pp. 222-38; Raoul Manselli, "La 'Lectura super apocalypsim' di Pietro di Giovanni Olivi," *Studi storici*, fasc. 19-21(Rome, 1955):3-5.

34. Christian of Stavelot or Christianus Druthmar, *Expositio in Matthaeum euangelistam*, chap. 56, *PL* 106:1456. See D. M. Dunlop, *The History of the Jewish Khazars*, pb. ed. (N.Y., 1967), p. 121, n. 10; and Richard E. Sullivan, "Khan Boris and the Conversion of the Bulgars: A Case Study of the Impact of Christianity on a Barbarian Society," *Studies in Medieval and Renaissance History* 3(1966):55-139.

35. Edmond Pognon, ed. and trans., *L'an mille* (Paris, 1947), pp. vii-viii; Henri Focillon, *The Year 1000*, pb. ed. (N.Y. & Evanston, 1971), pp. 39-72.

36. Ernst Sackur, *Sibyllinische Texte und Forschungen* (Halle, 1898), pp. 60-95. On the Syrian and Greek versions see Paul Alexander, "Medieval Apocalypses as Historical Sources," *AHR* 73(1968):997-1018.

37. Sackur, *Sibyllinische Texte*, pp. 177-87.

38. Ibid., pp. 104-13; Focillon, *The Year 1000*, pp. 54-59.

39. Abbot Joachim of Fiore, *Liber introductorius in Apocalypsim*, published with the *Expositio in Apocalypsim* (Venice, 1527; repr. Frankfurt, 1964), chap. 6, f. 6ᵛ. Joachim equated the seven seals of Revelation 5:1 with the seven divisions of the first *tempus*, and the seven *etates* of the second age with the openings (*apertiones*) of the seals in his brief *De septem sigillis*, ed. M. J. Reeves and B. Hirsch-Reich, "The Seven Seals in the Writings of Joachim of Fiore with Special Reference to the Tract *De septem sigillis*," *RTAM* 21(1954):239-47.

40. *Liber introductorius*, chap. 6, ff. 6ᵛ-9ʳ. The *Liber figurarum*, ed. L. Tondelli, M. J. Reeves, and B. Hirsch-Reich, *Il libro delle figure*, 2d ed. (Turin, 1953), 2:tav. 1-4, 7, 10, repeatedly illustrates the parallel series of seven times and wars as does the *De septem sigillis*. In their *The "Figurae" of Joachim of Fiore* (Oxford, 1972), pp. 4-5, M. J. Reeves and B. Hirsch-Reich bring together their research on the *Liber figurarum* which in their opinion significantly clarifies Joachim's varied schemes of history.

41. In Daniel 7, the fourth beast has ten horns in addition to a small eleventh one. In Revelation, the dragon (12:3- 4) and the beast (13:1) each have ten horns. In Rev. 17, the beast is ridden by the harlot, Babylon, and the seven heads and ten horns are said to be kings. Joachim consistently takes this group of texts as interlinked.

42. Joachim justifies his expectation of two antichrists in the *Liber introductorius*, chap. 7, ff. 9ᵛ-10ʳ. Tav. 14 of the *Liber figurarum* accounts for the two by identifying the first with the seventh head of the dragon, and the second (*ultimus antichristus*) with the dragon's tail. See M. J. Reeves and B. Hirsch-Reich, *Figurae*, pp. 146-52.

43. Apoc. 13:3. Joachim, *Expositio in Apocalypsim*, pt. 4, ff. 164ᵛ; *Liber figurarum*, tav. 14.

44. Joachim, *Liber figurarum*, tav. 14; *Expositio in Apocalypsim*, pt. 3, ff. 134ᵛ, says that the *Mauri* are vulgarly called *Meselmuti*. This would seem to refer to the origin of *Mesemothus*, probably meaning Almohads.

45. Joachim of Fiore, *Concordia noui ac ueteris testamenti* (Venice, 1519), bk. 3, pt. 2, chap. 4, f. 40ᵛ.

46. Ibid., bk. 3, pt. 2, chap. 6, f. 41ᵛ.

47. Runciman, *History of the Crusades,* 2:362-473.
48. Ibid., 3:3-79.
49. *Liber introductorius,* chap. 8, f. 10^{r-v}.
50. *Liber figurarum,* tav. 14.
51. The dates of the version of the *Liber introductorius* printed at Venice and the other introductory works to Revelation which Joachim wrote remain uncertain (see M. J. Reeves, *The Influence of Prophecy in the Later Middle Ages: A Study in Joachimism* [Oxford, 1969], p. 513). The editors of the *Liber figurarum* conclude that the collection dates from c. 1200 and was either Joachim's own work or done by one of his immediate disciples under his direction (M. J. Reeves and B. Hirsch-Reich, *Figurae,* pp. 75-98).
52. In my opinion the most accurate account of this interview is in Roger of Hoveden, *Gesta regis Henrici (RS* 49, 2:151-55). This particular account has been attributed to Abbot Benedict of Peterborough; however, Hoveden's authorship is defended by D. Stenton, "Roger of Howden and Benedict," *English Historical Review* 67(1953):574-82. Roger wrote a second version of this interview in his *Chronica, RS* 51, 3:75-78. Among the varied later continental chronicles see Robert of Auxerre, *Chronicon, MGH, SS.* 26, an. 1190:254-55. On the date of the interview see Runciman, *History of the Crusades,* 3:41-42. See also Evelyn Jamison, "The Sicilian Norman Kingdom in the Mind of Anglo-Norman Contemporaries," *Proceedings of the British Academy* 24(1938):237-85, especially 263-66.
53. Ps. Benedict-Roger of Hoveden, *Gesta,* 2:151-52. The list is identical to that of tav. 14 of the *Liber figurarum* except that the fifth name is spelled Melsemutus rather than Mesemothus. See also *Expositio in Apocalypsim,* pt. 2, f. 116^v.
54. Ps. Benedict-Roger of Hoveden, *Gesta,* 2:153.
55. *Expositio in Apocalypsim,* pt. 3, f. 134^v. This and the texts cited in notes 58 and 59 below are excerpted in E. R. Daniel, "Apocalyptic Conversion: The Joachite Alternative to the Crusades," *Traditio* 25 (1969), appendix, sel. 4-5:149-51.
56. Ibid., f. 134^{r-v}.
57. Ibid., pt. 4, f. 164^v. Cf. *Liber introductorius,* chap. 6, f. 8^{r-v}.
58. *Liber introductorius,* chap. 7, f. 9^v.
59. See for example, Joachim of Fiore, *Tractatus de vita et regula Benedicti,* ed. Cipriano Baraut, "Un tratado inedito de Joaquin de Fiore: De uita sancti Benedicti et de officio divino secundum eius doctrinam," *AST* 24(1951), chap. 42, p. 82; chap. 45, pp. 84-85. Joachim linked these coming orders with the Benedictine and Cistercian monks from whom the transitional monks were to come. Usually he linked the two orders of *uiri spirituales* with the transitional period, the single *ordo monachorum* with the third *status* itself. One of the two orders of *uiri* is characterized as eremitical, devoting itself to prayer and contemplation, the other as a preaching order. See M. J. Reeves, *Prophecy,* pp. 135-44.
60. *Concordia,* bk. 2, pt. 2, chap. 5, f. 21^{r-v}; ibid., bk. 5, chap. 50, f. 85^r; *Expositio in Apocalypsim,* pt. 3, f. 137^{r-v}. Frequently Joachim uses the figure of a circle, i.e., the gospel came from the Jews to the Greeks to the Latins and in the third *status* it will proceed from the Latins to the Greeks and finally to the Jews.
61. *Liber figurarum,* tav. 14, 22. See M. J. Reeves and B. Hirsch-Reich, *Figurae,* pp. 170-73. Freedom and contemplation are here to be understood as

the monastic *libertas* and *contemplatio* (Herbert Grundmann, *Studien über Joachim von Floris* [Leipzig & Berlin, 1927], pp. 119-56).

62. *Liber figurarum,* tav. 14.

63. M. J. Reeves, *Prophecy,* pp. 28-44; M. W. Bloomfield and M. J. Reeves, "The Penetration of Joachism into Northern Europe," *Speculum* 29(1954):772-93.

64. M. J. Reeves, "The Abbot Joachim's Disciples and the Cistercian Order," *Sophia* 19(1951):355-71; idem, *Prophecy,* pp. 56, 145-58. The *Super Hieremiam* was printed at Venice in 1525 and 1526, and at Cologne in 1577. All references here are to the last of these editions.

65. Salimbene de Adam, *Chronica,* ed. Oswaldus Holder-Egger, *MGH SS* 32:236-37. The companion work to the *Super Hieremiam,* a commentary on portions of Isaiah called the *Super Esaiam,* is of even more uncertain date, but stems from the same circle and reflects the same ideas. It was printed at Venice in 1517, preceded by a group of *figurae* known as the *Praemissiones.*

66. *Super Hieremiam,* chap. 20, p. 285.

67. Ibid., praef. 4-5; chap. 1, pp. 15-32; chap. 20, pp. 277-92.

68. Ibid., chap. 20, pp. 291-92 (text in E. R. Daniel, *Apocalyptic Conversion,* appendix, sel. 11, pp. 153-54).

69. Ibid., chap. 11, pp. 151-52 (text in Daniel, *Apocalyptic Conversion,* appendix, sel. 8-9, pp. 152-53).

CHAPTER II

1. Bonaventure, *Legenda maior sancti Francisci,* prol., sect. 1, *AF* 10:557.

2. H. Denifle, "Das Evangelium aeternum und die Commission von Anagni," *ALKG* 1(1885):101; P. Stephanus Bihel, "S. Franciscus, fuitne angelus sexti sigilli? (Rev. 7:2)," *Antonianum* 2 (1927):59-90.

3. Cajetan Esser, *Origins of the Franciscan Order,* trans. Aedan Daly, O.F.M. and Irina Lynch (Chicago, 1970), pp. 203-51.

4. M. J. Reeves, *The Influence of Prophecy in the Later Middle Ages: A Study in Joachimism* (Oxford, 1969), pp. 16-27; Ernst Benz, *Ecclesia spiritualis* (Stuttgard, 1934; repr. Stuttgart, 1964), pp. 4-48; P. Ilarino da Milano, "L'incentivo escatologico nel riformismo dell'ordine francescano," *L'attesa* 3:283-337. Abbot Odo of Cluny had earlier combined reform and eschatology. See Raffaello Morghen, "Monastic Reform and Cluniac Spirituality," ed. Noreen Hunt, *Cluniac Monasticism in the Central Middle Ages* (London, 1971), pp. 11-28; and K. Hallinger, "The Spiritual Life of Cluny in the Early Days," ibid., pp. 29-55.

5. M. J. Reeves, *Prophecy,* pp. 135-44; Norman Cohn, *The Pursuit of the Millennium,* 2d ed., rev. (N.Y., 1970), pp. 15-18, 108-09. Cohn defines millennialism as the belief that there will occur in the imminent future a collective, earthly, total transformation of the present imperfect condition into an actualized perfection by means of divine intervention rather than human efforts. Joachim was not a millennialist since his third *status* was to be the full realization of God's historical plan rather than the sudden interruption by the millennium of the downward course of history.

6. Gerhart B. Ladner, *Idea of Reform,* pb. ed. (N.Y. & Evanston, 1967), pp. 9-34.

7. Ibid., pp. 319-424.

8. Jacques de Vitry, *Epistola prima* (Genoa, October 1216) in *Lettres de Jacques de Vitry,* ed. R.B.C. Huygens (Leiden, 1960), pp. 75-76. Cf. *Epistola sexta* (Spring 1220), *Lettres,* pp. 131-33.

9. Idem, *Historica orientalis,* excerpts ed. H. Boehmer, *Analekten zur Geschichte des Franciscus von Assisi* (Tübingen & Leipzig, 1904), pp. 102-06.

10. *Catalogus sanctorum fratrum minorum,* ed. L. Lemmens, *Fragmenta minora* (Rome, 1903), p. 1.

11. Thomas of Celano, *Vita prima s. Francisci,* pt. 2, chap. 1, sect. 89, *AF* 10:68.

12. St. Francis, *Testamentum, Opuscula,* p. 79.

13. Esser, *Origins,* pp. 203-51.

14. Bonaventure, *Legenda maior,* prol., *AF* 10:558.

15. Salimbene de Adam, *Chronica,* ed. Oswaldus Holder-Egger, *MGH SS* 32:309-10.

16. Bonaventure, *Itinerarium mentis ad deum,* prol., sect. 2, *OTS* 5:179-80.

17. Ibid., chap. 7, sect. 1, 5:211-12.

18. Ibid., sect. 6, 5:213-14.

19. Ibid., sect. 3, 5:180.

20. Ibid., chap. 7, sect. 2, 5:212.

21. Ibid., prol., sect. 1, 5:179. Cf. sect. 3, 5:180.

22. Two versions of the *Collationes* have survived. One was edited in the *OO* 5:329-449, the other by F. Delorme, O.F.M., *Bibliotheca franciscana scholastica* 8(Quaracchi, 1934). Bonaventure developed the pattern of sevens in colls. 15 and 16, *OO* 5:400-08; Delorme, visio 3, colls. 3-4, pp. 172-93.

23. See E. R. Daniel, "St. Bonaventure: Defender of Franciscan Eschatology," *S. Bonaventura, 1274-1974,* 5 vols. (Grottaferrata, Rome, 1973-4): 793-806; Joseph Ratzinger, *The Theology of History in St. Bonaventure,* trans. Zachary Hayes, O.F.M. (Chicago, 1971); Bernard McGinn, "The Abbot and the Doctors: Scholastic Reactions to the Radical Eschatology of Joachim of Fiore," *CH* 40 (1971):30-47; M. J. Reeves, *Prophecy,* pp. 175-81. Both Ratzinger and McGinn interpret the *Collationes* as a moderate adaptation of Joachim's theology of history.

24. Tullio Gregory, "Escatologia e Aristotelismo nella scolastica medievale," *L'attesa,* 3:262-82; idem, "Sull' escatologia di Bonaventura e Tommaso d'Aquino," *Studi medievali,* 3rd series, 6, no. 2 (1965):79-94; David Burr, "The Apocalyptic Element in Olivi's Critique of Aristotle," *CH* 40(1971):15-29; Ratzinger, *Theology of History,* pp. 119-63.

25. Bonaventure, *Collationes in Hexaëmeron,* coll. 22, sects. 21-23, *OO* 5:440-41; Delorme, visio 4, coll. 3, p. 256.

26. Bonaventure, *Itinerarium,* chaps. 6-7, sect. 1, *OTS* 5:209-12.

27. Bonaventure, *Quaestiones disputatae de perfectione euangelica,* question 4, art. 2, *conclusio, OO* 8:186.

28. Ibid., question 1, 8:117-18.

29. Ibid., 8:119; question 2, art. 1, 8:126.

30. Ibid., question 2, art. 1, 8:127.

31. Conrad Harkins, "The Authorship of a Commentary on the Franciscan Rule Published among the Works of St. Bonaventure," *Fran. Studies* 29(1969):189-91. The date of David of Augsburg's *Expositio* is uncertain, but he died in 1272.

32. Harkins, "Authorship," attributes the work to John Pecham rather

than to St. Bonaventure, but while his arguments have made Bonaventure's authorship doubtful, they have not succeeded in demonstrating that it was the work of Pecham. Harkins contends that the *Expositio* faithfully mirrored the thought of St. Bonaventure (pp. 246-48).

33. Bonaventure [?], *Expositio super regulam fratrum minorum,* chap. 1, sect. 1, *00* 8:393; chap. 10, sect. 1, 8:431; chap. 12, sects. 1-2, 8:436.

34. D. E. Sharp, *Franciscan Philosophy at Oxford in the Thirteenth Century* (N.Y., 1964), pp. 175-76.

35. John Pecham, *Canticum pauperis pro dilecto,* ed. PP. Collegii s. Bonaventurae, *BFAMA* 4:133-205. The identity of the senior has been debated. Possibly it was St. Bonaventure.

36. Ibid., pp. 133-41.

37. Ibid., pp. 193-96.

38. Ibid., pp. 202-5.

39. *Meditatio pauperis in solitudine,* ed. F. M. Delorme, O.F.M., *BFAMA* 7. On the authorship and date see pp. xii-xxii.

40. Ibid., pp. 1-134.

41. Ibid., pp. 134-35.

42. Ibid., pp. 136-80.

43. Ibid., pp. 94-95, 115-19.

44. Ibid., pp. 180-272.

45. Ibid., pp. 272-365.

CHAPTER III

1. *Scripta Leonis, Rufini et Angeli sociorum s. Francisci,* ed. and trans. Rosalind B. Brooke, Oxford Medieval Texts (Oxford, 1970), chaps. 79, 82, pp. 226-27, 230-33. Prof. Brooke argues that the text of MS. 1046 of the Biblioteca communale of Perugia (originally "La 'Legenda antiqua s. Francisci' du MS. 1046 de la bibliothèque communale de perouse," ed. F. Delorme, *AFH* 15[1922]:23-70, 278-332) combined with excerpts from various other manuscripts is the best possible reconstruction of the original notes sent in by Brothers Leo, Rufinus, and Angelo in 1246 with the covering letter which is now found in manuscripts of the *Legenda trium sociorum* (for the text of the letter see *Scripta Leonis,* pp. 86-89). Brooke contends rightly that chaps. 111-17 of the *Scripta* which are independently known as the *Verba sancti Francisci* are later than the original collection. She dates them to the resignation of John of Parma and the beginning of the generalship of St. Bonaventure, c. 1257, but in my opinion there is no evidence to confirm this date. Chaps. 66-77, known separately as the *Intentio regulae,* apparently belonged to the original collection.

2. St. Francis, *Testamentum, Opuscula,* pp. 77-78; Thomas of Celano, *Vita prima s. Francisci,* pt. 1, chap. 17, sect. 45, *AF* 10:35.

3. Bonaventure, *Legenda maior s. Francisci,* chap. 8, sect. 1, *AF* 10:592.

4. St. Francis, *Testamentum, Opuscula,* p. 77.

5. Thomas of Celano, *Vita prima,* pt. 1, chap. 10, sect. 23, *AF* 10: 19-20; Cajetan Esser, *Origins of the Franciscan Order,* trans. Aedan Daly, O.F.M. and Irina Lynch (Chicago, 1970), pp. 204-8.

6. Thomas of Celano, *Vita prima,* pt. 1, chap. 12, sect. 29, *AF* 10:23-24.

7. Ibid., chap. 13, sect. 32-33, *AF* 10:25-27.

8. Ibid., chap. 15, sect. 36, *AF* 10:29.
9. St. Francis, *Regula bullata,* chap. 9, *Opuscula,* p. 71.
10. Idem, *Regula prima,* chap. 3, *Opuscula,* p. 28.
11. Ibid., chap. 17, p. 46.
12. Ibid., chap. 16, p. 44.
13. Hugh of Digne, *Expositio Hugonis super regulam fratrum minorum,* ed. Alessandra Sisto, *Figure del primo francescanesimo in Provenza: Ugo e Douceline di Digne* (Florence, 1971), pp. 319-21. Sisto provides a biography which includes editions of Hugh's *Expositio, De finibus paupertatis,* and *Disputatio inter zelatorem paupertatis et inimicum domesticum eius.*
14. Odulphus Van der Vat, *Die Anfänge der Franziskanermissionen und ihre Weiterentwicklung im nahen Orient und in der mohammedanischen Ländern während des 13. Jahrhunderts* (Werl in Westf., 1934), p. 35, n 31, quotes the *Expositio* of chap. 12 from Cod. Lat. 8826 of the Münchener Stattbibliothek:

" Quicumque fratrum diuina inspiratione uoluerint ire inter Saracenos et alios infideles,' hereticos et in fide errantes ex simplicitate, ad predicandum eis fidem uel ad exercitandum se in pressuris exsilii, paupertatis et uarie despectionis, uel pro palma martyrii acquirenda, uel pro fidelibus, si qui morantur inter eos, in fide roborandis–petant inde licentiam a suis ministris prouincialibus uel etiam a generali ministro si uolunt. Ministri uero nullis eundi ad tales licentiam tribuant nisi eis, quos ratione etatis, scientie, probitate uirtutis, discretionis, fortitudine corporis, et aliarum utilium conditionum ad hoc ideoneos uiderint ad mittendum. Nisi enim talibus fuerint conditionibus prediti, et exemplares esse studeant in uita, plus possunt ibi obesse quam prodesse. Precipue tamen expedit tales esse deuotos, qui per orationis usum a deo familiariter adherentes obtinere ualeant ad ea, que magis expediunt, et a contrario amoueri."

15. *Declaratio super regulam* in *Speculum minorum,* pt. 3, ff. 105^V-106^r.
16. St. Francis, *Verba admonitionis,* no. 6, *Opuscula,* pp. 9-10.
17. St. Francis, *Regula prima,* chap. 22, *Opuscula,* pp. 51-52; idem, *Epistola prima, Opuscula,* pp. 92-94.
18. Idem, *Regula prima,* chap. 16, *Opuscula,* pp. 45-46.
19. The instructions with regard to the two modes of converting the infidels and the concluding admonitions were omitted from the twelfth chap. of the *Regula bullata (Opuscula,* pp. 73-74). Van der Vat, *Die Anfänge,* pp. 25-29, argues that the omissions indicated a change in the views of the ministers rather than an alteration of St. Francis's view, but it is more likely, in my opinion, that the changes were made simply to decrease the length of the Rule.
20. Thomas of Celano, *Vita prima,* pt. 1, chap. 20, sect. 55, *AF* 10:42.
21. Ibid.; John Moorman, *A History of the Franciscan Order from its Origins to the Year 1517* (Oxford, 1968), pp. 24-25.
22. Thomas of Celano, *Vita prima,* pt. 1, chap. 20, sect. 56, *AF* 10:43; Giulio Basetti-Sani, O.F.M., *Mohammed et St. François* (Ottawa, 1959), pp. 27-60, 157-212.
23. Thomas of Celano, *Vita prima,* pt. 1, chap. 20, sect. 56, *AF* 10:43.
24. Moorman, *History,* pp. 48-49; Thomas of Celano, *Vita prima,* pt. 1, chap. 20, sect. 57, *AF* 10:43-44; idem, *Vita secunda s. Francisci,* pt. 2, chap.

4, sect. 30, *AF* 10:149. Golubovich, *Biblioteca* 1:1-104 brings together all the sources through the fifteenth century for this journey of Francis.

25. *Passio sanctorum martyrum fratrum Beraldi, Petri, Adiuti, Accursii, Othonis in Marochio martyrizatorum, AF* 3:593; *Chronica 24 generalium, AF* 3:21.

26. Giordano of Giano, *Chronica*, sects. 7-8, *AF* 1:3-4.

27. Raphael M. Huber, O.F.M. conv., *St. Anthony of Padua* (Milwaukee, 1948), pp. 9-10.

28. *Sancti Antonii de Padua legenda prima*, ed. Leon de Kerval, *S. Antonii de Padua uitae duae quarum altera hucusque inedita*, Collection d'études et de documents, 5(Paris 1904), chap. 5, p. 29. Kerval regards this as the earliest extant life of Antony.

29. Ibid., chap. 5, p. 29.

30. Ibid., chap. 6, pp. 33-34.

31. *Chronica 24 generalium, AF* 3:78.

32. Ibid.; *Vita Aegidii* in Walter Seton, *Blessed Giles of Assisi, BSFS* 8 [Manchester, 1918], chap. 19, pp. 86-87, and Brooke, *Scripta Leonis*, chap. 18, p. 346.

33. Ibid.

34. Blessed Giles of Assisi, *Dicta beati Aegidii assisiensis*, ed. PP. Collegii S. Bonaventurae, Appendix 1, *BFAMA* 3:93-94.

35. Ibid., p. 99.

36. Seton, *Blessed Giles*, pp. 13-20; *Vita Aegidii*, chaps. 8-10, in Seton, *Blessed Giles, BSFS* 8:64-70, and Brooke, *Scripta Leonis*, pp. 328-35.

37. Giordano of Giano, *Chronica*, sects. 5, 17, 18, *AF* 1:3, 6-8.

38. Ibid., sects. 17-18, *AF* 1:6-8.

39. *Passio sanctorum fratrum Danielis, Agnelli, Samuelis, Donnuli, Leonis, Nicolai, Hugolini ordinis fratrum minorum, AF* 3:614.

40. Ibid., pp. 614-15.

41. Ibid., p. 613.

42. *Chronica 24 generalium, AF* 3:186-87, 221, 227; Robert I. Burns, "Christian-Islamic Confrontation in the West: The Thirteenth Century Dream of Conversion," *AHR* 76(1971):1396-97.

43. Burns, "Christian-Islamic Confrontation," *AHR* 76:1395.

44. See below, chap. 6.

45. See above, p. 44.

46. Thomas of Celano, *Vita prima*, pt. 1, chap. 20, sect. 56, *AF* 10:42.

47. Ibid., sect. 56, *AF* 10:43; Giulo Basetti-Sani, O.F.M., *Mohammed et St. François*, pp. 27-60, 157-212.

48. Thomas of Celano, *Vita prima*, pt. 1, chap. 20, sect. 57, *AF* 10:43-44.

49. Ibid., pt. 2, chap. 2, sects. 91-95, *AF* 10:69-73.

50. Julianus de Spira, *Vita s. Francisci*, chaps. 3, 5, 7, 11, *AF* 10:342-43, 347-48, 351-52, 363.

51. Ibid., chap. 7, *AF* 10:353, chap. 11, 10:362.

52. Moorman, *History*, p. 111.

53. Thomas of Celano, *Vita secunda*, pt. 1, chap. 6, sects. 10-11, *AF* 10:137.

54. Bonaventure, *Legenda maior*, chap. 1, sects. 5, 6, *AF* 10:562-63; ibid., chap. 2, sect. 4, *AF* 10:565.

55. Ibid., chap. 3, sect. 3, *AF* 10:567-68.

56. Ibid., chap. 4, sects. 3, 7, *AF* 10:572, 574; chap. 5, sect. 1, *AF* 10:577.

57. Ibid., chap. 9, sects. 5-9, *AF* 10:599-601.

58. Ibid., chap. 13, sects. 1-3, *AF* 10:615-16.

59. Ibid., sect. 10, *AF* 10:620.

60. The portrait of St. Francis in the *Legenda maior* is reinforced by the *Itinerarium mentis ad deum*, where Bonaventure took the saint as the model of Franciscan spirituality. See E. R. Daniel, "The Desire for Martyrdom: A Leitmotiv of St. Bonaventure," *Fran. Studies* 32(1972):75-76.

61. Bonaventure, *De triplici uia*, prol., *DO*: 3.

62. Ibid., chap. 2, sects. 8-11, *DO:* 16-19.

63. Ibid., chap. 3, sect. 1, *DO:* 20-21.

64. Ibid., sect. 2, *DO:* 22.

65. Ibid., sects. 3-5, *DO:* 23-26.

66. *Manus quae contra omnipotentem tenditur,* ed M. Bierbaum, *Franz. Stud.,* Beihefte 2:38-168. Gerard entitled his reply, *Contra aduersarium perfectionis christianae.* It has been edited by Sophronius Clasen, O.F.M., in "Tractatus Gerardi de abbatisuilla, 'Contra aduersarium perfectionis christianae,' " *AFH* 30(1938):276-329; 31(1939):89-200.

67. J. Guy Bougerol, *Introduction to the Works of Bonaventure,* trans. Jose de Vinck (Paterson, N.J., 1964), pp. 176, 178. Bonaventure had earlier composed the *Quaestiones disputatae de perfectione euangelica* in reply to Guillaume de St. Amour's *De periculis nouissimorum temporum* (E. Gilson, *The Philosophy of St. Bonaventure,* trans. Dom Illtyd Trethowan and Frank J. Sheed [Paterson, N.J., 1965], pp. 11-12, 21).

68. *Manus,* chap. 3, p. 48; chap. 4, pp. 59-60.

69. *Contra aduersarium,* bk. 1, pp. 291-303.

70. Bonaventure, *Apologia pauperum,* chap. 3, sects. 2-3, *OO* 8:244-45.

71. Ibid., sect. 4, *OO* 8:245.

72. Ibid., sect. 7, *OO* 8:246.

73. Ibid., chap. 4, sects. 1-3, *OO* 8:252-53.

74. Fr. Jacobus Mediolavensis or Fr. James of Milan, *Stimulus amoris,* ed. PP. Collegii S. Bonaventurae, *BFAMA* 4:1-129. The *Stimulus* emphasized the contemplative life rather than mission, but admitted the friars' obligation to their neighbors (see chap. 21, pp. 120-22). The anonymous *Mediatatio pauperis in solitudine,* ed. F. M. Delorme, O.F.M., *BFAMA,* vol. 7, placed greater emphasis on the mission of the Order.

75. Hugh of Digne, *Expositio,* chap. 12, p. 321.

76. *Expositio super regulam,* chap. 12, sects. 1-2, *OO* 8:436. See above, chap. 2 .

CHAPTER IV

1. A complete critical edition of Bacon's works is needed. The *Opera hactenus inedita,* ed. Robert Steele, 16 vols. (Oxford, 1909-1940), does not contain the works addressed to the pope. The *Opus maius* was edited by J. H. Bridges, 3 vols. (Oxford, 1897-1900; repr. Frankfurt, 1964); but for Pt. 7, it has been superseded by Eugenio Massa, *Rogeri Baconis moralis philosophia* (Turin, 1953). The translation of the *Opus maius* by Robert B. Burke, 3 vols. (Philadelphia, 1928) was based on Bridges's edition. The *Opus tertium, Opus minus* and *Compendium studii philosophiae* ed. J. S. Brewer, *Opera quaedam hactenus inedita, RS* 15, must be supplemented by A. G. Little, *Part of the*

Opus tertium of Roger Bacon (Aberdeen, 1912). The *Compendium studii theologiae* was edited by Hastings Rashdall, *BSFS* 3. References will be to the above-cited editions except that the *Rogeri Baconis moralis philosophia* will be used instead of Bridges's edition, and references to Little's portion of the *Opus tertium* will be cited as *Opus tertium* (Little).

2. Stewart C. Easton, *Roger Bacon and His Search for a Universal Science* (N.Y., 1952), pp.9-34.

3. Thomas of Eccleston, *Tractatus de adventu fratrum minorum in Angliam,* ed. A. G. Little (Manchester, 1951), pp. 17-18. *Chronica 24 generalium, AF* 3:130, 229-30, says that Adam and St. Anthony of Padua were sent to study theology at Vercelli and then, at the Chapter General of 1238 or 1239, led the opposition to Brother Elias. Adam cannot have studied at Vercelli, however, if he only joined the Order in 1232 (see Rosalind Brooke, *Early Franciscan Government* [Cambridge, Eng., 1959], pp. 27-45, 161-67).

4. Thomas of Eccleston, *Tractatus de aduentu,* p. 50; Easton, *Roger Bacon and his Search,* p. 93; A. G. Little, *The Grey Friars at Oxford* (Oxford, 1892), p. 136.

5. Little, *Grey Friars,* p. 138, dates his death November 18, 1258.

6. *Opus tertium,* chap. 22, p. 70.

7. Easton, *Roger Bacon and His Search,* pp. 87-97.

8. J. M. Bridges, *The Life and Work of Roger Bacon* (London, 1914), pp. 16-17, 25, dates his entrance into the Order c. 1245-50. Edward Lutz, *Roger Bacon's Contribution to Knowledge* (N.Y., 1936), p. 4, cites 1250; Albert Garreau, *Roger Bacon, frère mineur* (Paris, 1942), p. 29, cites 1251. Theodore Crowley, *Roger Bacon, the Problem of the Soul in his Philosophical Commentaries* (Louvain, 1950), p. 18, pushes the date to 1257. A. C. Little, "On Roger Bacon's Life and Works," *Roger Bacon Essays* (Oxford, 1914) p. 5, and Easton, *Roger Bacon and His Search,* pp. 97-98, 118, leave the date open.

9. Easton, *Roger Bacon and His Search,* pp. 118-26, suggests that Bacon both needed financial support for his scientific studies and was attracted by the moral ideal of the Franciscans. Little, "Life and Works," p. 5, and Emile A. Charles, *Roger Bacon* (Paris, 1861), pp. 19-20, cite the influence of Adam Marsh.

10. *Opus tertium,* chap. 3, p. 15. Brewer quotes a passage from the *Opus minus* not found in the surviving fragmentary manuscript that would seem to imply that he suffered some form of imprisonment (*Opera quaedam hactenus inedita, RS* 15:xciv). The *Opus tertium* speaks only of *impedimenta.*

11. On Gerard see below, chap. 5.

12. Easton, *Roger Bacon and His Search,* pp. 126-43; E. R. Daniel, "Roger Bacon and the *De seminibus scripturarum,*" *Mediaeval Studies* 34(1972): 462-67.

13. *Opus tertium,* chap. 10, pp. 32-34.

14. Ibid., chap. 15, p. 91; *Opus maius,* pt. 3, chap. 3, 3:88-89.

15. S. A. Hirsch, "Roger Bacon and Philology," *Roger Bacon Essays,* pp. 101-02.

16. Robert Grosseteste, *Epistolae,* no. 57, ed. Henry Luard, *RS* 25:173-78.

17. D. E. Sharp, *Franciscan Philosophy, BSFS* 16(Oxford, 1930), p. 5.

18. Lee Max Friedman, *Robert Grosseteste and the Jews* (Cambridge, Mass., 1934), p. 8; Francis S. Stevenson, *Robert Grosseteste: Bishop of Lincoln* (London, 1899), p. 105.

19. Stevenson, *Robert Grosseteste,* pp. 225-29.

20. Ibid., p. 21; S. Harrison Thomson, *The Writings of Robert Grosseteste, Bishop of Lincoln, 1235-1253* (Cambridge, Eng., 1940), pp. 121-22, 131-32.

21. Robert Grosseteste, *Epistolae,* no. 5, *RS* 25:33-38; Friedman, *Robert Grosseteste,* pp. 11-18. The Dominicans constructed a *domus conuersorum* in Oxford c. 1231-33.

22. Friedman, *Robert Grosseteste,* pp. 23-25.

23. Vida Scudder, *The Franciscan Adventure* (N.Y., 1931), p. 102; A. G. Little, *Grey Friars,* p. 137.

24. Adam Marsh, *Epistolae,* no. 43, *RS* 4, pt. 1:146-47.

25. Ibid., no. 246, *RS* 4, pt. 1:413-37.

26. Easton, *Roger Bacon and His Search,* pp. 144-66. The *Opus maius* was followed by the *Opus minus* and the *Opus tertium.* Bacon's original project, the *Scriptum principale,* was apparently left unfinished. The letter written by Clement IV in 1266 can be found in Brewer, ed., *Opera quaedam hactenus inedita, RS* 15:1.

27. *Opus maius,* pt. 1, 1:3-4.

28. *Compendium studii theologiae,* pt. 1, chap. 2, pp. 28-34.

29. *Opus maius,* 1:266; *Opus tertium,* p. 208; Daniel, "Roger Bacon and *De seminibus,*" *Mediaeval Studies,* 34:464-65.

30. Easton, *Roger Bacon and His Search,* pp. 190-91.

31. *Compendium studii philosophiae,* pp. 395-404.

32. *Opus maius,* pt. 5, 2:164-66.

33. Ibid., pt. 3, chaps. 13-14, 3:120-25.

34. *Opus maius,* pt. 2, chaps. 1, 9-14, 3:36, 53-68; *Opus minus,* pp. 357-59; *Opus tertium,* chap. 23, pp. 73-74.

35. *Opus tertium,* chaps. 1, 5, 24, pp. 3, 4, 20, 81.

36. *Opus maius,* pt. 2, chaps. 18-19, 3:75-79.

37. *Opus tertium,* chaps. 10, 25, pp. 32-33, 89-95.

38. Ibid., chaps. 30, 65, pp. 106-7, 268-70.

39. *Opus tertium* (Little), p. 10; *Opus maius,* pt. 4, 1:249-53.

40. *Opus tertium,* chap. 54, p. 204; *Opus tertium* (Little), p. 10.

41. *Opus maius,* pt. 4, 1:301-4.

42. Ibid., 1:266-69, 309, 365.

43. *Moralis philosophia,* pt. 1, pp. 3-31.

44. Ibid., pt. 4, pp. 187-88.

45. Ibid., pp. 189-93; *Opus maius,* pt. 4, 1:253-66. In the *Opus maius* Bacon lists the Jews, Chaldeans, Egyptians, Muslims, Christians, and the sect of antichrist. In the *Moralis philosophia* he at first includes the pagans, idolaters (Buddhists), Tartars, Saracens, Jews, and Christians, but then gives another list that omits Islam and adds antichrist.

46. *Moralis philosophia,* pt. 4, pp. 195-223.

47. *Opus maius,* pt. 4, 1:253-86.

48. *Chronica 24 generalium, AF* 3:360; Easton, *Roger Bacon and His Search,* pp. 192-202.

49. Easton, *Roger Bacon and His Search,* pp. 202-5; *Compendium studii theologiae, BSFS* 3.

50. The *Vita beati Raymundi Lulli* or *Vita coetanea* was edited by B. de Gaiffier, "Vita beati Raimundi Lulli," *Analecta bollandiana* 48 (1930):130-78. Gaiffier's text and the *Vida coetania* or Catalan version are printed on facing pages in Ramon Llull, *Obras literarias,* ed. Migual Batllori, S.I., and Migual Caldentey, *T.O.R. Biblioteca de autores christianos* (Madrid, 1948), pp. 46-77.

References to the Latin text will be to Gaiffier's version while the Catalan will be cited in the version of Batllori and Caldentey.

51. E. Allison Peers, *Ramon Lull: A Biography* (London, 1929), pp. 4-7; *Vita,* chap. 2, p. 47; but see J. N. Hillgarth, *Ramon Lull and Lullism in Fourteenth-Century France* (Oxford, 1971), p. 2, n.9, who contends that Llull was not a page.

52. *Vita,* chap. 5, p. 148; *Vida,* chap. 5, 49; Peers, *Ramon Lull,* pp. 12-13.

53. Peers, *Ramon Lull,* pp. 15-16.

54. *Vita,* chaps. 2-9, pp. 146-50; *Vida,* chaps. 2-9, pp. 47-51.

55. Peers, *Ramon Lull,* p. xv.

56. *Vita,* chap. 10, p. 150; *Vida,* chap. 10, p. 51.

57. Peers, *Ramon Lull,* pp. 34-36.

58. *Vita,* chaps. 11-13, pp. 151-52; *Vida,* chaps. 11-13, pp. 51-53.

59. Armand Llinares, *Raymond Lulle: philosophe de l'action* (Paris, 1963), pp. 90-91.

60. Peers, *Ramon Lull,* pp. 45-46.

61. *Vita,* chap. 14, pp. 152-53; *Vida,* chap. 14, p. 53.

62. *Vita,* chap. 16, p. 154; *Vida,* chap. 16, p. 55; Llinares, *Raymond Lulle,* p. 95. On Bertrandus see the *Chronica 24 generalium, AF* 3:387, 391.

63. *Vita,* chap. 17, pp. 154-55; *Vida* chap. 17, p. 55; Peers, *Ramon Lull,* pp. 128-37.

64. Llinares, *Raymond Lulle,* pp. 95-96; Golubovich, *Biblioteca,* 1:365.

65. Peers, *Ramon Lull,* pp. 135-36, gives a brief résumé of the later history of Miramar.

66. Peers, *Ramon Lull,* pp. 142-54; Llinares, *Raymond Lulle,* pp. 96-97.

67. *Vita,* chaps. 18-19, pp. 155-56; *Vida,* chaps. 18-19, pp. 55, 57; Llinares, *Raymond Lulle,* pp. 101-2.

68. Luke Wadding, *Annales minorum,* ed. PP. Collegii S. Bonaventurae, 32 vols. (Quaracchi, 1931; 3d ed., 1964), ad annum 1290, 5:268; A. Rubio Lluch, *Documents per l'historia de la cultura catalana mig-eval,* 2 vols. (Barcelona, 1908, 1921), 1:9-10; Llinares, *Raymond Lulle,* p. 125, 125n.

69. *Vita,* chap. 19, pp. 155-56; *Vida,* chap. 19, p. 57. Hillgarth, *Ramon Lull,* p. 54, says that it is "virtually certain" that Llull used this authorization.

70. *Vita,* chaps. 20-32, pp. 156-66; *Vida,* chaps. 20-32, pp. 57-67.

71. *Vita,* chaps. 32-43, pp. 166-74; *Vida,* chaps. 32-43, pp. 67-77; Peers, *Ramon Lull,* pp. 268-69; Llinares, *Raymond Lulle,* pp. 114-15, 120-21.

72. *Vita,* chap. 44, p. 174; *Vida,* chap. 44, p. 77; Llinares, *Raymond Lulle,* pp. 120-22.

73. On the implementation of this decree see Berthold Altaner, "Raymundus Lullus und der Sprachenkanon (Canon 11) des Konzils von Vienne (1312)," *Historisches Jahrbuch* 53(1933):190-219; idem, "Die Durchführung des Vienner Konzilsbeschlusses über die Errichtung von Lehrstühlen für orientalische Sprachen," *ZKG* 52(1933):223-36; Roberto Weiss, "England and the Decree of Vienne on the Teaching of Greek, Arabic, Hebrew, and Syriac," *Bibliothèque d'humanisme et renaissance* 14(1952):1-9.

74. Llinares, *Raymond Lulle,* pp. 122-24.

75. Ibid., pp. 124-26; Peers, *Ramon Lull,* pp. 371-75; Hillgarth, *Ramon Lull,* pp. 134, 369n. Llinares believes that Llull died in Majorca and was not a martyr. Peers thinks that he was stoned but lived until he arrived in Palma. Hillgarth regards the martyrdom as an unfounded legend.

76. Llinares, *Raymond Lulle,* p. 125; Peers, *Ramon Lull,* p. 375.

77. Peers, *Ramon Lull*, p. 45.
78. William of Rubruck, *Itinerarium*, ed. Wyngaert, *Sinica francescana*, chap. 13, 1: 196.

CHAPTER V

1. Salimbene de Adam, *Chronica*, ed. Oswaldus Holder-Egger, *MGH SS* 32: 231, 233, 236, 237. Salimbene himself, Hugh of Digne, John of Parma, Gerard of Borgo San Donnino, and Bartolomaeus Guiscolus are among those described as Joachites or *maximi Ioachitae*, those whom Salimbene regarded as disciples of the Abbot Joachim. Clearly in Gerard's case, less certainly where Hugh and John of Parma are concerned, Salimbene's use of the word indicated expectation of the coming third *status* and the assignment to Frederick II of the role of antichrist.

2. E. R. Daniel, "Roger Bacon and the *De seminibus scriptuarum*," *Mediaeval Studies* 34(1972):462-64, summarizes the current theories about the authorship and date of the *De seminibus* as well as its content. See also B. Hirsch-Reich, "Zur 'Noticia saeculi' und zum 'Pauo,'" *MIOG* 38(1921-22): 580-610; 40 (1924-25):317-25; idem, "Alexander von Roes Stellung zu den Prophetien," *MIOG* 57 (1959):306-16. I have used the text in Cod. Vat. lat. 3819, ff. 1^r-18^v, and am indebted to the Manuscripta microfilm project at St. Louis University and to the Vatican Library itself for use of the microfilm copy of this text. Dr. Hirsch-Reich was working on an edition of the *De seminibus* for the *MGH QzG*, but her death left it unfinished. I have accepted her hypothesis that the author was a monk at Michelsberg in Bamberg.

3. Bonaventure, *Collationes in Hexaëmeron*, coll. 15, sect. 25, *OO* 5:401-2, ed. F. Delorme, O.F.M., *Bibliotheca franciscana scholastica* 8 (Quaracchi, 1934), visio 3, coll. 3, sects. 24-25, pp. 176-77.

4. Adam Marsh, *Epistolae*, ed. J. S. Brewer, *RS*, no. 43, 4:146-47. Adam wrote to Robert Grosseteste that he was sending him some "paucas particulas de uariis expositionibus abbatis Ioachim," which Adam had received a few days earlier from an unnamed friar who had carried them from the continent. He wanted Grosseteste's opinion on Joachim's prediction of the imminence of the "immutabilis prouidentiae dies formidandi." Salimbene, *Chronica, MGH SS* 32:233-34, lists both Adam and Robert among the intimate friends of Hugh of Digne. M. W. Bloomfield and M. J. Reeves, "The Penetration of Joachism into Northern Europe," *Speculum* 29(1954):785-86, argue that Adam's interest in Joachim must have come from contact with Hugh.

5. Paschalis's source was probably the papal bull, *Cum hora (iam) undecima*, issued originally by Pope Gregory IX, June 11, 1239, and reissued by Innocent IV, Alexander IV, Nicholas IV, Clement V, and John XXII, becoming the foundation of the privileges of the mendicant missionaries. The bull began by asserting that it was now the eleventh hour when the *plenitudo gentium* had to be realized before the salvation of Israel could occur. See the version of Clement V, July 23, 1307, in *BF*, no. 84, 5:35-37.

6. Alexander Minorita, *Expositio in apocalypsim*, ed. Alois Wachtel, *MGH QzG*, 1:436-37, 493-95, 509. On the date of Alexander's commentary, see M. J. Reeves, *The Influence of Prophecy in the Later Middle Ages: A Study in Joachimism* (Oxford, 1969), pp. 177-78.

7. See E. R. Daniel, "A Re-examination of the Origins of Franciscan Joachitism," *Speculum* 43(1968):671-76; and M. J. Reeves, *Prophecy,* pp. 175-90.

8. Salimbene, *Chronica, MGH SS* 32:44, 236; Daniel, "Re-examination," *Speculum* 43:672-73.

9. Salimbene, *Chronica, MGH SS* 32:236-37.

10. Ibid., pp. 239-53. The two Franciscans were Joannes Gallicus and Johanninus Pigulinus. The Dominican was Peter of Apulia, a lector at Naples. F. Russo, "Gioachinismo e Francescanesimo," *MF* 41(1941):71-73, notes the evidence of Joachitism at Naples and contrasts it with the lack of similar evidence of Joachitism among the contemporary Franciscans of Calabria.

11. Salimbene, *Chronica, MGH SS* 32:298; Daniel, "Re-examination," *Speculum* 43:674.

12. Salimbene, *Chronica, MGH SS* 32:234; Rosalind Brooke, *Early Franciscan Government: Elias to Bonaventure* (Cambridge, Eng., 1959), p. 221, n.2 See above chap. 3, and below, Appendix I.

13. Daniel, "Re-examination," *Speculum* 43:674-75.

14. The *Liber introductorius* was excerpted by the Commission of Anagni; the protocol was edited by H. Denifle, *Evangelium aeternum.* B. Töpfer, "Eine Handschriften des *Evangelium aeternum* des Gerardino von Borgo San Donnino," *Zeitschrift für Geschichtswissenschaft* 7(1960):156-63, argued that Dresden, Sächs, Landesbibl., A. 121, is a copy of Gerard's work, containing most of his glosses but not the introduction. On the excerpts made by the secular masters at Paris see Ernst Benz, "Joachim Studien II: Die Excerptsätze der pariser Professoren aus dem *Evangelium aeternum,*" *ZKG* 51 (1932):415-55. M. M. Dufeil, *Guillaume de Saint Amour et la polémique universitaire parisienne, 1250-1259* (Paris, 1972) gives the conventional view of Gerard.

15. Salimbene, *Chronica, MGH SS* 32:236-37. Angelo of Clareno in *Historia Septem Tribulationum,* trib. 3, ed. F. Ehrle, "Die Spiritualen, ihr Verhältnis zum Franziskanerorden und zu den Fratricellen," *ALKG* 2(1886):268-69, states that Gerard made the same prediction in Constantinople at the time of St. Louis's capture in 1250, while Gerard was accompanying John of Parma on the latter's embassy.

16. Delno West, "The Re-formed Church and the Friars Minor: The Moderate Joachite Position of Fr. Salimbene," *AFH* 64(1971):273-84; idem, "The Present State of Salimbene Studies with a Bibliographic Appendix of the Major Works," *Fran. Stud.* 32(1972):225-41.

17. E. R. Daniel, "Apocalyptic Conversion: The Joachite Alternative to the Crusades," *Traditio* 25(1969):142-44, 146-48; Salimbene, *Chronica, MGH SS* 32:492-95.

18. See the Bibliographical essay; M. J. Reeves, *Prophecy,* pp. 191-228; John Moorman, *A History of the Franciscan Order from its Origins to the year 1517* (Oxford, 1968), pp. 188-204. Moorman has little sympathy for the Spirituals' Joachitism but is more favorable to their stand on poverty. M. D. Lambert, *Franciscan Poverty* (London, 1961), treats the poverty question by studying the legal issues. On the relationship between poverty and spirituality see E. R. Daniel, "Spirituality and Poverty: Angelo da Clareno and Ubertino da Casale," *Medievalia et humanistica,* n.s. 4(1973):89-98.

19. Salimbene, *Chronica, MGH SS* 32:301-4, 309-10, 322, 456, 553; Angelo Clareno, *Historia,* trib. 3, ed. F. Ehrle, pp. 268-69; ibid., trib. 4, pp.

271-87. On the position of St. Bonaventure with respect to St. Francis see E. R. Daniel, "St. Bonaventure, a Faithful Disciple of St. Francis? A Re-examination of the Question," *S. Bonaventure, 1274-1974*, 5 vols. (Grottaferrata Roma, 1972-), 2:171-87; published also in *The Cord* 23(1973):292-304. See also E. R. Daniel, "The Trial of John of Parma" (delivered at the Eighth Conference on Medieval Studies, Kalamazoo, Mich., May 1973).

20. Peter John Olivi's *Lectura super apocalypsim* has never been printed. I have used Cod. Vat. Borgh. 38, ff. 1^r-154^r, which unfortunately breaks off at Rev. 19:17. The Commission established by Pope John XXII in 1319 compiled excerpts and these have been edited by E. Baluze, *Miscellaneorum* (Paris, 1678), 1:213-67. Ign. von Döllinger, *Beiträge zur Sektengeschichte des Mittelalters*, 2 vols. (repr. ed., N.Y., 1960), 2:527-85, is accessible, but Döllinger's inaccurate transcriptions are compounded by his failure to distinguish clearly the actual excerpts from his own summaries and comments. My references will be to Cod. Vat. Borgh. 38 (Cod.) and Baluze (Bal.).

Joachim had used *status* for the threefold scheme only, employing *tempus* or *etas* for his divisions into two's or seven's. Olivi employs *status* for the seven *etates* of Joachim, but distinguishes these seven *status ecclesie* from the three general *status*. See *Lectura*, Cod., prol., f. 10^{ra-va}, partly excerpted in Bal., no. 4, p. 217; Cod., chap. 3, ff. 42va-43rb/Bal., nos. 13-15, pp. 223-25; Cod., chap. 6, f. 69^{ra-va}/Bal., nos. 22-23, pp. 228-29; Cod., chap. 7, ff. 72va-73rb/Bal., no. 28, pp. 235-36; Bal., chap. 21, nos. 59-60, pp. 266-67; Raoul Manselli, *La 'Lectura super apocalipsim' di Pietro Giovanni Olivi*, Studi Storici, fasc. 19-21 (Rome, 1955):141-44, 162-67, 170-71, 179, 185-92; Ernst Benz, *Ecclesia spiritualis* (Stuttgart, 1934; repr., 1964), pp. 256-332; idem, "Joachim Studien 1: Die Kategorien der religiösen Geschichtsdeutung Joachims," *ZKG* 50(1931):89-97.

21. Olivi, *Lectura*, Cod., prol., f. 2^{va-vb}; Manselli, '*La Lectura*,' 192-235; Benz, *Ecclesia spiritualis*, pp. 265-85.

22. Olivi, *Lectura*, Cod., prol., f. 2va/Bal. 1, pp. 214-15; Cod., prol., f. 11^{ra-va}/Bal., no. 5, p. 218; Cod., prol., f. 18va/Bal., no. 9, p. 221; Cod., chap. 6, ff. 69ra-75vb/Bal., nos. 23-31, pp. 229-41; Cod., chap. 6, f. 79^{rb-vb}/Bal., no. 32, pp. 241-42.

23. Ibid., Cod., prol., f. 6rb/Bal., no. 3, pp. 216-17; Cod., prol., f. 10^{ra-va}/Bal., no. 4, p. 217; Cod., prol., f. 17va/Bal., no. 8, p. 220; Cod., prol., f. 19ra/Bal., no. 10, p. 221; Cod., chap. 3, f. 45rb/Bal., no. 19, pp. 226-27; Cod., chap. 5, f. 55^{rb-va}/Bal., no. 20, p. 227; Cod., chap. 6, f. 68va/Bal., no. 21, pp. 227-28; Cod., chap. 8, f. 85vb/Bal., no. 33, p. 242; Cod., chap. 9, ff. 86va-94ra/Bal., nos. 34-37, pp. 243-46.

24. Ibid., Cod., chap. 10, ff. 97va-98ra/Bal., no. 38, pp. 246-47. Critical text in David Flood, *Peter Olivi's Rule Commentary: Edition and Presentation*, Veröffentlichungen des Instituts für europäische Geschichte Mainz, Abteilung abendländische Religionsgeschichte, ed. Joseph Lortz, bd. 67 (Wiesbaden, 1972), pp. 192-93.

25. Olivi, *Lectura*, Cod., prol., vol. 2va/Bal., no. 1, pp. 214-15; Cod., prol., f. 10^{ra-va}/Bal., no. 4, p. 217; Cod., prol., f. 11^{ra-va}/Bal., no. 5, p. 218; Cod., chap. 3, ff. 42va-43rb/Bal., nos. 13-15, pp. 223-25; Cod., chaps. 10-11, ff. 98ra-104va/Bal., nos. 39-43, pp. 247-51; Cod., chap. 21/Bal., nos. 59-60, pp. 266-67.

26. Ibid., Cod., chap. 3, ff. 42va-43rb/Bal., no. 13, p. 223.

27. Ibid., Cod., chap. 8, ff. 79vb-80rb. Olivi's seventh *status* appears to

resemble that of St. Bonaventure's *Collationes in Hexaëmeron* in its emphasis on the contemplative attainment of the seventh *status.* See above, chap. 3.
28. See above, n. 26.
29. Peter John Olivi, *Expositio super regulam,* chap. 12, *Speculum minorum,* pt. 3, ff, 123ᵛ-124ᵛ; Flood, *Rule Commentary,* 192-93.
30. Karl Balthazar, *Geschichte des Armutsstreites im Franziskanerorden bis zum Konzil von Vienne* (Münster, 1911), pp. 236-47; Abbé Vidal, "Un ascète du sang royal: Philippe de Majorque," *Revue des questions historiques* 88(1910):361-403; Mercedes van Heuckelum, *Spiritualistische Strömungen an den Höfen von Aragon und Anjou während der Höhe des Armutsstreites* (Berlin & Leipzig, 1938). The circle included the two sons of Charles II of Naples, Robert and Ludwig, as well as Philip of Majorca, Frederick III of Sicily, Jaime II of Aragon, and the cardinals, Jacob Colonna, Peter Colonna and Napoleon Orsini. The most important document is the process brought against a member of the circle, Adhemar de Mosset (Vidal, pp. 396-99).
31. *De statibus ecclesie,* ed. José M.a. Pou y Marti, *Visionarios, beguinos y fraticelos catalanes (siglos xiii-xv)* (Vich, 1930), pp. 483-512. Article 24 is found on p. 503. The extracts were made by Fr. Pedro de Palude, O.P. and the Carmelite Guiu Terrena, bishop of Majorca, 1321-32. On the Béguins see also Raoul Manselli, *Spirituali e Beghini in Provenza,* Studi storici, fasc. 31-34 (Rome, 1959).
32. Moorman, *History,* pp. 307-8.
33. Golubovich, *Biblioteca,* 3:407-13, 424-52.
34. Lambert, *Franciscan Poverty,* p. 175; D. Pacetti, "I codici autografi di S. Bernardino da Siena della Vaticana a delle comunale di Siena," *AFH* 27(1934):224-58, 565-84; 28(1935):253-72, 500-516; idem, "Gli scritti di S. Bernardino da Siena, in *S. Bernardino da Siena* (Milan, 1945), pp. 109-30; Peter John Olivi, *Quaestiones quatuor de domina, BFAMA* 8:30-41; P. Victorinus Doucet, "De operibus manuscriptis Fr. Petri Ioannis Olivi in biblioteca universitatis Patavinae asservatis," *AFH* 28(1935):156-97, 408-42.
35. Decima L. Douie, *The Nature and the Effect of the Heresy of the Fraticelli* (Manchester, 1932), pp. 132-42.
36. On Ubertino's use of Olivi's *Lectura* see R. Manselli, "Pietro di Giovanni Olivi ed Ubertino da Casale," *Studi medievali,* 3rd series 6, fasc. 2 (1965):95-122. Ubertino, however, incorporates material from other sources and in certain respects sharpens the thrust of Olivi's eschatology.
37. Ubertino da Casale, *Arbor uitae crucifixae Iesu,* bk. 5, chaps. 1, 3, 8, 9, 12.
38. F. Callaey, "Les idées mystico-politiques d'un franciscain spirituel," *RHE* 11(1910):721-27; idem, "L'influence et la diffusion de l'*Arbor uitae* d'Ubertin de Casale," *RHE* 17(1921):533-46. The *Arbor uitae* is also found on ff. 1-134 of ms. no. 88 of the Cathedral of Valencia (D. Elias Olmos y Canalda, *Catalogo descriptivo: codices de la catedral de Valencia* [Valencia, 1943], pp. 71-72).
39. E. Blondeel d'Isegem, "L'influence de'Ubertin de Casale sur les écrits de S. Bernardino de Siene," *Collectanea franciscana* 5(1935):5-44.
40. Library of Congress, Rare Book Room, Incun. 1485, U14, bk. 5, chap. 18, marginal note.
41. Angelo Clareno, *Expositio regulae fratrum minorum,* ed. L. Oliger (Quaracchi, 1912), pp. 226-28. See below, chap. 6.
42. Herbert Grundmann, "Die Papstprophetien des Mittelalters," *Archiv*

für Kulturgeschichte 19(1928):77-138; M. J. Reeves, Prophecy, pp. 401-6; idem, "Some Popular Prophecies from the 14th to the 17th Centuries," *Studies in Church History*, ed. G. J. Cuming and Derek Baker, 8(Cambridge, Eng., 1971):107-34; Friedrich Baethgen, "Der Engelpapst," Schriften der Königsberger Gelehrten Gesellschaft, Geisteswiss. Kl. 10, no. 2 (1933):75-119. "Angelic pope" meant a pope or popes who would reform the papacy and the church as if they were angels, or who would lead lives so holy as to be worthy of the adjective, angelic. None of these prophecies envisioned actual angels themselves taking the papal throne.

43. Roger Bacon, *Opus tertium*, ed. J. S. Brewer, *Opera quaedàm hactenus inedita, RS* 15:86.

44. Idem, *Compendium studii philosophiae*, ed. J. S. Brewer, *Opera*, pp. 402-3.

45. *Oraculum angelicum Cyrilli*, ed. Paul Piur, *Briefwechsel des Cola di Rienzo*, Teil 4, in *Vom Mittelalter zur Reformation*, ed. Konrad Burdach, bd. 2 (Berlin, 1912):223-343. The *Oraculum* was attributed to a carmelite named Cyril of Constantinople, and included a prologue by Fr. Gilbertus Anglicus, letters from Cyril to Joachim and from Joachim to Cyril, the *Oraculum* itself, and a gloss attributed to Joachim. Except for the prologue, the *Oraculum* dates from between 1280 and 1290 (see M. J. Reeves, *Prophecy*, pp. 522-23).

46. The *Introductio in librum Joachim de semine scripturarum* has been edited by Raoul Manselli, "La religiosità d'Arnoldo da Villanova," *Bulletino dell' Istituto storico italiano per il medio evo e archivio muratoriano,* 63(1951):43-59.

47. The *Tractatus de tempore de aduentu antichristi* was partially edited by H. Finke, *Aus den Tagen Bonifaz VIII: Funde und Forschungen,* 2 vols. (Münster, 1902), 2:cxxix-clix. Franz Pelster, "Die Quaestio Heinrichs von Harclay über die zweite Ankunft Christi und die Erwartung des baldigen Weltendes zu Anfang des XIV. Jahrhunderts," *Archivio italiano per la storia della pietà* 1(1951):25-82, describes the controversy.

48. Moorman, *History*, pp. 198-99; Angelo Clareno, *Historia*, trib. 6, ed. F. Ehrle, p. 129.

49. On these Catalan and Italian versions see the reading list at the end of the chapter. On the Béguins see above, n.31.

50. Benz, *Ecclesia spiritualis*, pp. 368-71.

51. Manselli, "La religiosità," pp. 15-39; Benz, *Ecclesia spiritualis*, pp. 373-82; idem, "Die Geschichtstheologie der Franziskanerspiritualen des 13. und 14. Jahrhunderts nach neuen Quellen," *ZKG* 52(1933):109-10; Gordon Leff, *Heresy in the Later Middle Ages,* 2 vols. (N.Y., 1967), 1:176-85. Arnau's *Expositio super apocalipsim* survives in three manuscripts, Cod. Vat. lat. 5740, pp. 1-105, Cod. Ottob. lat. 536, and Cod. Vat. lat. 1305. All references are to the first. On Arnau's seven *tempora* see *Expositio*, pp. 9-10, 14-24, 32-33, 37-42, 64-67; *Confessio de Barcelona* in *Obres catalanes*, ed. M. Batllori and J. Carreras i Artau, 2 vols. (Barcelona, 1947), 1:114; and *De mysterio cimbalorum,* Cod. Vat. lat. 3824, f. 80^v.

52. Arnau de Vilanova, *Obres catalanes,* 1:218-22; idem, *Tractatus de aduentu antichristi*, ed. Finke, *Aus den Tagen Bonifaz,* 2:cl-cli; idem, *Allocutio super significatione nominis tetragrammaton,* ed. J. Carreras i Artau, *Sefarad* 9(1948):100-101. In his *Sobre la mort de Bonifaci VIII*, partially edited by Finke, *Aus den Tagen Bonifaz,* 2:cxc, Arnau said to Pope Boniface XI, "Admoneris etiam inuitare paganos et infideles atque scismaticos ad

audiendum pacifice uerbum Christi, quoniam tempus conuersionis et reconsiliationis ipsorum accelerat." See also Hillgarth, *Ramon Lull,* pp. 53-58, 70-71, 95-98, 129-33.

53. Arnau de Vilanova, *Obres catalanes,* 1:223-43; Manselli, "La religiosità," pp. 21-22.

54. Arnau de Vilanova, *Tractatus de aduentu antichristi,* ed. Finke, *Aus den Tagen Bonifaz,* 2:cxxxii-cxxxiii. In the *De mysterio cimbalorum,* Cod. Vat. lat. 3824, ff. 95ᵛ-96, the prophecy entitled *Ve mundo in centum annis* predicted that a *uespertilio* would lead the Greeks back to the Catholic faith.

55. Arnau de Vilanova, *Obres catalanes,* 1:223-43; Manselli, "La religiosita," pp. 5-6.

56. J. Carreras i Artau, "Les obres theologiques d'Arnau de Vilanova," *AST* 12(1936):218. Among the works translated were the *Allocutio;* the *Dyalogus de elementis catholicae fidei;* the *Philosophia catholica;* the *Eulogium;* the *Lliço de Narbona;* a tract called *De la humilitat i paciencia de Jesucrist* of which only the Greek version survives; the *Tractatus de caritate;* and the *Per cio che molti.* The codex formerly belonged to St. Germain des Près but after the French Revolution was taken to Russia and is now in the National Library of Leningrad. For a description see M. Victor le Clerc, "Raymond de Meuillon," *Histoire littéraire de la France,* 20 (Paris, 1842):261-65. According to J. Carreras i Artau, "Una versió grega de nou escrits d'Arnau de Vilanova," *AST* 8 (1932):127-34, the translator was Arnau himself and the translations were connected with Arnau's interest in the monks of Mt. Athos. M. Batllori, ed., "Les versiones italianes medievals d'obres religioses de mestre Arnau de Vilanova," *Archivo italiano per la storia della pietà* 1(1951):400-410, agrees with Carreras i Artau and adds that the Italian versions of three of the same works were probably intended for use by the Spirituals of Tuscany. Both groups of translations would then date from the last years of Arnau's life, c. 1305-1311. See also M. Batllori, "Els textes espirituals d'Arnau de Vilanova en llengua grega," *Quaderni ibero-Americani* 14(Turin, 1953):358-61.

57. Arnau de Vilanova, *Expositio,* pp. 38-40; see *Tractatus de aduentu antichristi,* ed. Finke, *Aus den Tagen Bonifaz,* 2:cxli-cxlii, where Arnau interprets Acts 1:6, "Domini, si in hoc tempore restituas regnum Israel" as a reference to the "consummatione seculi uel ultima conuersione Iudeorum ad Christum." See also idem, *Allocutio,* J. Carreras i Artau, "Arnaldo de Vilanova, apologista antiiudaica," *Sefarad* 7(1947):49-61; Arnau de Vilanova, *Informació espiritual, Obres catalanes,* 1:234-35.

58. Antonino de Stefano, *Federico III d'Aragona, re di Sicilia* (Palermo, 1937), pp. 14-16, 83-88; Douie, *Nature and Effect,* p. 16; Finke, *Acta aragonensia,* 2:661-72, 695-99.

59. Herbert Grundmann, "Liber de Flore: Eine Schrift der Franziskaner-Spiritualen aus dem Anfang des 14. Jahrhunderts," *Historisches Jahrbuch* 49(1929):33-91, contains a partial edition of the *Liber de flore.* See also M. J. Reeves, *Prophecy,* pp. 402-6. A portion of an apparent commentary from the later 14th century on the *Liber de flore* survives in MS Car C. 26 (#241), 15th century, of the Zentralbibliothek in Zurich, f. 34ᵛ, inc. "Celi enarrant gloriam dei." There is a third work called the *Horoscopus,* purportedly translated by one Dandalus of Lerida from the Hebrew; Grundmann argued that this work closely resembles the *Vaticinia* but has an astrological character not found in the papal prophecies (*Liber de flore,* pp. 38-41).

60. The *Vade mecum*, written in 1356, was edited by Edward Brown in the appendix of his edition of the *Fasciculus rerum expetendarum et fugienda-rum* of *Ortuinus Gratius* (London, 1690), 2:496-508. See pp. 497-501; and J. Bignami-Odier, *Etudes sur Jean de Roquetaillade* (Paris, 1952), pp. 71, 77-81, 94, 98, 116-18, 124, 143-45, 170.

61. Bignami-Odier, *Etudes*, pp. 81-85, 88-89, 95, 103, 142, 163, 170, 172; *Vade mecum*, pp. 497-502, 506.

62. Lynn Thorndike, *A History of Magic and Experimental Science*, vols. 2 & 3 (N.Y., 1923, 1934), 3:354-55.

63. *Vade mecum*, pp. 497-98, 506; Bignami-Odier, *Etudes*, pp. 65, 100-103, 124-25, 142, 163. The *Vade mecum* was Jean's most popular work. Some eighteen manuscripts survive (see Bignami-Odier, *Etudes*, pp. 245-46), and French, German, and Catalan translations also are preserved (ibid., pp. 241-42, 246-48, 251). There is a Castilian translation at the University of Salamanca in Sal. MS. 1877, ff. 237^v-251, described by Guy Beaujouan, *Manuscrits scientifiques médiévaux de l'université de Salamanque et de ses 'colegios mayores,'* (Bordeaux, 1962), pp. 82-83.

64. Emil Donckel, "Studien über die Prophezeiung des Fr. Telesphorus von Cosenza," *AFH* 26(1933):29-104, 282-314; M. J. Reeves, *Prophecy*, pp. 324-31, 343-46, 423-24. The *De magnis tribulationibus et statu ecclesie* was published at Venice in 1516, ff. 8^v-44^r.

65. *De magnis*, ff. 10^r, 14^r-15^r, 18^r-^{v}, 20^r-21^v, 22^v-30^r, 32^r-35^r, 37^v-39^v.

66. M. J. Reeves, *Prophecy*, pp. 324-28, 424; Donckel, "Studien," pp. 33-49. In Bibliothéque nationale lat. 14669 at Paris, ff. 123^r-127^r, excerpts from the gloss attributed to Joachim on the *Oraculum angelicum Cyrilli*, chaps. 9-10, are followed by an extensive collection of notes by someone who made considerable use of Telesphorus (ff. 127^r-133^r, 135^v-145^v).

67. Luke's notebook is now in the Biblioteca nazionale centrale, Florence, Magl. XX, no. 59, provenienza Strozzi, 4^0, #652. On Luke see M. J. Reeves, *Prophecy*, p. 434. Ibid., pp. 534-40 describes some prophetic anthologies.

CHAPTER VI

1. See Bibliographical Essay, p. 157.

2. See E. R. Daniel, "Spirituality and Poverty: Angelo de Clareno and Ubertino da Casale," *Medievalia et humanistica*, n.s. 4(1973):89-98; Hilarin Felder, *Geschichte der wissenschaftlichen Studien im Franziskanerorden* (Freiburg im Breisgau, 1904), pp. 1-51; John Moorman, *A History of the Franciscan Order from its Origins to the year 1517* (Oxford, 1968), pp. 89-95, 113-54; P. Gratien, *Histoire de l'ordre des frères mineurs in xiiie siècle* (Paris and Gembloux, 1928), p. 110.

3. "Legenda s. Francisci assisiensis tribus ipsius sociis . . . adscripta," ed. Michael Faloci Pulignani (Foligno, 1898), re-ed. Guiseppe Abate, O.F.M., *MF* 39(1939):375-432. Abate's edition is used here. Clearly the *Legenda* is not the work of Leo, Rufinus, and Angelo described in the prefatory letter (see chap. 3). Its own provenance, however, is controversial. It is intended to be a *uita*, but its emphasis is on St. Francis's conversion and the career of the small group of companions through the confirmation of the primitive rule by Pope Innocent III in 1209. Moreover, it abbreviates considerably the remainder of St. Francis's life and omits any mention of his missionary journeys. F. C.

Burkitt, "The Study of the Sources for the Life of St. Francis," in *St. Francis of Assisi: 1226-1926, Essays in Commemoration* (London, 1926), p. 47, suggests that the *Legenda* was compiled to complete the *Speculum perfectionis*, a theory that would call for a date after 1317. John Moorman, *The Sources for the Life of St. Francis of Assisi* (Manchester, 1940; repr. Farnsborough, Hants., 1966), pp. 68-76, divides the *Legenda* into three parts: chaps. 2-60, 61-67, and 68-74. He dismisses the last two sections as later additions to the original work, but argues that the first section, although written later than the *Vita prima* of Thomas of Celano, uses the same sources in a more primitive fashion. Theophile Desbonnets, "La legende des trois compagnons; nouvelles recherches sur la geneologie des biographies primitives de s. François," *AFH* 65(1972):66-106, contends that the *Legenda* was written after Thomas of Celano's *Vita prima*, the *Vita* by Julianus of Spira, and the Perugian *Scripta Leonis* but before Thomas of Celano's *Vita secunda* because it apparently made no use of this last nor of St. Bonaventure's *Legenda maior*. He dates it therefore between 1235 and 1248, possibly in 1246. However, the fact that the *Legenda* did not use the *Vita secunda* or the *Legenda maior* does not prove that it was written earlier than either of them.

The speech of the Bishop of Assisi appears in sect. 48, pp. 414-15.

4. Ibid., sects. 5-8, pp. 379-82; sects. 11, 13-14, pp. 384-88.

5. Ibid., sects. 25, 28-29, pp. 397-400.

6. Ibid., sects. 30-31, pp. 400-401.

7. Ibid., sect. 36, pp. 404-5.

8. Ibid., sect. 58, pp. 421-22.

9. Ibid., sect. 40, pp. 407-8; sect. 57, pp. 420-21.

10. Ibid., sect. 41, pp. 409-10; sects. 68-70, pp. 430-31.

11. *Speculum perfectionis seu s. Francisci assisiensis legenda antiquissima auctore fratre Leone,* ed. Paul Sabatier (Paris, 1898), rev. ed. by Sabatier, *Le Speculum perfectionis ou Mémoires de frère Léon,* 2 vols. *BSFS* 13, 17(Manchester, 1928, 1931; repr. Farnborough, Hants., 1966). The second edition is used here. The date of its composition is now accepted as 1318 (see Moorman, *Sources,* p. 131).

12. For the effort of Elias and the ministers to protest the new rule, see the *Verba s. Francisci,* ed. Rosalind Brooke, *Scripta Leonis, Rufini et Angeli, sociorum s. Francisci, Oxford Medieval Texts* (Oxford, 1970), chap. 113, pp. 285-87.

13. *Speculum perfectionis,* chaps. 2-26, pp. 4-76, especially chap. 26, pp. 72-76.

14. Ibid., chaps. 27-38, pp. 77-100; chap. 48, pp. 126-28; chaps. 68-73, pp. 194-218.

15. Ibid., chaps. 91-97, pp. 267-81; chap. 65, p. 183.

16. The edition of the *Fioretti* used here is *I fioretti de s. Francesco,* ed. G. Battelli, *Collezione di classici italiani* 13(Turin, 1944). The *Actus beati Francisci et sociorum eius* were edited by Paul Sabatier, *Collection d'études et de documents* 4(Paris, 1902). The *Actus* may be the work of Br. Ugolino di Monte Santa Maria, c. 1270-1342. On the sources employed in the *Actus* see Moorman, *Sources,* pp. 159-67. The anonymous translator of the *Fioretti* also wrote the *Considerazioni sulle sacri stimmate* which are usually printed with the *Fioretti* (Battelli, pp. 126-74).

17. *Actus,* chaps. 1, 6, 13, pp. 1, 20, 23; *Fioretti,* chaps. 1, 7, 13, 25, pp. 3, 20, 31, 57-60.

18. *Actus*, chap. 4, pp. 16-17; *Fioretti*, chap. 5, pp. 15-16.

19. *Actus*, chap. 7, p. 27; *Fioretti*, chaps. 5, 8, 36, 44, pp. 15-17, 22-24, 83-84, 100-101.

20. *Considerazioni*, pp. 145-47.

21. *Actus*, chaps. 16, 60, pp. 55-59, 179; *Fioretti*, chap. 16, pp. 37-41.

22. Moorman, *History*, pp. 396-97. Bartholomew arranged the *conformitates* according to the image of a tree from which extended twenty branches, each bearing two *conformitates* or *fructus*. See Bartholomew, *De conformitate uitae beati Francisci ad uitam domini Iesu*, Prologus secundus, *AF* 4:16-18.

23. On his sources see Bartholomew, *De Conformitate, AF* 5:xxxiv-xliv.

24. Ibid., Fr. 1, pt. 2, *AF* 4:33-60; Fr. 8, pt. 2, *AF* 4:189; Fr. 12, pt. 2, *AF* 4:622-23; Fr. 38 (bk. 3, Fr. 10), pt. 2, *AF* 5:467-69; Fr. 5, pt. 2, *AF* 4:117-20; Prol. secundus, *AF* 4:7.

25. Ibid., Prol. secundus, *AF* 4:8; Fr. 1, pt. 2, *AF* 4:39-40; Fr. 10, pt. 2, *AF* 4:480-83; Fr. 25 (bk. 2, Fr. 13), pt. 2, *AF* 5:289; Fr. 27 (bk. 2, Fr. 15), pt. 2, *AF* 5:316-17; Fr. 31 (bk. 3, Fr. 3), pt. 2, *AF* 5:377; Fr. 36 (bk. 3, Fr. 8), pt. 2, *AF* 5:456.

26. Ibid., Fr. 8, pt. 2, *AF* 4:324; Fr. 8, pt. 2, *AF* 4:253; Fr. 8, pt. 2, *AF* 4:332-33; Fr. 8, pt. 2, *AF* 4:333-34.

27. Ibid., Fr. 25 (bk. 2, Fr. 13), pt. 2, *AF* 5:290; Fr. 31 (bk. 3, Fr. 3) pt. 2, *AF* 5:393, 410; Fr. 36 (bk. 3, Fr. 8), pt. 2, *AF* 5:456.

28. Iohannes de Plano Carpini, *Ystoria Mongolorum*, ed. Van den Wyngaert, *Sinica franciscana*, 4 vols. (Quaracchi, 1929), 1:27-130; Benedictus Polonus, *Relatio*, ibid., 1:135-43; Guillelmus de Rubruc, *Itinerarium*, ibid., 1:164-332. All three works have been translated by Christopher Dawson in *The Mongol Mission* (London, 1955; repr. as *Mission to Asia*, N.Y. & Evanston, 1966).

29. All three letters of John of Monte Corvino are edited by Van den Wyngaert, *Sinica franciscana*, 1:340-55. Golubovich, *Biblioteca*, 3:87-93 prints the second and third letters (those of 1305 and 1306 respectively) but calls them the first and second letters. For a translation see Dawson, *Mission*, pp. 224-31.

30. Golubovich, *Biblioteca*, 3:86.

31. Third letter (1306), Golubovich, *Biblioteca*, 3:92/Van den Wyngaert, *Sinica franciscana*, 1:354-55.

32. Second letter (1305), Golubovich, *Biblioteca*, 3:89/Van den Wyngaert, *Sinica franciscana*, 1:350.

33. Golubovich, *Biblioteca*, 3:94.

34. Ibid., 4:244-48/Van den Wyngaert, *Sinica franciscana*, 1:499-506.

35. The *Cantici spirituali* were edited in "I cantici spirituali del B. Ugo Panziera da Prato dei frati minori," in the *Miscellanea pratese di cose inedite o rare, antiche e moderne* 3(n.p. 1861). Hugo's treatises appeared at Firenze in 1492 from the press of Antonio Miscomini. *Questi sono li dolori de la mente di Cristo* was edited by Don Guiseppe de Luca, *Prosatori minori del trecento*, 1:*Scrittori di religione*, *La letteratura italiana: storia e testi*, 12, no. 1 (Milano e Napoli, 1954), pp. 31-35.

36. *Cantici spirituali*, pp. 7-15.

37. See Appendix.

38. Marcellinus da Civezza, ed., *Storia universale delle missione francescane*, 11 vols. (Rome, 1857-1895), 3:366-72.

39. Ibid., 3:369-71.

40. In addition to the editions by F. Tocco, "Le due prime tribolazioni dell' ordine francescano," *Rendiconti della reale accademia dei lincei,* 17 (Rome, 1908):3-32, 97-131, 221-36, 299-328, of tribulations 1 and 2, and F. Ehrle, "Die Spiritualen, ihr Verhältnis zum Franziskanerorden und zu den Fraticellen," *ALKG* 2(1886): 127-64, 256-327, of tribulations 3-7, *Historia septem tribulationum* was edited by Ign. von Döllinger, *Beiträge* 2:417-526. Golubovich, *Biblioteca,* 1:341-50, edited the fifth tribulation. Angelo gave a briefer account of his missionary activities in his *Epistola excusatoria,* ed. F. Ehrle, "Die Spiritualen," *ALKG* 1:521-33. The extensive collection of Angelo's letters has been edited in part by F. Ehrle, ibid., pp. 533-69, but a complete critical edition is needed.

41. Moorman, *History,* pp. 188-89, 193. See above, chap. 5.

42. *Historia,* Döllinger, pp. 421-22.

43. Ibid., pp. 417-27, 431, 437-38; trib. 1, Tocco, pp. 101-3/Döll., pp. 441-42.

44. *Historia,* Döll., pp. 426-29, 433-34, 438-39; trib. 1, Tocco, pp. 112-19/Döll., pp. 450-55.

45. *Historia,* trib. 1, Tocco, pp. 122-27/Döll., pp. 457-59.

46. *Historia,* Döll., p. 417; trib. 7, Ehrle, pp. 148-53.

47. *Historia,* Döll., pp. 418-24.

48. Ibid., pp. 417-28; trib. 1, Tocco, pp. 101-8/*Döll., pp. 441-47.*

49. Historia, Döll., pp. 420, 431, 437, 439.

50. Angelo of Clareno, *Expositio super regulam,* ed. L. Oliger (Quaracchi, 1912), pp. 222-25.

51. *Chronica 24 generalium, AF* 3:412-15, 515-27, 529, 535-36, 554-56, 564-65; Bartolomaeus, *De conformitate,* Fr. 8, pt. 2, *AF* 4:332-36; Golubovich, *Biblioteca,* 1:325, 342; 2:66, 69-71; 3:211-13.

52. *Passio,* in *AF* 3:597-613. Thomas is the same friar who had been imprisoned with the Spirituals of the March of Ancona and later worked in Armenia and Persia as a missionary (see above, chap. 5). A chronology of his career is given by Golubovich, *Biblioteca* 3:219-21.

53. *Chronica 24 generalium, AF* 3:540-43.

54. On the printer see *Catalogue of Books Printed in the Fifteenth Century now in the British Museum* (London, 1913), 3:776. The *Tractatus de martyrio sanctorum* is Hain #10864. I have used a copy now in the Bibliothèque mazarine in Paris (#1333). Inc. "Querenti mihi ac diligenter perstrutanti christiane ecclesie fundamentum." The foliation is my own.

55. *Tractatus,* chap. 12, f. 35^v; chap. 17, ff. 50^v-51^r; *Excusatio,* ff. 56^v-57^v; Golubovich, *Biblioteca,* 5:290-97.

56. *Tractatus,* chap. 9, ff. 23^v-24^r; chap. 17, f. 51^{r-v}; Golubovich, *Biblioteca,* 5:291-92.

57. J. M. Hussey, ed., *Cambridge Medieval History,* vol. 4: *The Byzantine Empire,* pt. 1: *Byzantium and its Neighbours* (Cambridge, Eng., 1966), pp. 736-75.

58. *Tractatus,* Prologue, f. 2^{r-v}.

59. Ibid., ff. 2^r-3^r.

60. Ibid., chap. 1, ff. 3^v-6^r.

61. Ibid., chap. 2, f. 6^{r-v}.

62. Ibid., chap. 3, ff. 8^r-9^r.

63. Ibid., chap. 4, ff. 9^r-10^v.

64. Ibid., chaps. 5-7, ff. 10^v-18^v.

65. Ibid., chap. 9, ff. 20^r-24^r.
66. Ibid., chap. 11, f. 28^{r-v}.
67. Ibid., ff. 28^r-30^v.
68. Ibid., chap. 12, ff. 35^r-40^r.
69. Ibid., chap. 14, ff. 43^r-45^r.
70. Ibid., chap. 15, ff. 45^r-47^v.
71. Ibid., chap. 16, ff. 47^v-49^r. The text of this chapter is given partially by Golubovich, *Biblioteca,* 5:294-95.
72. *Tractatus,* chap. 17, ff. 49^r-56^r. Excerpts in Golubovich, *Biblioteca,* 5:295.
73. *Tractatus,* chap. 11, ff. 30^v-35^r.
74. Ibid., *Excusatio,* f. 56^v; chap. 16, f. 48^v.

Bibliographical Essay

The following bibliography lists basic works of scholarly value pertaining to my subject as a whole. Works of more narrowly defined interest are listed after the appropriate chapter.

A solid foundation for Franciscan history was established during the later years of the nineteenth century and the first half of the twentieth. In 1894 Paul Sabatier published his *Vie de Saint François d'Assise* at Paris. Four years later he edited the *Speculum perfectionis (Speculum perfectionis seu s. Francisci assisiensis legenda antiquissima auctore fratre Leone,* Collection de documents pour l'histoire religieuse et littéraire de moyen age, 1 [Paris]) which he believed was a confirmation of his original insights. He later revised it as *Le Speculum perfectionis ou mémoires de frère Léon sur la seconde partie de la vie de St. François d'Assise,* 2 vols. *BSFS* 13, 17 (Manchester, 1928; repr. Farnsborough, Hants., 1966). Sabatier was a liberal French Protestant whose interpretation of the Order's early history was colored by his sympathy for St. Francis and anticlericalism; he believed that an institutionalized order had been imposed on the saint's personal religious ideal.

A. G. Little helped to found the *British Society of Franciscan Studies* but devoted most of his research to the English scholastics, Robert Grosseteste, Adam Marsh, and Roger Bacon. John Moorman (*A History of the Franciscan Order from its Origins to the Year 1517* [Oxford, 1968], and *The Sources for the Life of St. Francis of Assisi* [Manchester, 1940; repr. Farnsborough, Hants., 1966]), Rosalind Brooke (*Early Franciscan Government: Elias to Bonaventure* [Cambridge, Eng., 1959] and *Scripta Leonis, Rufini et Angeli, sociorum s. Francisci,* Oxford Medieval Texts [Oxford, 1970]), and M. D. Lambert (*Franciscan Poverty* [London, 1961]) have continued to develop Sabatier's interpretation with some modifications.

The Order produced its own historians almost from the beginning. Giordano of Giano, *Chronica, AF* 1:1-19, Thomas of Eccleston, *Tractatus de aduentu fratrum minorum in Angliam,* ed. A. G. Little (2d ed., Manchester, 1951), and the Italian Joachite, Salimbene de Adam, *Chronica,* ed. Oswaldus Holder-Egger, *MGH SS* 32, were followed in the fourteenth century by Angelo of Clareno, *Historia septem tribulationum* (see chap. 6, n. 40), and the *Chronica 24 generalium* (*AF* 3). The "official" *vitae* by Thomas of Celano, *Vita prima s. Francisci* (*AF* 10:1-126) and *Vita secunda s. Francisci* (*AF* 10:127-268), and St. Bonaventure, *Legenda maior* (*AF* 10:555-652), were complemented by the rolls compiled by Brother Leo, used later in the *Scripta Leonis* and the *Speculum perfectionis.* Bartolomaeus of Pisa joined biography and history in his *De conformitate uitae beati Francisci ad uitam domini Iesu* (*AF* 4-5).

Luke Wadding, *Annales minorum,* 32 vols. (Quaracchi, 1931-1964), 3d ed., and J. H. Sbaralea, followed by Conrad Eubel, *Bullarium franciscanum,* 8 vols. (Rome, 1759-   ) assembled many of the documents. Herbert Holzapfel, *The History of the Franciscan Order,* trans. Antonine Tibesar and Gervase Brinkmann (Teutopolis, Ill., 1948), Hilarin Felder, *Geschichte der Wissenschaftlichen Studien im Franziskanerorden bis um die Mitte des 13. Jahrhunderts* (Freiburg-im-Breisgau, 1904) and *The Ideals of St. Francis,* trans. Berchmans Bittle (New York, 1925), and P. Gratien, *Histoire de la fondation et de l'évolution de l'ordre des frères mineurs au xiiie siècle* (Paris and Gembloux, 1928) became classical works. More recently Cajetan Esser, *The Origins of the Franciscan Order,* trans. Aedan Daly, O.F.M., and Irina Lynch (Chicago, 1970) and *Das Testament des heiligen Franziskus von Assisi* (Münster, 1949), has begun to reinterpret the Order's development.

Since the late nineteenth century, the center for historical study within the Order has been the Collegio S. Bonaventurae, formerly at Quaracchi near Florence and recently relocated at Grottaferrata near Rome. The *Analecta franciscana,* the *Archivum franciscanum historicum,* and the *Bibliotheca franciscana ascetica medii aevi* have combined to print many of the most important materials for the thirteenth and fourteenth centuries.

The first attempt to write a history of the Franciscan mission was made by Dominikus de Gubernatis in his *Orbis seraphicus: de missionibus inter infideles* (Rome, 1689). Marcellino da Civezza, *Storia universale delle missione francescane,* 11 vols. (Rome, 1857-95), is still the only comprehensive history. Girolamo Golubovich, *Biblioteca,* collected source materials and edited them together with articles on most of the missionaries of the thirteenth, four-teenth, and fifteenth centuries. No words can adequately convey its contribution. Anastasius Van den Wyngaert, *Sinica franciscana*, vol. 1 (Quaracchi, 1929) edited the reports of the missionaries to China. Leonhard Lemmens, *Geschichte der Franziskanermissionem* (Mün-ster in Westf., 1929), *Die Heidenmissionen des Spätmittelalters (Franz. Stud.* Beihefte 4), and Odulphus Van der Vat, *Die Anfänge der Franziskanermissionen und ihre Weiterentwicklung im nahen Orient und in der mohammedanischen Ländern während des 13. Jahrhunderts* (Werl in Westf., 1934), clarified the history of the medieval mission. P. Alphonsus Schnusenberg, ed., *Historia mis-sionum ordinis fratrum minorum,* 2 vols. to date (Rome, 1967-   ), treats the medieval period briefly. Noè Simònut, *Il metodo d'evangelizzazione dei francescani tra Musulmani e Mongoli nei secoli xiii-xiv* (Milan, 1947) and Giulio Basetti-Sani, *Mohammed et saint François* (Ottawa, 1959) were pioneer efforts in studying the Franciscan approach to mission.

The history of the Dominicans in the thirteenth century is covered by R. P. Mortier, O.P., *Histoire des maîtres généraux de l'ordre des frères prêcheurs,* vol. 1 (Paris, 1903). R. F. Bennett, *The Early Dominicans* (Cambridge, Mass., 1937), is especially valuable for its treatment of study and poverty. Marie-Humbert Vicaire, O.P., *St. Dominic and his Times,* trans. Kathleen Pond (New York, 1964), is the standard biography. William A. Hinnebusch, O.P., *The History of the Dominican Order: Origins and Growth to 1500,* 2 vols. to date (Staten Island, N.Y., 1966-   ), has so far devoted itself to the constitution and organization of the Order. Although Dominican missions were widespread during the thirteenth and fourteenth centuries, historians have largely neglected this topic; the pioneer work by Berthold Altaner, *Die Dominikanermissionen des 13. Jahrhunderts* (Habelschwerdt, 1924), remains the only attempt at such a study. The missionary colleges have attracted more attention. The most accessible work is Robert I. Burns, "Christian-Islamic Confrontation in the West: The Thirteenth Century Dream of Conversion," *AHR* 76(1971):1386-434.

One should begin any study of Joachim of Fiore with Morton W. Bloomfield, "Joachim of Flora: A Critical Survey of his Canon, Teachings, Sources, Biography and Influence," *Traditio* 13 (1957):249-311, George La Piana, "Joachim of Flora: A Critical Survey," *Speculum* 7 (1932):257-82 and Jeanne Bignami-Odier,

"Travaux récents sur Joachim de Flore," *Le Moyen Age* 58 (1952): 145-61. Henry Bett's *Joachim of Flora* (London, 1931) and E. Jordan, "Joachim de Flore," *DTC* 8, pt. 2:1425-58, are now dated. The groundwork was done during the 1920s and 1930s by a group of German and Italian scholars. Ernesto Buonaiuti, *Gioacchino da Fiore: I tempi, la vita, il messagio* (Rome, 1931): Herbert Grundmann, *Studien über Joachim von Floris* (Leipzig & Berlin, 1927); idem, *Neue Forschungen über Joachim von Fiore* (Marburg, 1950); Ernst Benz, *Ecclesia spiritualis* (Stuttgart, 1934; repr., 1964); "Joachim-Studien 1: Die Kategorien der religiösen Geschichtsdeutung Joachims," *ZKG* 50(1931):24-111; "Joachim-Studien 2: Die Excerptsätze der pariser Professoren aus dem Evangelium aeternum," *ZKG* 51 (1932):415-55; "Joachim-Studien 3: Thomas von Aquin und Joachim de Fiore; Die katholische Antwort auf die spiritualische Kirche und Geschichtsanschauung," *ZKG* 53 (1934):52-116; "Die Geschichtstheologie der Franziskanerspiritualen des 13. und 14. Jahrhunderts nach neuen Quellen," *ZKG* 52(1933):90-121; and "Die Kategorien der eschatologischen Zeitbewusstseins: Studien zur Geschichtstheologie der Franziskanerspiritualen," *Deutsche Vierteljahreschrift für Literaturewissenschaft und Geistesgeschichte* 11 (1933):200-229 represented a more radical interpretation suggesting that Joachim's third *status* was implicitly heterodox. J. C. Huck, *Joachim von Floris und die ioachitische Literatur* (Freiburg-im-Breisgau, 1938), and Francesco Foberti, *Gioacchino da Fiore* (Florence, 1934) and *Gioacchino da Fiore e il Gioacchinismio antico e moderno* (Padua, 1942) defended Joachim's orthodoxy. For the most part subsequent studies have added little to these earlier works. Antonio Crocco, *Gioacchino da Fiore* (Naples, 1960), is valuable for its study of Joachim's doctrine of the trinity while Henri de Lubac, *Exégèse médiévale: le quatre sens de l'écriture*, 4 vols. in 3(Paris, 1959-64), 2, pt. 1:437-559, treats Joachim's exegesis carefully. Marjorie Reeves and Beatrice Hirsch-Reich, *The 'Figurae' of Joachim of Fiore* (Oxford, 1972), is however, a major analysis of the abbot's understanding of history.

Joachim's works were printed in Venice (*Expositio in apocalypsim* with the *Liber introductorius* in 1527; *Concordia noui ac ueteris testamenti* and *Psalterium decem chordarum* together in 1519; all three reprinted Frankfurt a. M., 1964). Ernesto Buonaiuti edited the *Tractatus super quatuor euangelia*, Fonti per la storia d'Italia, 67 (Rome, 1930), and some of the shorter works in *Scritti minori*, 1, Fonti per la storia d'Italia 78(Rome, 1936). Leon Tondelli, M.

Reeves and B. Hirsch-Reich edited the *Liber figurarum, Il libro delle figure di Gioacchino da Fiore,* 2 vols., rev. ed., Turin, 1953). Arsenio Frugoni has edited the *Aduersus Iudeos,* Fonti per la storia d'Italia, 95(Rome, 1957). The *Tractatus de uita et regula Benedicti* has been edited by Cipriano Baraut in "Un tratado inedito de Joaquin de Fiore: De uita sancti Benedicti et de officio diuino secundum eius doctrinam," *AST* 24(1951):33-122. The varied editions promised by German scholars have so far failed to materialize.

On Joachitism, Marjorie J. Reeves has brought together her research in *The Influence of Prophecy in the Later Middle Ages: A Study in Joachimism,* (Oxford, 1969), and *The Figurae of Joachim of Fiore,* written with Beatrice Hirsch-Reich, (Oxford-Warbung Studies (Oxford, 1972), pp. 262-369, works which synthesized and expanded her own and others' previous studies. The articles by H. Denifle and F. Ehrle remain the starting point for a study of the Franciscan Spirituals (H. Denifle, "Das Evangelium aeternum und die Commission von Anagni," *ALKG* 1 (1885):49-142; F. Ehrle, "Die Spiritualen, ihr Verhältnis zum Franziskanerorden und zu den Fraticellen," ALKG 1(1885):509-69; 2(1886):106-64, 249-336; 3(1887):553-623; 4(1888):1-190; idem, "Zur Vorgeschichte des Concils von Vienne," ALKG 2(1886):353-416; 3(1887):1-195; idem, "Petrus Iohannis Olivi, sein Leben und seine Schriften," ALKG 3(1887):409-552. Karl Balthazar, *Geschichte des Armutsstreites im Franziskanerorden bis zum Konzil von Vienne* (Münster, 1911), René de Nantes, *Histoire des spirituels dans l'ordre de Saint François* (Paris, 1909), and D. S. Muzzey, *The Spiritual Franciscans* (New York, 1907), are now dated. Decima L. Douie, *The Nature and Effect of the Heresy of the Fraticelli,* (Manchester, 1932), remains useful and important. Raoul Manselli in his *La 'Lectura super apocalipsim' di Pietro Giovanni Olivi,* Studi storici, fasc. 19-21(Rome, 1955), and numerous articles has worked particularly with Peter John Olivi and Arnau de Villanova.

Index of Biblical Citations

Index

Actus beati Francisci, 107, 109; possible authorship of, 152 n.16
Adalbert, Saint, 6
Adam Marsh, O.F.M., 55-56, 142 n.3; influence on Roger Bacon, 56-57; and Joachim's prophecies, 145 n.4
Alexander of Bremen, O.F.M.: *Expositio super Apocalypsim*, 77
Al-Malik al-Kamil I, Sultan, 42
angelic popes, 60, 91-97, 148-49 n.42
Angelo Clareno, O.F.M., xiii-xiv, 87, 88, 127; maintains Franciscan understanding of mission, 90-91, 114-17; *Expositio super regulam*, 90-91, 116-17; *Historia septem tribulationum*, 81-82, 90, 115-16
Anthony of Padua, Saint, 42-43
antichrist: Augustinian understanding of, 13; in Franciscan eschatology, 28-29, 31, 33; Joachite expectations of, xii, 16, 18-20, 84, 89, 93, 95-96, 97; in medieval prophetic works, 14; Roger Bacon discusses, 60, 65
apocalyptic conversion: definition of, 12-13; encourages toleration of Jews, 13, 58, 94, 133 n.32; tradition independent of Joachitism, 76-77, 112. *See also* Joachitism
Armenia, 11; Spiritual-Conventual controversy in, 87-89
Arnau de Vilanova, 98, 150 n.52-56; and apocalyptic conversion of Israel, 150 n.57; predicts angelic popes, 92-94; *Informació espiritual*, 94; *Tractatus de tempore . . . antichristi*, 92

Augustine of Hippo, Saint: eschatology developed by, 13-14, 20, 28-30, 35; *De ciuitate dei*, 3; *Rule* (attributed to), 125
Averroes (Ibn-Rushd), 7, 70
Avignon, papacy at, 96-97

Bartholomew of Pisa, O.F.M., xiii, 109; *De conformitate*, 109, 153 n.22
Bartolomaeus Guiscolus, O.F.M., 77-79, 145 n.1
Béguins, 82, 86, 89, 93
Bernard of Clairvaux, Saint, 8, 133 n.32
Bernard of Quintavalle, O.F.M., 42, 49, 103, 108
Bernardino of Siena, Saint, 89, 90
Bonaventure, Saint: formulates Franciscan eschatology, 30-34; influenced by Joachite eschatology, 31, 76, 82; and martyrdom, 48-53; Spiritual or Conventual, 27, 81-82; *Apologia pauperum*, 51-53; *Collationes in Hexaemeron*, 31-32, 77, 137 n.22-23; *De triplici uia*, 50-52; *Expositio super regulam*, 33-34, 53, 137-38 n.32; *Itinerarium mentis ad deum*, 30-31, 32, 141 n.60; *Legenda maior*, 26, 29-30, 37, 48-50, 109, 127, 151-52 n.3; *Quaestiones disputatae de perfectione euangelica*, 32-33, 141 n.67
Boniface VIII, Pope, 94; and Ramon Llull, 70; role in Spiritual-Conventual controversy, 87, 91-92